CRASH!
BANG!
WALLOP!

Twenty20: A History Of The Brief Game

Martyn Hindley

KNOW THE SCORE BOOKS SPORTS PUBLICATIONS

CRICKET	Author	ISBN
ASHES TO DUST	Graham Cookson	978-1-905449-19-4
CRASH! BANG! WALLOP!	Martyn Hindley	978-1-905449-88-0
GROVEL!	David Tossell	978-1-905449-43-9
MOML: THE ASHES	Pilger & Wightman	1-905449-63-1
MY TURN TO SPIN	Shaun Udal	978-1-905449-42-2
WASTED?	Paul Smith	978-1-905449-45-3

CULT HEROES	Author	ISBN
CARLISLE UNITED	Mark Harrison	978-1-905449-09-7
CELTIC	David Potter	978-1-905449-08-8
CHELSEA	Leo Moynihan	1-905449-00-3
MANCHESTER CITY	David Clayton	978-1-905449-05-7
NEWCASTLE	Dylan Younger	1-905449-03-8
NOTTINGHAM FOREST	David McVay	978-1-905449-06-4
RANGERS	Paul Smith	978-1-905449-07-1
SOUTHAMPTON	Jeremy Wilson	1-905449-01-1
WEST BROM	Simon Wright	1-905449-02-X

MATCH OF MY LIFE	Editor	ISBN
DERBY COUNTY	Nick Johnson	978-1-905449-68-2
ENGLAND WORLD CUP	Massarella & Moynihan	1-905449-52-6
EUROPEAN CUP FINALS	Ben Lyttleton	1-905449-57-7
FA CUP FINALS 1953-1969	David Saffer	978-1-905449-53-8
FULHAM	Michael Heatley	1-905449-51-8
LEEDS	David Saffer	1-905449-54-2
LIVERPOOL	Leo Moynihan	1-905449-50-X
MANCHESTER UNITED	Ivan Ponting	978-1-905449-59-0
SHEFFIELD UNITED	Nick Johnson	1-905449-62-3
STOKE CITY	Simon Lowe	978-1-905449-55-2
SUNDERLAND	Rob Mason	1-905449-60-7
SPURS	Allen & Massarella	978-1-905449-58-3
WOLVES	Simon Lowe	1-905449-56-9

GENERAL FOOTBALL	Author	ISBN
2006 WORLD CUP DIARY	Harry Harris	1-905449-90-9
BEHIND THE BACK PAGE	Christopher Davies	978-1-84818-506-7
BOOK OF FOOTBALL OBITUARIES	Ivan Ponting	978-1-905449-82-2
BURKSEY	Peter Morfoot	1-905449-49-6
HOLD THE BACK PAGE	Harry Harris	1-905449-91-7
MY PREMIERSHIP DIARY	Marcus Hahnemann	978-1-905449-33-0
OUTCASTS	Steve Menary	978-1-905449-31-6
The Lands That FIFA Forgot		
PARISH TO PLANET	Dr Eric Midwinter	978-1-905449-30-9
A History of Football		
TACKLES LIKE A FERRET	Paul Parker	1-905449-47-X
(England Cover)		
TACKLES LIKE A FERRET	Paul Parker	1-905449-46-1
(Manchester United Cover)		

RUGBY LEAGUE	Author	ISBN
MOML WIGAN WARRIORS	David Kuzio	978-1-905449-66-8

FORTHCOMING PUBLICATIONS IN 2008

MATCH OF MY LIFE	Editor	ISBN
BRIGHTON	Paul Camillin	978-1-84818-000-0
IPSWICH TOWN	Mel Henderson	978-1-84818-001-7

GENERAL FOOTBALL	Author	ISBN
FORGIVE US OUR PRESS PASSES	Football Writers' Association	978-1-84818-507-4
JUST ONE OF SEVEN	Denis Smith	978-1-84818-504-3
MAN & BABE	Wilf McGuinness	978-1-84818-503-6
PALLY	Gary Pallister	978-1-84818-500-5
PLEASE MAY I HAVE MY FOOTBALL BACK?		
	Eric Alexander	978-1-84818-508-1

RUGBY LEAGUE	Author	ISBN
MOML LEEDS RHINOS	Caplan & Saffer	978-1-905449-69-9

CRASH! BANG! WALLOP!

Twenty20: A History Of The Brief Game

Martyn Hindley

www.knowthescorebooks.com

First published in the United Kingdom
by Know The Score Books Ltd, 2008
Copyright Martyn Hindley

Know The Score Books Limited
118 Alcester Road, Studley, Warwickshire, B80 7NT
01527 454482   info@knowthescorebooks.com   www.knowthescorebooks.com

A CIP catalogue record is available for this book from the British Library
ISBN: 978-1-905449-88-0

Jacket design by Graham Hales

Printed and bound in Great Britain
By Cromwell Press, Trowbridge, Wiltshire

Photographs reproduced by kind permission of the International Cricket Council

ACKNOWLEDGEMENTS

I've always thought the 'acknowledgement' section in a book is the most hyperbolic one: how could it take so many people to contribute to one person's work, at the end of the day? It is only in writing one that I really understand that every single person who has ever gone to print must have skimped on the number of people they have thanked because I have been lucky enough to have the help and support of so many that I am likely not to remember all of them here. For that, I apologise in advance.

I owe a debt of gratitude to each person who agreed to be interviewed for this book: for the time they gave up and the unswerving support they gave for the project. Brad Hodge was interviewed in mid rain-break at Old Trafford, Rana Naved gave nervous glances out to the middle at Liverpool whilst his Sussex team-mates were losing wickets and hastening his arrival at the crease and Stuart Law gave up time in his holidays at almost 10 in the evening. Most of that was orchestrated by Rebecca Trbojevich who, as well as restoring my faith in communications departments of the sporting world, has been a great motivator and is a good friend.

Most press departments have gone above and beyond the call of duty to help out: Rhonda Kelly and her team in the Stanford 20/20 offices, Colin Maynard's valued help, kindness and assistance at Lord's, Gareth Thomas at Zee TV, Ruweida Kandan in South Africa and Eivion Bowen of Cricket Victoria. For help and advice in what has been a new and quite daunting assignment for me, I have been fortunate enough to have the guidance of Andy Wilson, Graham Hardcastle, Andrew McGlashan and Phil Caplan, who might now be regretting his forthright insistence that "every person has something to tell in print and it's up to others to judge whether it's any good or not." John Bradley pushed my career in the right direction years before that and for that, I'm grateful. Support has always been granted unswervingly by my Dad, Paul and step-mother Janet and I'm not sure they realise just how important that it has always been.

Of course, wickets would never have been pitched had it not been for patient and very understanding employers. Ever since joining TWMC, company owner Tim White has allowed me to be flexible with my working time, something that has greatly benefited this book and as a cricket fan himself, I hope the end product justifies the faith he has shown in me. Gary Hickson at BBC Radio Lancashire has also been a great ally and thanks also go to Phil Bird and Gary Hunt for their support. It goes without saying that without the hard work, trust and faith of both Simon Lowe and Andrew Searle at Know the Score, this book wouldn't have seen the light of day either.

All of this has of course meant that my family have been largely neglected for more than twelve months so I would like also to apologise to them all and especially thank the long-suffering Claire for putting up with me. Her enthusiasm and tender loving care for the minutiae of the book has known no bounds and without her, I would have given up after the first few obstacles. She is a true star and the end result is as much her persistence and hard work as mine.

Finally, the thanks must go to Martin Crowe, John Carr, Stuart Robertson et al – the forward-thinking ones who gave Twenty20 to the world and offered up something so fascinating to talk about. In doing so, perhaps they saved cricket outside the international sphere from the financial abyss.

Martyn Hindley, April 2008

To my mother, Karen. I hope I make you proud.

CONTENTS

We Twenty Kings

"Now bring on the bang bang club."

Robert Houwing,
Wisden Cricketer (SA edition; Aug/Sept '07)

AJAY BRISTLED WITH FEAR AND radiated anxiety. In the beginning, he had nimbly skirted his wiry frame around the Tavern block of the Liberty Life Wanderers Stadium, unfurling the amber-white-green standard of his nation and inciting fellow Indians to bellow out in support of their side. With his thin, reedy moustache and long-sleeved, smart blue shirt, he seemed a curious chant master but his lively outbursts during India's innings suffocated Pakistan's support by comparison. His opening gambit of "Twinkle, twinkle, little star, India: you're my shining star" was received with a certain amount of local ridicule but the younger members of the crowd had clutched at the baton. With their team now defending 157 in the first ever World Twenty20 final, those same youngsters clamoured around Ajay and implored him to rally the troops once again.

Their enthusiasm and unnerving belief in their heroes had been dimmed by Pakistan's threat to march back into a game that had appeared beyond them. When Yasir Arafat took a huge heave at Irfan Pathan and heard the emphatic dismantling of his stumps, Pakistan still required 53 runs off 24 balls and were reeling from the loss of their seventh wicket. But Misbah ul-Haq was still there, a relative unknown before the competition but the man who had dug Pakistan out of a ropey predicament when these big rivals had met in the group stage, helping to force a tie.

Ajay hadn't travelled from Hong Kong to witness defeat against the old enemy. He had chaperoned his fiancée to illustrate the fervency of India-Pakistan scraps. She sat beside me in a delightful aquamarine sari, sparkling and stimulated by the realisation that she was witnessing a classic. "I think this is a good game, great game," she understated.

Misbah pressed the play button on Pink's *Get This Party Started* by propelling Harbhajan Singh back over his head for a maximum and soon endorsed his own decision to refuse singles and not give the strike to Sohail Tanvir by clobbering another couple of weighty sixes. Nineteen came from the over and fuelled Ajay's tendency to fear the worst.

His concerns were matched by those of Mahendra Singh Dhoni, the Indian skipper in the absence of both Rahul Dravid and a credible alternative. Dhoni waddled thirty metres or so to advise his fast bowler Sreesanth after Tanvir welcomed him to the eighteenth over by biffing the opening ball over the fence at long-on: twenty-nine required. His wisdom either wasn't taken on board or just didn't work. Sreesanth looked tight under pressure and bowled a big wide then missed with a shy at the stumps at the bowlers end trying to curtail Tanvir's frantic search for a leg bye. By this time, every Indian fan in the ground applauded anything that didn't involve a boundary.

Misbah kept them clapping with just a single from the next two deliveries and then Tanvir hushed them again by thumping to deep backward square leg for six. All of a sudden, twenty runs off the last thirteen balls seemed very gettable, making the eruption a volcanic one when Sreesanth calmed his nerves to clean up Tanvir next ball and leave Pakistan eight down.

With Misbah on strike though, Dhoni's irritability was palpable at the start of the nineteenth over and it was starting to transfer to the sidelines. On the grassed bank bordering the chute that deposits players to the arena from the dressing rooms, they waved their Indian flags but made relatively little noise. Dhoni watched as RP Singh was milked for a single and then the wicket-keeper fumbled a slower ball and the batsmen got through for a bye that returned Misbah to strike. Singles weren't enough but Misbah took one anyway, exposing Umar Gul who was bowled and the whole game looked over again, just as it had fifteen minutes before. Last man Mohammed Asif had a brutal scything swing at the last ball of the over and managed to beat short third man for four runs that left thirteen needed to win off the final six balls.

I suddenly felt anxious now. Twelve runs wasn't unheard of in desperation but I panicked that this fabulous contest – just like the one in Durban, the first meeting of the teams in this competition – would be settled on penalties. I didn't care who won but just didn't want the tie-breaker, the lottery. At least both teams were well versed in the rules and regulations if it came down to it.

In Durban Harbhajan had bowled impeccable yorkers, but in the final, the slightest inaccuracies in length saw him pilfered for 36 runs in just three overs. So Dhoni turned instead to Joginder Singh to bowl the crucial twentieth over. Singh was immediately wayward with an off-side wide. Twelve runs required. Next up, Misbah lunged forward and threw himself into a cover drive but only connected with fresh air. Any Indian advantage from the dot ball was erased with interest next ball, which disappeared towards the golf course for six runs that halved the task.

Ajay held his hands on his head and gave the general impression that his world had just collapsed around him. So did the lion's share of the Tavern. His fiancée wore a one-smile-fits-all expression that suggested she didn't mind what came next. Out in the middle Misbah had a brain fade to rescue the mood of her intended, running to the off-side to confront Joginder's next ball whereupon he shovelled it over his left shoulder. Immediately, he knew the connection wasn't good enough and turned to watch the ball dip after thirty metres of travel and drop comfortably into the hands of the calm Sreesanth. It could quite easily have been Kolkata or Mumbai as the huddles of Indians whooping and screaming in unbridled delight started to rock the Wanderers. India were world kings in a form of cricket that their administrators didn't like and their players barely knew. This would take some celebrating. Beaten by five runs, the Pakistanis trudged disconsolately away from the scene of the party.

* * *

HAVING TRAVELLED SUCH A distance, I was pleased for Ajay that his day would be memorable for the right reasons. It represented a fairytale end to the beginning of Twenty20 as a type of cricket, preparing the ground for potential wholesale changes to the way cricket is structured and run across the globe. But that is for the future. Now perhaps for the first time, it was fair to analyse what this brief form of the game has already brought to the sport and at what cost.

My first experience of Twenty20 came at its christening: a group stage match between Yorkshire and Leicestershire in the first season of the English domestic cup. The weight of numbers turning up offered a contradictory tale but watching the Phoenix and the Foxes play out a reasonable game left me unfulfilled. Every other ball either seemed to be a boundary or an unsightly swipe looking for one so it seemed as though the art form was lost. Like university degrees, they lose veneer and a little significance if everyone has one. This was cricket without context similar to watching a highlights package with boundaries and wickets and little in between to determine the tactics, the phoney wars and the mini-battles emerging between batsman and bowler. No sense of the change of fields just lustful attention to rope-hopping. To me, it was as interesting as watching a full day of Test cricket in which each and every delivery was blocked. Despite being a university student at the time and loathe to feel that I'd wasted precious pounds and pence, I left at the interval, completely unenthralled.

Yet Twenty20's inception was exciting because this was precisely how I had had my love for the game accelerated by playing it as a youngster. After every Monday and Thursday at school, I would cross the fields from home and head to Astley and Tyldesley Cricket Club to play in the junior ranks of the Bolton Association, where, over the course of four summers, I determined only that my talents in the sport were cripplingly few. One incident did stand out for me though and flashed before my mind's eye when I started to commentate on Twenty20 a good decade or more later.

Stuck in first, the under-13s were batting against Blackrod on a gloomy Monday and I was opening. Or rather, trying to. My first few shots punished whatever fresh air clung around nearby, pushing, prodding and slogging my way to the same result: I couldn't lay bat on ball. I had managed to see off a few partners but only had five or six to my name in the eighth over by which time, the coach (stood as the umpire at square leg as always happened in these games) bellowed out in a gruff and patronising way that if I didn't start hitting the bloody thing, he'd retire me and get someone in who could. I got quite angry quite quickly at that age. The next ball was thrashed through the covers quite well for four but it made me far too excited and I suddenly thought I could do that with every ball. I threw my weight onto the front foot to the next delivery too but it was shorter and I just plopped a drive off the shoulder of the blade into the hands of cover, who must have been quite sad to see me get out. I could hear the coach cursing me on my way off. We were all out for forty odd and lost the match with about twelve overs to spare.

I might have been physically weak and talentless, but still the episode taught me to respect those professionals whose mantras would include things like 'score off every ball' by the time Twenty20 had celebrated its third birthday. But at the time of the Yorkshire episode, I carried too many conservative and stick-in-the-mud views to appreciate the potential for entertainment. Thankfully, that soon changed.

By the eve of the first World Twenty20 in South Africa in September 2007, so much had happened in "short-form cricket" that coaches, players and pundits alike were all doing it the good service of attaching scientific thought to it; treating it in much the same way as a Test match. In fact, some would maintain Twenty20 at its highest level to be the form of the game that best compared and prepared individuals for the Test arena in that one mistake or piece of brilliance could be the difference between success and failure in much the same way as the elongated, more revered version of the game. The dawning of a new age of cricket appeared very much on the horizon with the launch of the megabucks Indian Premier League (IPL) in April 2008, just six months after India had been crowned as the brief game's first World Champions, sparking a fervour and a clamour for more of this instant gratification.

Despite the odd dissenting voice, now every nation had stakeholders wanting a slice of the new pie. Through Twenty20 a different generation of cricket fan had been inducted, drawing new brands of advertisers towards the sport and making it richer as a by-product. New investors came flocking to the table with fresh ideas and competitions that veered away from the traditional to such an extent that cricket faced a mini-crisis: that of establishing who owned the entire game? Did anyone have a right to put a monopoly on a game played and watched by so many people in the Test nations and the wider world? It produced power struggles: some producing a detrimental effect on the sport, others with the capacity to see cricket's audience and marketability developed across the globe. Has cricket graduated or regressed?

Converted from early cynicism, I have become fascinated by the quickfire evolution of Twenty20 and how different components of the game have changed in a relatively short timespan. A batsman now looks to score in innovative and unorthodox areas whilst bowlers face a struggle to expand their repertoire just to ensure they don't become fodder and ergo, an endangered species. The way that Umar Gul had bowled for Pakistan in the final that had rattled Ajay's cage so much had been on the point of perfection with the 'blockhole' delivery to suggest that he had the ball on a string. A special skill had been carefully honed to the point it could be called upon at will. So Twenty20 has gained intricacies that didn't seem possible in that opening season and this has affected a U-turn in the way that not only I see it but many others too, some of them inside the game. I enjoy it now and make no apology for that.

As a young and nerdy kid, I'd spend wet Sundays at county cricket grounds trying to devise a formula that would encourage people in to watch their sides. I was fed up of heading to Lancashire matches and finding myself to be one of the only people present not drawing a pension — it indicated a bleak future. One of my most hair-brained plans was to divide the County Championship into four regional pools, upping rivalries whilst lowering travel times for players and fans and culminating in a play-off style of grand finale in August and September to determine the national champions. Even my mates at school — some of them equally nerdy — thought I needed my head testing. I tore up my mini-doctrine and dreamily hoped that someone would inject some energy and funds some-how. Twenty20 would become that thing to herd people back inside county grounds and so long as the pound note is able to talk, it was immediately clear that professionals had to adapt to survive in their new surroundings. In England and South Africa, it would breathe life back into a dying sport beneath the international layer. In India and the West Indies, apathy for Twenty20 was revolutionised by entrepreneurs outside of the game whose motives were not primarily the betterment of cricket but whose impact in those areas will breed professionalism where none had previously existed.

It is difficult to assess when exactly the roots for Twenty20 were planted. Some may say they were there the very day the first league pitched up for an evening game of standard twenty over cricket after work or school. Others contend that it washed in from the horrendous Australian summer that ruined an Ashes series in 1970-71 and spawned the first ever one-day international as an unwanted lovechild.

Whatever the correct answer may be, Twenty20 had to fight from the incu-bator from the very beginning against both conservatism and the cynic. Ridicule spewed forth from many different quarters. In 2007, a group of jocular stewards at Old Trafford steadfastly refused to acknowledge that this new, exciting, short form of cricket could be the same as a 'proper' game.

"Twenty20? What's that," blustered one, "some kind of rounders isn't it?"

The group chuckled at the insinuation, I winced. Thankfully, others have given it a more broadminded approach and Twenty20 has grown to be well-planned and structured as a result. But the origins of the game in modern times probably stemmed from a much more liberal and less reactionary society than England: New Zealand.

Hitting To The Max

*"What in essence we did was to take the first ten overs
and the last ten overs of a standard one-day game and
take the crap bits out of the middle."*

Martin Crowe

A CANTANKEROUS WIND TORE ACROSS Auckland's confined oval at Eden Park but
still nobody left. Everyone believed. From the brute force of Mark Greatbatch and
Ken Rutherford in the New Zealand innings to the instinctively disguised varieties
of pace and bowling styles in defence, the home crowd were compelled to cheer,
hope, pray. For a nation bred on the powerful bullying their rugby players imposed
on others, the sniff of glory in a sport with more finesse was too thrilling.

In reaching the World Cup semi-final against Pakistan on 21 March 1992,
New Zealand had already eclipsed the endeavours of their great rivals from
across the Tasman, finishing top of the nine-team group phase with Australia
never finding consistency and landing up fifth, missing the semi-finals entirely. In
their semi, New Zealand's captain threatened more.

Crowe came to the crease with the Kiwis in a hefty portion of trouble at 39/2
and displayed as much enthusiasm for the situation as the crowd, lacerating the
Pakistani bowlers with crunching upper cuts and cover drives. In keeping with the
nearly-story that the 1992 World Cup was to become for New Zealand, his freedom of movement became blighted by a knee injury that forced Crowe to bat
with a runner and the ensuing confusion occasioned his run out after recording
an 83-ball innings of 91.

Ulltimately, it was in vain as Pakistan inched their way towards the 263 required with six balls and four wickets to spare. Crowe had scored more runs than any other player in the competition, at an astounding average of 114, having been dismissed just four times in nine amblings to the crease. But such thrill-a-minute outings were very rare in one-day international cricket and any love that Crowe may have had for it had long since disappeared.

* * *

WHATEVER THE DISAPPOINTMENTS OF Eden Park, Crowe had already underlined his potential as a cricketing innovator during those Finals. The skipper had been quick to spot the rewards of taking the pace off the ball by employing the likes of Chris 'Chipper' Harris to jumble up the rhythm of opposing batsmen but more radical had been the decision to give the new ball to off-spin artist, Dipak Patel, sensing that incoming openers would find it more difficult to settle against such a new and different threat. By the mid-nineties though, retirement on the field led to Crowe chancing his arm at real developments off it.

"It originated really through a chance meeting I had with the CEO at SKY Television," reflects the ex-captain who quickly became a respected commentator on the game.

"I had just retired, or was just about to, and he was a New Yorker who was very much into his baseball. He was looking into buying into cricket to alleviate what is known as 'churn' where people would subscribe to SKY for the rugby season and then switch it off again when that was finished. Cricket was seen as a better way to do it. That was all before SKY had the rights to international games for New Zealand so what we were looking at was a completely different package."

Crowe was asked whether the sport could be condensed into something that could be squeezed into a similar time frame to baseball and responded with Cricket Max.

"It was something that already appealed to me", he reflects, "because I'd been in the schools in the few years before and heard that a lot of kids at 14 and 16 years-old were giving up the game because it was slow to them and quite boring as well."

Looking back at the success of Max within New Zealand and the following evolution of Twenty20, such an admission from one of short-game cricket's founding fathers may seem a very obvious statement. After all, Crowe had to sell the prospect to his bosses at SKY Television at the time and, ten years or so later, he could claim the plaudits for what his forethought was to ultimately produce.

Cricket lovers across the world offer a confused grimace on learning of the concepts involved in Max Cricket, using the sport's traditionally conservative mindsets to see it as an overly contrived form of the game. It is best regarded as a wholly different sport.

The most far-reaching rules came in and around the 'Max Zone', a trapezium-shaped box painted straight down the ground, around sixty metres from the striking batsman. Straight shots would be rewarded by doubling their worth, meaning that a monster-six over the bowler's head would produce twelve runs instead of six. To encourage batsmen to hit through the ball rather than square of the wicket with cross-batted slogs, no fielders would be allowed in the zone when the ball was bowled and, even if they were to stray into the box under a skier the batsman could not be caught out there either. Crowe believed in his innovation enough to have it patented and having seen it in action, still believes it to have added a dimension further than the modern-day Twenty20.

"I branded Max with a MaxZone because I felt that it created more thought, more tactics and more strategy in what is a pretty fast and furious slogathon and it also enabled sides to come back from nowhere," he argues, his contention being that it produced fewer matches that would peter out towards the end with the result long having been obvious.

The format of the matches helped that as well. Whilst being twenty overs per side with each bowler permitted four of them, the innings were split into quarters to leave – effectively – a thrasharound Test Match. Each side would have all of their ten wickets available in each innings and the victor would be deduced from the aggregate totals.

Within the game came some new gimmicks that stuck and others that didn't.

Bowlers were encouraged to bowl as straight as the batting team were goaded into hitting so wides carried a two-run penalty and after over-stepping for a no-ball, the next delivery could be smashed anywhere with immunity from dismissal by any method apart from run outs. The latter seemed to be educational to developing players more than anything else and has survived to many forms of twenty-first century cricket.

"We created small grounds that would suit Max," continues Crowe.

"I think we tried a rugby league ground and a running track and modified them more to be like a cricket oval and it seemed to work. Five or six thousand were paying to come and watch but more importantly, because it was a Friday night league, SKY had more than double the audience figures for one-day cricket, so to that end, it was a great success."

SKY were big pawns in the whole game. The vacant slot for rugby was nicely filled with competitive sport and their cash provided sums of money that seemed almost implausible to the majority of players in the system who had never represented New Zealand at international level. The winning state of the first Max Cup Final in February 1997 landed NZ$14,000 with the loser still making NZ$7,000. More impressively to the individuals, NZ$5,000 was the prize for the competition's 'Most Valuable Player' – a points system run through the championship that added extra edge between Canterbury all-rounder Craig McMillan and Andrew Penn, of Central Districts, the two battling it out for the loot until their respective sides met in the Napier final.

Aside from cash, other figures were causing something of a stir in the opening season as well as a public still perceiving cricket as a game of attrition came to terms with strike rates that seemed perverse. In guiding Canterbury to a crushing win over Otago in a virtual semi in Carisbrook, McMillan crashed a century in just 29 balls that bizarrely involved seven conventional boundaries, one six, four eights and a twelve. Otago had themselves railed along at almost twelve runs an over in their first innings but their efforts were dwarfed and they were out of a match that contained almost five hundred and fifty runs in little more than three hours.

The only down side to the competition seemed to be the rapid turnaround between the initial stages and the final. Indeed, so under-prepared were Canterbury for their winning sequence that they had a nightmare trip to McLean Park for the final, having to endure a two-hour bus ride from Palmerston North because it was the closest city they could fly to at short notice, with all seats booked up between Christchurch and nearby Wellington.

* * *

AFTER STAGING THE FIRST domestic competition to reasonable national acclaim, it seemed only logical to host an international rival and try to give Max the oxygen of global publicity. In November 1997, England obliged.

Well, I say England but it wasn't quite the England-New Zealand battle that had taken place in Ahmedabad in the World Cup some eighteen months before. This was the New Zealand Max Black Caps against the English Lions, both parading squads of players fitting into the 'great domestic player' bracket at limited-overs level rather than truly international class. There were exceptions to that rule of course. NZ opener Craig Spearman had blasted a ton against England's supposed finest in that World Cup and Robin Smith, Chris Lewis and Phil DeFreitas in the visiting camp boasted almost four hundred international caps between them.

"Before we went, the lads met up at the end of the cricket season and we had a brief discussion," says Lancashire all-rounder Ian Austin, one of the fringe internationals selected for the tour. "We said 'let's just go out there and have a bit of fun' and that's what we did. We just had a Beano whilst we were out there — a five-day jolly. Of course we were competitive when we were on the pitch but we weren't slow to buy each other a few beers afterwards."

Of course it's difficult for any player to take a brand new concept so seriously especially one that seemed such a blatant bastardisation of the sport that had been their lifeblood for years beforehand. The itinerary hardly helped the situation — four games crammed into a tour that lasted little more than a week from leaving English terra firma to hitting it again. Three of the matches were internationals.

England won the first in Auckland but as Austin was to remember, "I'm not quite sure how. They batted better and fielded better and perhaps had a plan B where we just went out and played."

The Kiwis hurled down the gauntlet with a challenging 121/6 first up, prising out an eight-run advantage after Dominic Ostler's unbeaten half-century. But both sides upped the ante exponentially in the second half, England breaking the then-Max record by chasing 136 in the fourth innings off just 9 overs: not bad for a side still feeling the effects of a 33-hour flight to the furthest reaches of the globe.

In the *Daily Telegraph*, Mark Nicholas gushed about the new format.

"New Zealand's custom-built cricket max team, shorn mind you of the four or five players who would have been chosen had the Test team not been touring Australia, reeled from an onslaught that these talented English cricketers reserved for their one-off opportunity to prove that they might have been chosen for the more important, more acceptable perhaps we should say, tours of the busy winter ahead," he scribed.

Not only was it the on-field action that captured Nicholas' imagination but also the marketing of it from the broadcast team who turned Max into reality, marvelling that "Sky and Crowe are now a team, running a well-supported first-class domestic competition and selling this first international series to three television networks around the world." Listening to the immaculately turned-out Nicholas presenting modern cricket to the world on these television networks adds to the sense that the former Hampshire batsmen isn't easily impressed, especially by gimmicks. His praise thus acquires further gravitas.

The remainder of the mini-series drifted away from the visitors though, starting with a day game in Hamilton. Surreally though, the 'Lions' went into the last over with half a chance of winning the game needing 42 – thanks to the existence of the MaxZone. Gloucestershire's Mark Alleyne spotted an opportunity for rare history and cleared the boundary with the first three balls going for two sixes and a twelve, only for his side to land up thirteen runs short.

"It was good in terms of encouraging good and exciting cricket but it might have gone too far with the gimmicks and all that," says Alleyne, not a fan of Max despite his apparent natural aptitude for it.

"It didn't encourage traditional batting techniques so if you wanted to do well then sometimes you had to compromise that. As time went on though, it was just like anything else new, you just reverted to your old habits and the basics."

Ludicrously, 'England' were asked to maximise the potential crowd by playing the following day – a Sunday. The already-weary touring side flew down to Wellington on the North Island's southerly tip early in the morning, played in the late evening and then boarded a flight the morning after to start their marathon return journey. Unsurprisingly, they were thrashed by ten wickets in what turned out to be the decider.

"I couldn't see it taking off around the world," Ian Austin recalls, "but once we were out there playing, it did seem pretty appealing. It was one of those things that you had to push to the right people and see if they got behind it. We played the last game of that series on the Test ground in Wellington but it was just a shame that it was done a bit too quickly. Like anything, there's only so much money that you can be paying out at once and the matches came thick and fast for the public to shell out for.

"We did take a group of very good one-day cricketers there from the counties and we had a reasonable amount of experience between us. The good thing was that the crowds did turn up as well and we had about six or seven thousand in for one of the games which was on an echoey old football or rugby ground where the noise bounced off the stands at both sides."

Despite the qualified enthusiasm of those involved — either reporting or playing — the Max brand struggled to make an impact worldwide. A West Indian side lazily branded with the clichéd "Caribbean Calypsos" tag were hammered at Jade Stadium in Christchurch in 1999-2000 by a New Zealand outfit who had, by this time, had enjoyed four seasons' worth of exposure to Crowe's concept. A home win by 8 wickets and with almost a full three overs to spare would have done little to encourage West Indians to embrace the format.

The longer the game took to lift-off on the global scale, the less chance it had of being adopted by the ICC's other Full Members. Primarily, New Zealand were too good at it and it was likely that few other nations would ever beat them at it as rookies. Secondarily, most of the television networks with the cash to make a real difference across the cricket playing world had the rights to Test and ODI cricket in its fifty-over format so they barely needed to gamble with Max at all.

"The sticking point with Max seemed to be that it was too contrived to some people and 'just not cricket' and I understand that," says Crowe.

"I've always believed that cricket should be a four innings game and that we should try to provide some continuity between the Test match game and other forms as well. They designed a two-innings game to give both sides an opportunity to drag it back in the first place if they started badly — a second chance. We want the fairest way of deciding a match and I think we got that with Max cricket.

"I think that New Zealand Cricket were becoming a bit frustrated though because only New Zealand were playing it but they didn't put one cent of funding into it — that all came from SKY TV. There wasn't an overall ownership of Max, so it just fizzled out."

The death of Max – if that is the right phrase for something that never endured a full and trouble-free birth – was gradual. In 2000, the State Max competition saw it's one hundredth match in the discipline but with interest internationally showing no sign of an insurrection, the domestic programme became a pre-season curtain-raiser for fans and batsmen alike to get something of an eye in before the serious stuff kicked off.

The international Max matches were seen as perfect season-openers from some quarters as well with influential figures like Richard Hadlee believing they could assume the same prestigious place on the calendar as the Lilac Hill match in Australia or the MCC taking on the tourists ahead of a series in England.

India kicked off their tour of New Zealand at Jade Stadium in 2002 on a freezing night where the seasonally typical drizzle and light breeze combined to produce conditions more associated with rugby: ironic given that Max was intended to replace rugby in the television schedules over the summer months.

Still, ten thousand turned up in Christchurch and were treated to some vintage Sachin Tendulkar as he adapted his inimitable style to exploit the Max Zone and force 72 off 27 balls before perishing in the first innings with the scoreboard reading 108/2 in the eighth over. The Indians eked out a ten-run advantage that proved insufficient as batting became more difficult and the hosts cruised to a 21-run win.

On the face of it, it seemed like any ordinary Max International but the truth couldn't have been further away. The backdrop was troublesome with the New Zealand Cricket Players' Association locked in a stoic dispute with the national governing body that claimed the Provincial A tournament (for 2nd XI teams) and the State Max as collateral. Both were cancelled in the midst of a Players' strike – a blow for Max organisers hoping to trial the competition without the zone that many thought was hampering attempts at international popularity.

"Ironically, the players who had been so enthusiastic in the way they played Max, killed it with the strike," argues Crowe, "because time soon got on to the next year and then other things were already in place. It might be that Max cricket was five years or so ahead of it's time."

The strike may have sounded the death knell for Cricket Max but, as would later be the case with its big brother, Twenty20, the broadcasters had to be fully behind it too because the colour of media money was to be the coping stone of the short cricket house. In New Zealand, attentions had drifted away from Max and with it's new-found status as a pre-season tournament, it could hardly compete with international cricket when SKY secured the rights to the Kiwis' matches soon after the turn of the millennium.

As Joseph Romaros typed in the New Zealand Listener: "The game survived for a few years partly because SKY TV did not have the rights to regular domestic cricket and needed something to screen. It leapt at Max, praising the ultra-abbreviated version of the game in extravagant terms … Now that SKY TV screens all the one-day internationals and Test Matches played in New Zealand, it no longer needs Cricket Max." Like a prostitute instantaneously dumped by her previously eager partner, Max was ditched as an attractive proposition and left to sob with no support and it's metaphorical mascara running.

Max had taken flight outside of New Zealand too but it hardly threatened world awareness, never mind domination. Crowe's team worked with Cricket Australia to merge the brand with their 'Super Eights' competition, retaining the Max Zone but renaming it 'Super Max' to incorporate the Australians.

Allen Border became a fellow advocate of short-form cricket and joined Crowe in presenting to the ICC in 1998, formats of the abridged game to play in teams of either eight or eleven. Their booklets and pamphlets were met with a real buzz of approval, especially from the England and Wales Cricket Board (ECB). However, there was to be one sticking point and the ECB representatives remained unequivocal in their stance: "you'll never get one of those Max zones at Lord's."

Getting It Off The Square

"In simple marketing terms, we saw it in the same way as the Fun-Size Mars bar. Mars wouldn't dream of making one that looked and tasted different to the real thing and neither did we with Twenty20."

Stuart Robertson

IAN AUSTIN SEEMED TO HIT the nail on the head when he commented that Cricket Max and tradition just couldn't go hand in hand and it seemed to contribute to the creation of the halfway house brand that was to become the Twenty20 Cup for the first time in England in 2003. Whatever the successes and failures of Max in competition though, it can retrospectively be seen to have paved the way for Twenty20's existence by raising some pretty important issues to those protecting sources of revenue into cricket around the world.

Primarily, the numbers attending cricket matches were dwindling rapidly. Whilst in New Zealand, Crowe's brainchild came to the fore at a time when attendances were declining steeply even in Test Matches, England hadn't quite got that far but the counties were feeling the pinch.

Up steps John Carr, a former top order bat with Middlesex turned ECB Director of Cricket Operations. As another ex-county pro, Steve James, was to argue in the *Daily Telegraph*, Carr was the somebody who "had the courage of his convictions to keep telling the counties that it [short-form cricket] was viable at the professional level." Essentially, what eventuated in the Twenty20 Cup was the same as I had played modestly as a weakling 11 year-old behind the tennis courts at Astley and Tyldesley. Only then, few of us could hit the ball as far as "outside the circle" and we would be lucky to have parents' car headlights rather than floodlights to prevent stinging injuries if we were so unfortunate as to end up batting second.

"We got the approval of the First Class Forum to run a pilot competition for 'short-form cricket' as we knew it then, in 1999," says Carr. "We came up with a format that the counties playing first class cricket in 2000 should be split into six groups of three teams and play one home match each in a round-robin format. The counties weren't as confident and thought that dropping the Benson and Hedges Cup was a high-risk strategy so rather than replace it, the pilot allowed them to dip their toes in the water. But we decided it wasn't fair. It wasn't fair on the players to add another few matches and an additional tournament into an already busy schedule and one match per county wasn't a fair test. The media were likely to see it that way too."

Taking a step backwards and committing wholeheartedly to a competition that everyone wanted perhaps saved the life of Twenty20 before it had even been born. Instead, the steps were planned tentatively. On 21st June 1999, Glamorgan and Worcestershire were persuaded to play an early-evening friendly to test the logistics of a condensed match, played over 25 overs. Around a thousand spectators arrived to cast their eyes over proceedings – more than a fair return for a game with nothing riding on it. From the experiment, the ECB learned that the game would be better served by clipping the 'top and tail' of the playing times to leave a 5.30pm to 8.15pm game, adjusting it to twenty overs a side, as Crowe had done only this time in one innings. By bringing forward the close of play by fifteen minutes, Twenty20 matches would have the necessary benefit of finishing in natural daylight. Carr's idea had moved on a stage but it could only bear fruit because it had somebody to sell it.

"I was looking at the consumer appetite to cricket," recalls Stuart Robertson, at the time, the ECB's Marketing Manager in the Commercial Department, "and just from looking at the data from the individual counties, there was a considerable consumer decline – something like 17% in the five seasons leading up to 2001. So I worked hard to try and get the money to pick up the consumer research and see exactly why that was. There was a pot of money Channel 4 worked with as the terrestrial broadcaster at the time and we ring-fenced some of that cash to do a research study."

To get the punters in, the administrators believed that either "the product" had to improve or the way it was sold to the public had to change. Yet only a couple of years before, no such revolution had seemed necessary.

Robertson adds: "Martin Crowe came over and had a chat about his Cricket Max which had already started in New Zealand and given what had happened over there, Keith Pont and myself were asked to join a working party to see what we could come up with. David Acfield was the Chair of the Committee and I think Dermot Reeve [the former Sussex, Warwickshire and England all-rounder, later to form part of the Channel 4 commentary team] might have been on there too but the round table came to nothing. There seemed to be no real appetite to bring together short-form cricket and no weight of argument behind it."

But counties were struggling with County Championship matches up and down the land being played in eerie, secluded grounds with onlookers adding decoration between the swathes of empty plastic seats. What they needed was a financial lifeline. The four-year agreement with insurance company Frizzell as title sponsors of the domestic four-day competition was reportedly worth around £1million, hardly a sustaining amount and in 2002, Lancashire – one of the best-supported counties in England – could entice an aggregate of just 747 non-members through the gates for their three home ties in the Benson and Hedges Cup. So Robertson had a job on his hands to change the perception of cricket.

That became clear from the first stage of research he embarked upon, a 'desk audit' of attitudes among broadcast audiences that – surprise, surprise – painted a picture of the average cricket-goer as a middle-aged, middle-class, white male.

"It hardly took a rocket-scientist to work it out but that meant we weren't engaging with the 16 to 34 year-olds, women, children, ethnic minorities and huge sections from the inner city population," continues Robertson.

"So the next stage of research was the 'qualitative research' where we took thirty or so groups of people nationwide – a chunky piece of research by anyone's standards. We wanted to develop an insight into what people thought about a wide range of issues such as nicknames, coloured clothing, floodlights etcetera. The key word around the responses was 'accessibility' or the lack of access that many felt they had to cricket. Some of it was physical – where games were played, on which days and at what times. Some of it was social too because some people were under the impression that you had to be a member to watch cricket or be seconded or go in a shirt and tie."

Looking from the outside, the general view of cricket was always one of a somewhat exclusive club but now the people on the inside were getting to grips with that as well, they could chart the course for change. All that remained was to see how many people might be swayed by a change of marketing.

"We did an omnibus survey of 4,100 respondents by an in-home question-naire," recalls Robertson. "The first question was 'what do you think of cricket?' It had a variety of responses from 'I love it' to 'I hate it' or 'I dislike it intensely' but once people said that they hated it, we left it there because they were people who we put into the bracket of 'cricket rejecters'."

Robertson and his team identified that if people couldn't stand cricket then their perception was unlikely to change with a different marketing strategy so the remainder of the questionnaire was designed to find out how many people could be persuaded. Despite his own admission that branding a person either a 'rejecter' or 'tolerator' of the sport was crude, it was the best way of assessing who might be keen on going along to a game if the product suited them. Around a third of the respondents were tolerators. That meant nineteen million people could be talked into watching cricket.

Of course, they couldn't all be expected to sit through over a hundred overs in a day of Championship cricket as an hors d'oeuvre. Furthering the research, Robertson defined the game on offer to be one weighted ridiculously in favour of the social upper classes from the older age groups. When the ques-tionnaire asked for people's views on a three-hour game to be played in the early evenings of summer, there was a surge of optimism from previously luke-warm quarters.

"It's not a difficult concept and seems even more straightforward now," reflects Robertson. "It's too long and on at times when people can't watch it. So make it shorter and put it on at times when they can go. It made sense, so that's what we did."

Now that an abbreviated form of cricket had been hit upon as an idea, adding the gloss had many people purring as Robertson gathered together stake-holders in the game to glean their thoughts on what the competition should be and how it should be played. Whereas Crowe's concept was born around the desire to fill a gap in SKY TV scheduling in New Zealand, broadcasters were still going to be mightily influential in England too. Arguably without them, it couldn't get off the ground in England either so BSkyB's Executive Producer for cricket, Barney Francis, was an integral part of the panel.

SKY Sports had developed their cricket coverage since arriving on the scene at the start of the nineties but despite devoting time and money to cover overseas Test Matches and one-day internationals, they didn't have a product that seemed made for them in the same way as rival sports. In football, the Premiership went hand-in-hand with Monday night live matches and injected so much kudos, publicity and cash into the competing clubs as to make it the place to be in football. Rugby league had the Super League brand developed with the switch to summer competition in 1996 and later, there would be Premier Leagues of Darts and Snooker to fill the Thursday night slots that had become relatively quiet in terms of live sport to broadcast. Now, this short-form of cricket with the prospect of people actually in the grounds seemed made for them.

"I went in there from the outset with a few big demands," remembers Francis. "I had an idea to try to create some new things and some of them got through and some of them didn't. One of the major things for us at SKY was that the ECB had instructed the county teams that the players had to be 'miked up' during the matches and that was a very big thing for us with a new product because once something is in place, it's then quite hard for television to go in and get changes and indeed, television doesn't always want to go in and get changes. The responsibility was with us to make sure it was good television and something a bit different."

Max had been thrown out for being too gimmicky so the committee were on shaky ground in proposing new ideas for what was to become the Twenty20 Cup. Still, it didn't stop some attempts at innovation.

Francis envisaged a golden over being called by the fielding captain, where ever run scored would be doubled.

"I thought that using the big screens and the loudspeakers and an announcement that this would be 'Boom-time', we would keep the crowd involved and that it would have something different but it was a bit too radical for the ECB.

"Back then, we didn't know what a good score might be and all that but as it happens, we didn't really need it because teams have been teeing off from the start and it's been great to watch."

Stuart Robertson was keen as well but was glad to have been persuaded against an idea that would have seen the umpires holding up golden cards to the crowd to indicate the start of this 'golden over'.

"The funny thing was speaking to either Duckworth or Lewis and asking them how they would adjust their system [for rain-affected matches] based on the golden over," Robertson remembers. "Whoever it was, their face lit up and they said it would be a fantastic problem to deal with!"

Francis was also of the opinion that people would come in to watch this form of cricket to see boundaries being hit and proposed a uniform size of outfield so that teams playing at The Oval could play an identical style of game to teams at Taunton, where the playing area is far smaller. Sixty yard boundaries with an inner circle of thirty yards would have given similar parameters to those seen on the rugby grounds and running tracks of Max Cricket but the idea didn't get off the ground. Neither did the proposal of a 'Hotseat' for the next batsman in, rejected because of the likelihood of coaches and captains being as flexible as possible with their batting orders to meet the demands of all situations.

Assessing which ideas made the cut and which ones didn't for the inaugural Twenty20 competition gives us a more rounded idea of what the ECB were looking to get out of the exercise in the long-term, which was a kind of introductory guide to the world of cricket at it's most hectic, something that could inspire visitors to the more traditional forms of the game in the future. The added bonus was that people would come and pay to watch it.

"It was never intended as an end in itself but as a means of getting people interested actively in watching cricket," confirms Robertson.

"The hope was that after watching one of these games then people new to the game might go on and take in a National League game or something like that. I think we kept the standard cricket rules to keep some continuity. We didn't want to bring people in, get them to understand the rules and then come to another game that was completely different so that's why we didn't take up the two-innings matches. We did have quite a bit of fun throwing new ideas forward and I suppose reducing the time for a new batsman to get to the crease [from two minutes to ninety seconds] was one of those."

Of course, for the idea to work it would have to have the wholehearted backing of the players who were updated on just about every nook and cranny of the planning operation through their collective union, the Professional Cricketers

Association (PCA). It doesn't take an investment of thousands to realise that fans only shell out their hard-earned cash to watch sport that is played in a competitive way between two sides wanting to win. Some pundits in New Zealand claimed by the end of Cricket Max that a lack of enthusiasm amongst the players helped bring about it's downfall (not a totally credible assertion given that the discipline gave even the modest stars a chance of a decent wage for the first real time outside of the international game) and the England and Wales Cricket Board wanted to avert such a possibility on their own shores.

"We held a vote with the First Class Forum (FCF) and they accepted it by eleven votes to seven so there were still a few people who were uncertain but the beauty of it overall was that the counties wanted it," enthuses Robertson, whose fascination with Twenty20 and the progress it has continued to make since he unleashed the notion on the sporting world can only be likened to that of a doting father.

"Before the final vote with the FCF, we presented to the marketing managers of all eighteen first-class counties who were unanimously in favour so it shows that the Chairmen found it more difficult to take on board. We also presented twice at the PCA AGM so the players knew all about it and were generally all in favour of it."

With broadcasters, players, administrators and a previously untapped public all largely onside with the idea behind Twenty20, all that was needed was an ironing out of the rules and a decision on a format that the inaugural tournament would take. The minimal opposition undoubtedly helped. Some traditionalists (a sizeable portion of whom were ex-players) were opposed to change and shouted their objections from the rooftops but with the current crop of professionals eager to give it a go, trial and error became the greatest yardstick of rules that would flop or float. At the Rose Bowl, Hampshire took on a Middlesex side in a couple of Twenty20 friendlies in one afternoon and met with Robertson over lunch to go through the finer points.

"I chaired a group of stakeholders to refine ideas on what the rules would be and also whether it would take place as part of a festival programme or on a more regular basis. The key drivers were the early evenings. Budgets were reasonably hard to predict for the first year because even though we were confident that Twenty20 would be a success, we couldn't have a situation where all the counties were expected to have floodlights because we had no proof that it would take off. The fixturing was quite easy from that point of view because we had to get our geographical calendar out and schedule it around the longest day in late June. We then put together the regional groupings – big local derbies are a great driver for bringing people in from a marketing perspective. We had these regional meetings as a kind of roadshow to talk about all of the issues."

The Twenty20 Cup would emerge onto the fixture lists in 2003 with the long-standing but weary Benson and Hedges Cup 50-over competition making way. With England's international side failing badly at the limited overs table, the other one-day cup had been standardised to fifty overs to ensure the up-and-coming players actually had some experience in it. With every effort made to allow Twenty20 to breathe without the oxygen of gimmicks on the field, off-field activities were prepared in earnest.

"We decided to work on developing a brand of Twenty20 and to resist a sponsor to see if a branded competition would work," Robertson finishes.

"We particularly wanted to work with sixteen to thirty-four year-olds and thought that music and activities were an important link."

If Robertson was the concept's father, it needed a mother figure too. A former ICC employee, Paula Warren, joined the team and struck gold with the idea of staging a "Finals Day" as an explosive jamboree of cricket to finish the championships with a flourish. The baby was ready to be born.

Lift Off

"It was more of a risk to the ECB from the point of view that we cover the events they put on. I was in no doubt that it would be a huge success. I think it was more about shaking up the quite sticky domestic system, so it wasn't a risk for SKY Sports at all."

Barney Francis,
Executive Producer, SKY Sports Cricket

THE TIMING OF THE Twenty20 Cup's arrival upon the British sporting calendar was, by both accident and design, just about perfect. Coming as it did in mid-June 2003 (the first five matches survived the obviously superstitious perils of being staged on Friday 13th), the schedulers avoided a collision with major footballing events such as the World Cup (staged the previous year) and the European Championships (scheduled twelve months later, in Portugal), which swamp the English culture up to and beyond the inevitable glorious failure.

Supporters of the national cricket team also had reason to feel quite buoyant – another typically English trait as they had actually achieved little. Hammered out of sight in Australia, the Ashes had proved elusive once again and the series Down Under had only been rescued by a fairly comprehensive win in the Sydney Test: a dead rubber. They left that series on a high and would involve themselves in a fascinating duel against South Africa that summer, a series that kicked into gear the Duncan Fletcher-Michael Vaughan feel-good factor leading all the way to the Ashes win in England two years later. Yes, England had fluffed their lines in the World Cup but they had the convenient excuse of the awfully handled no-show against Zimbabwe in Harare and all concerned appeared pretty delighted to bow out gracefully having pushed Australia all the way in Port Elizabeth, not withstanding their inability to skittle the would-be World Champions from 135/8 chasing 205.

So the public were largely positive about their cricket and far from demoralised with it when the Twenty20 Cup kicked off in earnest.

The format of the first competition depended heavily on the 'derby' matches, as implied by Stuart Robertson. The eighteen first-class counties were divided into three groups of six: a North Group, a South Group and a Midlands, Wales and West Group. Each team would face the others once with three matches at home and two away, or vice versa. The winners of each section would then make it through to the first ever Finals Day, joined by a concept known in other sports as the 'lucky loser'; the second-placed team with the best record.

It also relied heavily on a decent weather cycle across the summer, "The ECB has been lucky," reflected Tanya Aldred in the *Guardian* some four years later, "had the skies emptied in 2003, as they have done this year, the whole thing might have gone down on the long list of cricketing cock-ups." So whatever Robertson, Carr and Co managed to deduce in terms of strategy for Twenty20, external forces would have a significant role to play.

As Martin Crowe was to reflect, Twenty20 "was easy for people to get their heads around because it's such an easy derivative of 50-over cricket," and many of the rules remained the same. Fielding restrictions would be placed on the first 30% of a team's innings so for the first six overs in Twenty20, a fielding captain would be limited to placing two men outside of the thirty-yard circle and would be obliged to have two fieldsmen in catching positions, fifteen yards or closer to the bat. The free-hit rule was adopted from Cricket Max (it had already been a successful feature of the National Cricket League in England) and the essentials of deciding the winner – the team with the most runs – remained. It seemed straightforward.

"When we were launching Twenty20, the key stakeholders in the media got right behind it," remembers Robertson.

"BBC Radio Five Live were down at Worcester, I think, to present their breakfast show from down there and they had a mini-game on the breakfast show. SKY took it on board as well and covered it really well."

Robertson was also invited onto BBC Radio 4's *Today* programme to explain the thought behind short-form cricket, which soon turned into a debate when Brian Close was introduced to give this thoughts on Twenty20. A staunch Yorkshireman – a by-word for conservatism in cricket circles – the 72 year-old Close slammed the whole idea, the practical damage it would do to players' technique and what he saw to be an inevitable ruination of the game. With all due respect to a man who scored the lion's share of 35,000 first-class runs, Twenty20 organisers hardly had him in mind as their ideal target audience when they first sat down to thrash out the minutiae.

* * *

ROBERTSON TOOK HIS PLACE like a proud Dad at school Sports Day with over eight thousand others at The Rose Bowl on June 13 to watch Hampshire Hawks against Sussex Sharks on the opening night. Calculator-crunching and market research was all well and good but it was the simple number of bums on seats that would now decide whether Twenty20 was a route into the sport for the 'cricket tolerators' or not.

"When we talked about accessibility, I'll never forget how many people made it down to that first game," adds Robertson. "James Kirtley ran in to bowl the first ball and I think it was a wide. I remember he ran all the way back to his mark and that was the moment I thought 'yes, that's it: there's a full crowd here and the players have got it.'"

As a seam bowler who would be treated with far more respect by the South Africans in the Test Match arena just a couple of months later (he took 6-31 on a fairytale debut at Trent Bridge), perhaps Kirtley wasn't overwhelmed at the prospect of being lined up for big shots every other ball but still, he returned respectable figures of 1-17 in the 22 deliveries he sent down as Hampshire imploded from 66/0 to 153 all out with two balls of their 20-over allocation undelivered.

"Forget all that nonsense about the Twenty20 Cup being a bowlers' night-mare," proclaimed *The Argus*. "Sussex took all ten Hampshire wickets in 12 overs at the Rose Bowl last night, but they still ended up losing by five runs in a chaotic curtain-raiser to the new competition."

Hampshire collapsed after the blustering start afforded them by openers James Hamblin and Derek Kenway but as run-scoring was eclipsed by clattering wickets, the action remained non-stop. Wasim Akram thundered out of the dugout at the fall of the first wicket and such flexibility usurped the status quo to such an extent that he was announced to the crowd as Aussie left-hander Simon Katich. Unfettered, Wasim complemented his eight-ball cameo for 10 runs by cleaning up both Matt Prior and Murray Goodwin in successive balls at the start of the Sussex reply. The Sharks wriggled obstinately to free themselves from the shackles but were wounded by the early blows and landed up five runs short.

It had been a welcome little distraction for Sussex, away from the serious business of clutching the first County Championship in their history, which would come twelve weeks later. Their captain, Chris Adams, one of the English Lions to excel on the Cricket Max tour of 1997, lavished magnanimous praise on the concept despite defeat. More importantly, the media saw justification in the pre-tournament hype.

"A near-capacity crowd of 8,500 indicated the British public were willing to buy into the concept, much to the delight of the ECB Chief Executive Tim Lamb and Nick Pyke, Managing Director of the Rose Bowl," enthused the *Southern Daily Echo*. "Cricket virgins, families, members and regular fans piled in to watch Hampshire Hawks beat Sussex Sharks by five runs…and once the cricket was over, the youngsters were allowed to clamber onto the pitch for the pop concert to yell at headline performers, UK garage trio Mis-teeq."

Now that was a coup. I can't think how many county members at the inauguration of Twenty20 would regularly flick over to the music stations to listen to Mis-teeq between the shipping forecasts but it can't have been many. The very fact that the group had celebrated a number one hit since the turn of the century put them at polar opposites to the average paying fan for county cricket but a sexy female group shakin' their booty on the outfield couldn't quite deflect all criticisms on the first night.

"Worse were the Americanisms that simply do not belong in cricket — the music that blared out to greet the fall of wickets and also the arrival of batsmen," shrieked the *Southern Daily Echo*, realising that so soon after war in Iraq had started, the mere suggestion that anything could hail from the United States was tantamount to labelling it satanic or murderous. "Not to mention the public address announcer urging people to 'make some noise'. Please. Leave that at ice hockey, baseball arenas or Judge Jules. In fact, the whole evening reeked of the need to capture an audience through gimmicks and no substance."

Such a reaction was understandable as fans of any sport can accept subtle tampering with their favourite pastime so long as it isn't made unrecognisable, comparable perhaps to a seasoned library-goer enjoying a good book until their solitude is gate-crashed by a surly youth brandishing a loud ghetto-blaster. Stuart Robertson and the ECB had peered down the line at gimmicks but decided to steer well clear. The problem was that gradually phasing things such as music and crowd participation into the act is a difficult thing to do once the game is established as then, it has the potential to meet with disapproval from people within the sport who had weaned themselves onto Twenty20 as it had started. Furthermore, if a whole new image of cricket hadn't been presented at the start then crowds may not have been explosive enough to merit a continuation of the Twenty20 Cup to a stage where such parallel entertainments could be introduced. So the umbilical had to be cut, or rather, temporarily detached for three weeks in the season.

I recalled from my days at Leeds University how Trinity St.David's Church on the fringes of the campus had been at the fulcrum of local debate when it had been given a multi-million pound revamp and opened as a nightclub called Halo. The diversion from cricketing norms on the opening night of Twenty20 felt pretty similar.

* * *

AT FIRST-CLASS CHURCHES the length and breadth of England (and in Glamorgan), it appeared all counties were singing from the same hymnsheet as Hampshire and Sussex had in the South Group opener. Whilst their game had gone to the wire and provided a bucket-load of what the South Africans would go on to describe as "sportainment", it would prove to be nothing special in terms of team scores and personal milestones but statistically, it was almost the average game.

Team totals varied wildly on different nights as early evening conditions fluctuated in the temperate British summertime and nobody really knew what scores might prove to be competitive. The par score batting first turned out to be 156 in the first season – close to eight an over, a figure that rarely popped up in the one-day internationals that were breeding quickly to saturate the market. Crowe's analysis from Max still rang true in Twenty20 – the boring bits had been chopped from the middle. The players were having fun.

"Cricket had been becoming a quite scientific and highly pressurised so there was a very relaxed air about the first year," says Jeremy Snape, the Leicestershire all-rounder who would feature so prominently in the competition over the course of the first five seasons. "I was personally intent on having a structured plan on how we were going to play it because I'd heard a few senior pros from other counties say that they didn't even know what type of team they would be playing. I wanted to catch them cold."

The Leicestershire 'Foxes' were able to pick-pocket opposition sides thanks to their preparations and won all five of their first phase matches in the Northern Section but it made for a barely credible paradox with their progress in the more elongated versions of the game. With just one win from sixteen fixtures, the East Midlanders drifted out of the County Championship's top flight and also suffered relegation in the one-day league, albeit more narrowly.

As teams the world over would discover, four-day cricket or 50-over matches had a seriously accurate habit of breaking through individuals to detect weakness and punishing them for their inhibitions. In Championship cricket, an out-of-sorts batsman often behaves more tentatively because his ability to detect the bad ball is thrown off course by the over-riding concern to preserve his wicket. Of a one-day international in 2004, *Cricinfo's* Andrew Miller agreed, analysing that "for 20 tortuous overs against West Indies, England creaked to 59 for 3 with three of the country's most free-scoring batsmen, Marcus Trescothick, Michael Vaughan and Robert Key hamstrung by the need to survive, as well as push the score along." Twenty20 has never offered such a dilemma-strewn middle ground: there just isn't time to get so concerned.

So with trouble emanating from every traditional competition (the one-day league retained a half-feeling of tradition even though many of it's usual Sunday fixtures had been shunted to midweek at the behest of SKY Television), the Foxes all of a sudden found themselves on a level playing field with their rival counties and with no scope for excessive caution.

At the top of the order, they boasted one of the world's finest stroke makers in Brad Hodge, a Victorian who surprised onlookers by not playing for Australia until shortly before his thirty-first birthday but who still averaged 62 in the first-class season despite Leicestershire's travails. Hodge was the class act and would become arguably the world's best and most consistent Twenty20 exponent in both hemispheres over the first three years. Still, he needed support to push the Foxes through to Finals Day, an event that they would occupy with something akin to squatters' rights for the first four summers of the English competition.

It came from all quarters. The quirky and vocal wicketkeeper Paul Nixon bludgeoned crucial runs towards the end of the innings, perfected the reverse sweep and reacted with startling agility behind the stumps when opposition batsmen played the same strokes. Phil DeFreitas lent experience to the cause, Darren Maddy was to become labelled a 'Twenty20 specialist' and whilst second overseas player Virender Sehwag wasn't as explosive as many expected him to be with the bat, his off-breaks were delightfully effective. Indeed, spin overall emerged as a refreshingly useful tool. In one match against Yorkshire, the Foxes were defending 174/6 and looked in some bother when medium quick opener Charlie Dagnall disappeared for 40 runs off his four overs and DeFreitas eclipsed even that, his two overs costing 25. Sehwag didn't turn his arm over but Snape and Hodge teamed up to send down six overs between them, taking as many wickets for a miserly twenty runs as Yorkshire limped home short.

"I was surprised to be honest with how well the spinners were all doing," explains Snape, "I actually thought it might have been a bit of a fluke. By the second year, I thought it was a bit of PR but the trend continued because the spinners were working hard.

"I think one of my strengths as a bowler is in taking the pace off the ball and sending down some variation. So if I think a batsman's setting himself to play the sweep, I want to do what he wouldn't be expecting me to do and maybe try to turn the ball from middle to off or fire in a quicker, low full toss. If you looked at the balls I bowled in isolation using Hawkeye [the telemetry used on television to analyse bowlers' accuracy, speed and variations] it would just look rubbish but I think you have to be flexible with these things rather than stubborn because I'm confident I can think on my feet and challenge the batsmen that way."

Leicestershire turned their poor form in the other competitions to good effect to reach the last four but the other two group winners came from totally different backgrounds. Despite finishing behind Sussex and Lancashire in the County Championship, Surrey were arguably the team of 2003 and powered by the imagination of Adam Hollioake, soared to the top of the Southern standings. Gloucestershire were the one-day kings of the time having scooped seven one-day titles in one form or another since 1999 and unsurprisingly won all of their group games in the Midlands, Wales and West division.

"When Twenty20 came out, I think it helped us that were had plenty of young and independent thinkers in the squad and we were good at one-day cricket", says Mark Alleyne, then the Gloucestershire skipper.

"The game goes so quickly that a captain can't be in contact with his players all of the time so that's an advantage. We all knew in the field that you have to stop the other team from scoring first of all because that builds pressure in itself and you know in turn that will make the opposition want to take more risks and maybe lose a few wickets too."

If Gloucestershire's opponents lived by the same formula then they certainly found it a trickier business to carry out. Aussie all-rounder Ian Harvey blitzed the first ever Twenty20 ton at Edgbaston against Warwickshire, helping himself to three figures of just fifty balls and his side to their victory target of 135 in just the fourteenth over.

Warwickshire survived the shellacking to register 202-5 on the final night and squeeze through to Finals Day as the lucky losers, which would have been a record score had Gloucestershire not simultaneously gone on the rampage to hit Glamorgan for 221/7 at Bristol: more than eleven runs an over. Twenty20 had been alive for little more than two weeks and already the bar was being inched ever higher.

* * *

THE FIRST EVER FINALS DAY in Twenty20 set a new precedent for cricket anywhere in the world. The "fun-size Mars bar" referred to by Stuart Robertson on Twenty20's inception became King-sized for one-day only with plenty of other delectable treats on show which might have been unpalatable to fans of cricket's more established forms.

That would have been given a major test had the MCC's application to stage the inaugural Finals Day at Lord's have beaten the defences of Westminster City Council, who rejected their application for the required entertainment licence to stage a pop concert and erect floodlights. It certainly would have been a shock to the residents of the often becalmed St. John's Wood area had loudspeakers and live music gatecrashed the usually quaint and serene goings-on in NW8 but instead the event was relocated to Nottingham's international venue at Trent Bridge, a ground with almost half the capacity.

The idea behind the Finals Day was to celebrate the short form of the game by cramming three matches into a day-long festival. The first semi-final would be a morning start — as it turned out, a derby between Warwickshire and Leicestershire: West Midlands facing East. The other, kicking off in mid-afternoon, pitted Surrey against Gloucestershire after which there would be face-painting, hair-colouring and general mayhem ahead of the night-time final, to be played under lights. It was meant to epitomise the truly novel cricketing environment Twenty20 was supposed to be.

That was already reflected in the numbers passing through the turnstiles to get a glimpse of shackle-free batting in their early evenings. 80,000 people watched the first eighteen matches of Twenty20 in the first season, annihilating the crowds for the Benson and Hedges Cup, rendered anachronistic in the revolution. The previous year the B and H attracted 12,000 fewer people for a total of 45 matches and for many years the 'sold out' sign for the showpiece at Lord's had been gathering cobwebs: neglected.

"You get genuine cricket fans going to it," assessed Jeremy Snape, "and they book tickets months in advance, before they even know who's going to be in the final. I got to a Lord's final once with Gloucestershire against Glamorgan and it wasn't all about cricket fans because it seemed like half the valleys were down singing Welsh songs."

Snape's Leicestershire were in action first and with captain Phil DeFreitas winning the toss, they decided to bat first.

"For the first final there was a festival atmosphere," recalls Snape, who was uncharacteristically expensive in the semi. "Atomic Kitten were playing and I think most of our lads were too busy looking in the dressing room next door rather than concentrating on what was going on in ours! But there was a month or so between the group games and Finals Day and it just makes you lose your focus a bit if you've been doing something else like playing four-day cricket in between. I think we got caught up in the razzamatazz a bit and were three or four wickets down before we knew what had happened."

In front of a full house, the bowlers who had been categorised as mere accessories in this batsman's free-for-all trampled all over common perception. Pakistan's thunderous speedster Waqar Younis induced a leading edge from the dangerous blade of Virender Sehwag and the Foxes were 12/1. Knowing that he had to keep momentum under the fielding restrictions of the first six overs,

Trevor Ward played push-and-run to Dougie Brown at mid-off and lost the foot race: 12/2.

Arriving mid-carnage, Brad Hodge launched a little cameo of his own that essentially turned the first semi-final into a contest rather than the saturated squib it had threatened to be. Intertwining deft touches with forceful carving and occasional thrashing, the Victorian even managed to force two yorker-length deliveries to the boundary before holing out to mid-wicket and becoming Waqar's third victim for an entertaining 66. Without it, Leicestershire's eventual 162/7 would have been a pipedream and Atomic Kitten might have had to indulge in some light karaoke to fill the time before nightfall.

Instead, the game went down to the last over despite rarely looking like a contest. The Foxes' well-oiled machine creaked and ultimately fell apart under the incessant artillery pressure fired by Neil Carter and Nick Knight, who defied a sluggish start to raise Warwickshire's 50 in the fifth over. Captain DeFreitas relegated himself to specialist fieldsman after his solitary over had cost thirteen runs, Jamie Grove capitulated in a nine-minute over that cost twenty and even though both openers were joined in the pavilion by Ian Bell with the total still not in three figures, the rate was enough to see the Bears into the final by seven wickets with four balls unused. Leicestershire would be stronger for their experiences.

Fabulous bowling from Waqar's countryman, Azhar Mahmood would be the decisive feature of the second semi as well as Surrey maintained their unbeaten record in a closer contest against Gloucestershire that was much more suited to the fifteen thousand or so inside the ground and the hundreds of thousands in front of their television sets.

* * *

AROUND A QUARTER OF A million people in all watched Twenty20 cricket live in 2003, a figure that defies both logic and belief when the television coverage of the competition is taken into account. BSkyB, through their Sky Sports channels, screened almost a game a night and downgraded the importance of statistic-driven graphics to make way for character and personality.

"For many years before Twenty20, we'd been covering games in the then-Benson and Hedges Cup and also in the National League so one game a day was certainly nothing new," explains Barney Francis. "In fact for us, the logistics were much easier. Rather than being on-air from say four in the afternoon until eleven at night, we can be on for a bit more than three hours and then head off to the next place to get ready for the next broadcast."

The commentary team was often a compound of current players whose counties happened not to be in action that day along with the more regular faces and voices from coverage of other domestic cricket as well as internationals. Some were insightful, colourful, relaxed and funny. And then there was David Lloyd.

"With David, we have the infectious enthusiasm," continues Francis, "and a wonderful turn of phrase that I suppose is a great bonus to Twenty20 but it didn't come out in all forms of cricket before then so it's the perfect vehicle for him. I remember sitting on a plane on some England tour somewhere and thinking about who can put the wit into the coverage. I thought 'Bumble's nailed on for this'. The ECB were adamant that this was a young person's game that kids could come to after school so we needed to bear that in mind for televising it because of course, some of our other commentary options didn't perhaps fit the bill."

A walking textbook of salient points and on-the-money analysis for Test matches and one-day internationals, former England coach Lloyd got completely carried away by the whole Twenty20 rollercoaster. His giggly-schoolboy punditry earned him the affections of the new audiences that might not have even noticed him before when they flicked on the sports channels to see how the national side were doing – a kind of modern-day Ceefax with pictures. After the first season, banners crept into grounds up and down the country proclaiming 'Bumble is God' and 'David Lloyd for PM', he coined a new catchphrase –"Start the car" – heavily accented yet continually endearing with his Accrington twang and wasn't afraid to laugh at himself whether shot by the mini-pools at the boundary edge, alongside Bucking Broncos or in distress in a Taunton car park after inadvertently filling his motor with the wrong petrol before a Somerset game.

Lloyd's excitable approach went hand-in-hand with a new on-screen graphic for incoming batsmen, replacing the standardised obsession with statistics with off-field preferences such as favourite film, sports aside from cricket and bands.

"We had things like that to humanise players," adds Francis. "Along with the mics and the chats with players in mid-game, these players were coming into people's living rooms all of a sudden and a lot of people hadn't seen them before."

Francis concedes that there were obvious commercial spin-offs for players who could show their lighter, more personable side along with their sporting prowess and the participants weren't slow on the uptake. Whilst Jeremy Snape relished the opportunity to see inside the minds of opposite numbers through the television set, other players realised that professional sport has a limited shelf-life and cricketers have moderate earnings at county level so anything that would help boost the cash-flow in Twenty20 was an unplanned-for bonus. If local companies were watching and thought of a player as a good ambassador for their product then that could lead to lucrative advertising deals or after-dinner speeches in an ambassadorial role, in which case a few quick chats with cricket commentators in between deliveries would hardly become a heavy burden to shoulder. Seen in this light, the popularising of cricket through Twenty20 can be seen to have the potential to further the earnings of players just as Kerry Packer's World Series did and Crowe's Max to a lesser degree in New Zealand.

Just as forward-thinking an innovation – if more sparingly used – was the 'helmet-cam', paraded by Surrey opener Ian Ward on the first Finals Day at Trent Bridge.

"Barney asked me to do it and I had no problems with it at all as long as it didn't interfere with what I was doing," explains Ward, who admirably wandered from the commentary box after the first semi to play in the remainder.

"It was a much lighter helmet than I was used to wearing and the whole thing was completely wireless. All of the technology was done for me so I didn't have to worry about anything and I certainly wasn't trying to be a cameraman with it. The person I feel sorry for is James Lawton, whose job it was to sit in the truck and monitor the pictures from the helmet-cam. It was like staring at something out of *The Blair Witch Project* and after a while he had to step out of the truck because it was making him feel sick!"

On an afternoon golden enough to typify the entire debut summer of Twenty20, Ward – ably assisted by a handful of practical cameos – forced the Surrey Lions into a night-time stay at Trent Bridge with an innings of 49 that was made barely quicker than a run-a-ball but was to prove an essential contribution in a game where bowlers and batsmen enjoyed more parity than usual.

Ward would always be likely to lose limelight to the likes of his opening partner Ally Brown in Twenty20, whose razor retinas combined with not insignificant brawn made his tally of just sixteen career one-day internationals for England an inexplicably low return. Brown offered his pyrotechnics again by swatting fourteen runs in boundaries with the new ball before one mow too many went straight to Matt Windows on the boundary edge off the bowling of Jon Lewis.

From then on, the innings swung one way then the other and with 162 the losing first innings score in the first game, Surrey's existence on Finals Day flickered when they closed at 147/9. The batsmen just couldn't get away. Cunning old-stager Mike Smith halted the opening quest for an avalanche of runs by limiting Surrey to just eleven runs off the bat in his four overs. Ward tried to break the shackles but soon after launching his only six was duped by Ian Harvey and lost a stump, Mark Hardinges removed Rikki Clarke, Adam Hollioake and Azhar Mahmood shortly after all three had broken into double figures and then Harvey was back to prove his all-round worth with a deception of Graham Thorpe the ball after he had inched off the mark with a boundary.

It was only ever a simple chase if Gloucestershire avoided the clanging of early wickets but Surrey battled back. Azhar took two at the top, including the livewire Harvey, to have the Gladiators in disarray, worsened by the loss of Craig Spearman and Windows. From 35/4, Alex Gidman did everything to occasion the most unlikely of recoveries but back came Azhar to thud one into his timbers off the pads and the Gladiators floundered six runs shy of their victory target.

Surrey went on to win the final but as Anna Thompson was to reflect on BBC Sport Online, "it seemed many people could not care less about who won the final – except for the Surrey fans." Why would they? Girl-band Atomic Kitten had enlivened Trent Bridge whilst the Lions and the Bears were preparing to face off in the final, leaving the females to enjoy the music and the males to marvel at the kind of beautiful, slender bodies rarely attracted to County Championship cricket. The kittens were supported by the rather less feline United Colours of Sound whose remix of the 1978 10cc hit *Dreadlock Holiday* (including the lyrics "I don't like cricket – I love it') had been adopted as Twenty20's anthem and by this time, hadn't been overplayed enough during television coverage to avoid a live rendition.

As well as the free concert thrown in, the younger members of the crowd were able to witness three matches but still leave the cricket-a-thon early as Surrey eased home with 55 balls to spare and the adults were able to ease the hangovers that were coming to many of them after a long hot day in the glare of both the bar staff and the sun. The weather had certainly given Twenty20 the perfect conditions for it's entry into the world; an uncharacteristically blemish-free few weeks for the group stages and a beautiful day for the final ensuring that all forty-eight games would provide the results that the crowds had piled in to see.

Still, the players had the prestige of 'a first' at stake with their counties and there was a piece of silverware to be won. Warwickshire won the toss and opted to put runs on the board but soon found themselves paralysed with the loss of five wickets coming with just 33 runs chalked up. James Ormond bowled with accuracy and composure to return figures of 4/11 in four overs. The game was over with only the margin of Surrey's win to fight for. The Lions were chasing a paltry 116 and suffered their only hiccup at an insignificant stage, Ward stomping his way to fifty off just 27 balls before ending a century opening stand by gifting Waqar some catching practice and Graham Wagg a wicket.

"You might imply that we had a plan but that frankly isn't true," Ward says looking back on Surrey's title. "We just went out and played the game and I know that Mark Ramprakash and I had contrasting opinions on whether we should be looking for boundaries all the time or running it around at a run a ball for a while. I think any plan that we did have was a condensed version of the way that Adam Hollioake [then Surrey captain] played one-day cricket. I think it was about the third or fourth game when Ramps just said to me 'you're dead right Wardy, this is just about smashing it out of the park'.

"A lot of it was about performing in a more relaxed environment so we would turn up at the ground in jeans instead of a uniform or a tracksuit, it made a difference. But we had no idea how to play it at the start — it just all fell into place."

The Joke's Over

"Your average purist would argue that runs without context are about as pleasant as ... well, a dose of the runs."

Andrew Miller,
Cricinfo

WHILST SURREY MIGHT NOT HAVE been surprise winners of Twenty20's first edition on the English domestic scene, many of the statistical asides beggared belief. Okay, many of the players took the chance to relax and the form tables were reversed in some instances. But of the anomalous results that cricket buffs pride themselves on reciting, the bowlers' economy rates produced detail so random that purists would swear it came from either county scorers going on a two-week bender during the tournament or cobbling together a collective game of Owzthat and letting the die determine who performed and who didn't.

Of the five men to concede a tight-fisted five runs an over or fewer, only Dominic Cork, Mike Smith and Andrew Hall could call themselves genuine bowlers whilst Nick Knight qualified dubiously having sent down just five deliveries and Durham's Gordon Muchall returned the tidy figures of 1/8 in his two solitary overs but can scarcely dine out on it for life. The players and coaching staff involved all seem to be quite cagey about the seriousness of the first competition – or the lack of it that could produce such bizarre outcomes – but the added edge was tangible in the second season.

Part of the reason behind that was the realisation across the cricketing fraternity that Twenty20 had more in common with other forms of the game then they had originally been willing to admit. One false shot still ended a day's work for a batsman. A disastrous over for a bowler still ruined a spell and offered the initiative to the opposition, the only difference from standard practice being that the length balls outside off stump that used to be the stock delivery of every county journeyman now landed in the striker's hitting zone and would often be propelled out of the stadium. The captain still had to do his homework on the opposition and where they were likely to play their strokes, he still had to minimise the carnage whilst the fielding restrictions were in place. The only difference was that the happenings would be played out in the absence of a creepy echo and the lingering feeling of nearby tumbleweed.

Having salivated over the potential of Twenty20 from the outset, the media at large felt more than inclined to give itself a mascot-sized hug and a pat on the back at it's success. In the *Wisden Cricketer*, Emma John was positivity personified: "We were supposed to jeer as the ECB spent millions promoting a competition no one wanted to see, then mock as Atomic Kitten asked Mark Nicholas what a googly was anyway, and could they see his. Oh, for shame, we were wrong. The people of this happy isle are more giving, excitable, intelligent and extrovert than we tend to assume. The ECB – God bless it – put all its chips on number 20 and the croupier, for once, was pleased to pay out."

John adds that the tournament had been a success because players had combined serious competition with fun in perfect measures but the enjoyment was about to evaporate. Casually mentioning that Twenty20 was perhaps the lighter version of the game to Lancashire's Cricket Manager Mike Watkinson almost three years later, I received a glare that he would have struggled to replicate in his playing days had a number 11 harrumphed him over mid-wicket for a vertigo-inducing six. The thing is with big crowds is that they fetch hefty expectations inside their cooler bags. And nobody wants to lose beneath the beady eyes of the all-too-rare full houses in domestic cricket.

If the players were heading into Twenty20 with more intent in 2004 then so were marketing personnel across the eighteen counties, looking to maximise the offerings of the gift horse rather than passively staring it in the mouth. Essex had floodlit fixtures so could play host to female pop artists in the early evenings in an attempt to fill the ground earlier and attract lucrative revenue through the bars. A number of counties had speed-dating sessions and Glamorgan teamed up with a travel agent to host 'beanie-or-bikini' contests, with fans wearing the best beach and skiwear winning holidays. Worcestershire got into the summer feel by planting a hot-tub inside New Road and Warwickshire enrolled a celebrity (Tim Lovejoy, the male anchor of Sky Sports' whacky and extremely popular football show *Soccer AM*) to carry out their twelfth man duties.

In preparing for the very first season of Twenty20, Stuart Robertson recalls a Lashings against Gloucestershire Twenty20 that died a death with the public because it was "seen as a beer match". But the off-field gimmicks had the safety net of a competitive and entertaining sporting spectacle so they added to the fun rather than detracted from it. Almost shuddering at the thought that the first season was some kind of honeymoon period for Twenty20, the counties made sure that standards would hurtle upwards in the second edition and that short-form cricket would make attractive bedfellows.

The 2003 formula for Twenty20 was slightly expanded upon in the second year. Each division had seen just one team progress to Finals Day at the first time of asking but that rendered many matches dead for counties who might have lost their opening game or two or even seen their fixtures ruined by the weather, which was to be marginally less kind to the tournament in 2004. So the decision was taken to factor in a quarter-final stage, leaving two teams from six in each sector to qualify for the knockout stages plus the best two third-placed teams. Just one Monday night would be added to the fixture calendar and when each county was already suffering indigestion from the hefty portions of cricket they had to swallow, tagging on another dose of forty overs was hardly going to make a blind bit of difference.

"The only thing I thought was quite anomalous [about the format that was to develop in the Twenty20 Cup] was that there was an odd-grouping in the fixtures," reflects Stuart Robertson, illustrating the second-season dilemma of balancing popularity and the counties' need to cash in with the eternal worry of overkill. "It turned out that you would play some teams once and others twice so you lost part of the simplicity of it. If a 13 year-old knows another sport and comes along to a game to develop his or her interest in cricket, they would more likely than not be confused as to why it isn't simply home and away." The intensity of the second season often left the long-term picture projected by league tables of secondary importance when pitched against three-hour entertainment.

Having faltered in the Trent Bridge semi twelve months before, Leicestershire sprung out of the boxes quickly in the Northern Group and their originality on the field was replicated off it. The city newspaper, *Leicester Mercury* ran a competition, offering a 'home-from-home' on the boundary, the winners receiving tickets to watch a game at Grace Road seated between the boundary edge and the advertising hoardings, their comforts maximised with free drinks and pizza. When Leicestershire took on East Midlands rivals Nottinghamshire, the already giddy atmosphere was cranked up a notch.

"I'd always loved a crowd", then-Leicestershire medium quick Charles Dagnall would admit, "from the time I was at Warwickshire with Trevor Penney and Alan Richardson. It was funny that when the TV turned up, Trevor always promised me that he'd get a couple of run outs and entertain me. And he could do it as well! I've always been a bit of a showman and loved the limelight.

"It all kicked off for me though in that game against Notts when I won man of the match and all that but I was only playing because Daffy [Phil DeFreitas] pulled up half an hour before the start. He had a huge grin on his face when he told me but he was definitely injured and I thought with Kevin Pietersen playing, I was gonna get smashed. We ended up batting and getting 150."

With all due respect to Dagnall, he's a player who would command an average degree of attention from your average county cricket fan. No more. He's a showman but one who would often admit that his abilities in the game were never quite as extensive as his understanding or love of it. All of a sudden, this sportsman plying his trade in front of basic audiences was telegraphed into people's homes and relished the stage on which to perform. Defending an average score against a side packed with hitters, live on SKY Sports across the UK, here was a chance to make Charlie Dagnall a known quantity.

"Bilal [Shafayat] has hit me for four with the first ball," recalls Dagnall, "and then I've come back to get him and then Pietersen first ball. Hairs on the back of the hairs on the back of my neck are standing up by this time because the whole place is going crazy."

The atmosphere was tangible through television sets across the land. Players pulled faces and involved the crowd who were hyperactive on cricket and souped-up on life by the time Russell Warren came to the crease at Pietersen's ignominious exit. With little respect for Dagnall's ten minutes of fame, seasoned pro Warren took the attack to the bowling.

"It was a group of local cricketers in the end who won the local 'paper competition for the "best seats in the house". So Russell Warren's got down and swept me for six and it's gone well over Darren Maddy who's out at deep mid-wicket under the scoreboard. One of them leapt up, ran about twenty yards and caught it one-handed. Well, the whole place has gone mental and the only person who can't stand it is me because I've just been hit for six!"

The commentators were going bananas, namely Lloyd who swapped roles as Test commentator with all its associated gravitas to short-game nutcase as easily as you and I change underwear. One ball later, he was to trill his new catchphrase "STAARRRRRT the CAARRRR!" if not for the first time in anger than for a broadcasting baptism when Warren played a nothing shot and was bowled by Dagnall who, having held his nerve admirably, snatched the match award with 4/22 in a 40-run win.

The game was hardly more significant than any other in determining the sides progressing to the last eight but it is perhaps the best forty-over example of the radical switch in the game over a fifteen month stretch. Few of those present at Grace Road would have ever felt inclined to attend a game of cricket, let alone interact in one in such a way. Had a Benson and Hedges Cup match between the same two counties been playing to a finish after standard working hours on the same day, I'm sure that most of the SKY commentators getting inebriated on the feel-good of Twenty20, would have even bothered to switch on their sets at home. The point is that a shorter form of the game had aroused latent feeling towards a sport nose-diving almost voluntarily towards the shitheap. All of a sudden, a nursery for prospective Test and One-Day players co-existed with an entertainment industry that could pull in the punters and in some cases, unearth talent for a high-pressured environment if not the bread and butter of the four-day game. As Barney Francis once remarked, it also brought otherwise profile-less sportsmen into peoples' homes and made them marketable products.

"That game against Notts kinda made me," reflects Dagnall, "because I'd pulled a few faces, had some fun and some banter with the crowd and people had caught that on SKY. When I was out of the game injured, I was used then as an analyst on SKY the season after. More than that, because SKY used plenty of current players for their coverage, it gave players a view of the other side without taking them too far out of their comfort zone because they were on about something they were used to. By that time, I'd already been working for BBC Radio Leicester for a few years but I wanted to do more of it. In fact, one afternoon when I was discharged from hospital in June [2005] after an operation, there was a guy waiting to take me up to Old Trafford to do a Lancashire game against Yorkshire."

2004 as a year of Twenty20 cricket is best seen as a year through Leicestershire eyes purely as a story of topsy-turvy emotions that best epitomises sport. Form in the four-day brand had abandoned them and there had been a mid-season change of captain enshrined in mystery to the East Midlands public when veteran Phil 'Daffy' DeFreitas was succeeded at the helm by Brad Hodge – the Victorian who would later stake a claim to be the best Twenty20 batsman the discipline would know.

"For me personally, there were a few disappointments too", Dagnall adds on reflection. In the middle of the season, Daffy was replaced by Hodgey as captain and through one reason or another, nobody thought to invite him to the final. I was gutted because he'd mentored me. He'd been there with England in World Cups and all that but I wanted him to see me in my World Cup Final. It made me sad and I genuinely believe that others were upset by it too."

They might have been there the previous year but when the four camps pitched up at Edgbaston for the second Finals Day on a searing early-August morning, the Foxes were rated fourth-favourites by many of the bookies. In the first semi, the holders and master-blasters Surrey were up against Lancashire, emboldened by Andrew Flintoff's presence and about to embark upon relegation from the top tier of the Championship, eager to conjure the spirit of countless Lord's finals in the nineties that had elevated their already-lofty status as the Manchester United of domestic cricket: in the eyes of their members if nobody else. Following such a heavyweight arm-wrestle, Leicestershire and Glamorgan could play out their game with the same stakes but somehow, less pressure by weight of expectations to entertain.

Surrey had still never felt failure in Twenty20, without defeat in any of their completed matches over the first two summers. But from that pre-school came the sternest of plausible examinations.

The Lions batted first: big crowd, gorgeous day, the dinner party of Trent Bridge 2003 transformed into a casino party for Edgbaston 2004 with each invitee eager to bring their own chips to the table.

As is his wont, Ally Brown went hard at the ball with the blade and traded in boundaries and whilst none of the strokes were as lusty and lofted as those that had made his name (Brown had once made a double-ton in a 40-over Sunday

League match for Surrey at Guildford), they were equally effective, transporting him to 32 at better than two-a-ball before Flintoff tore in to disturb the furniture and send him packing. Benning had already been dismissed by James Anderson and Surrey's quest for a competitive total was consistently undermined by the clatter of constant wickets. Rikki Clarke was out-thought by the pensive left-arm twirl of Gary Keedy, the start of a spell that yielded the last 6 wickets for just 24 runs. All out for 133, the Lions' proud unbeaten record was staring down it's self-made barrel.

If another Twenty20 trend could be detected from the first innings of Finals Day though it was that multi-tasking had crept into cricket as player focus intensified. At one stage, Lancashire's Mark Chilton was in mid-full blown discussion with the SKY Television commentary box when Azhar Mahmood swatted Keedy down the ground and Chilton eased into a skidding catch throughout which he never looked like losing control of the ball. It was a sparkling dismissal and after it, Chilton picked up where he left off in the discussion as if he'd been rudely interrupted in a pub chat. Whilst obviously painting Chilton as an exceptional fieldsman, it also denotes quite a departure from the sensitivities of the traditional game where a batsman might withdraw from facing the next ball if the slip cordon is yapping pleasantries.

"When it [the 'miking up' of players] first came out, I think people were quite keen to embrace it," reflected Chilton ahead of a 2007 campaign that he would skipper for Lancashire.

"Even though it's a competition to win and that everyone wants to win, it fits into the easy-going nature of the game and the interaction is good for everyone. The technology side of things doesn't affect you things too much when you are playing but as a captain and a batsman, I'm not keen on it.

"Although you're having a conversation, you're definitely focusing on what your job is, as a cricketer for your county. I was fielding at deep mid-on and the captain had told me to field down there so that was the job I was doing for the team. I never thought of it being an issue at all."

For good measure, Chilton's panting was audible on international television as he skirted around the boundary to run out Phil Sampson with a sensational direct hit.

"It was quite funny really", says Chilton, "that they chose to come to me at that time and then I took a catch and a run out in an over. I suppose, looking back, it was quite freaky really! And it got a lot of playback on TV, which is good I suppose!"

The thrill of the chase was more intense than seemed possible with just 133 on the board. Andrew Flintoff opened but perished after a rapid opening stand of 22 and the inability to build meaningful partnerships tainted what seemed like a simplistic path to the evening game. Dominic Cork clouted into the dugouts for six and then to the cover-point boundary to make victory attainable for Lancashire, who bobbed and weaved around the run-a-ball-needed status by the death overs. Then, the Red Rose lost their heads and wilted one run shy.

Those who want to argue that Twenty20 has all the beauty of traditional cricket found a perfect example in Surrey's narrow win. The drama at the business end of the game was equal to that in an old Natwest Cup or Benson and Hedges match in England, the nuances of captaincy and variation bowling no dissimilar to that at the death of a gripping one-day international or a tight Test Match. Experienced medium-pace bowling played it's part, spin weaved an intricate, balanced and occasionally mesmeric thread around a so-called game for batsmen. Tension dominated. For those who could take it, two more instalments remained.

"It was the hottest day of the year and we were on second", recalls Leicestershire's Charlie Dagnall, "which was perfect for us because all the fans came down to see Surrey play Lancashire in the first match and they'd all started drinking at about half 10!

"As a player, I knew my limitations and looking back, I was never going to play for England because I probably wasn't quick enough. I always wanted to get to a Lord's Final because that would be the biggest crowd I'd ever have the chance of playing to and it was a reachable goal. A day like that, for the everyday Joe Cricketer like me, would be just incredible.

"We had a good game against Glamorgan and John Sadler took a storming catch. Here was a lad who had only just been taken on to the staff and wasn't really well known outside of Leicestershire but that piece of brilliance from him had got him noticed. By mid-afternoon, there was a great atmosphere and people were off their faces. I just remember thinking: 'this is what you play the game for.'

Only, people being "off their faces" at cricket matches had never been the order of the day for the traditionalist paying his or her membership subscriptions loyally to their counties seemingly forever. A respectable appreciation of the sport was commonplace throughout my youth and the applause for a fifty or a maiden over, viewed as sacrosanct. You would rapidly be condemned in the eyes of your elders should you commit the age-old sin of wandering from your seat before the end of an over. A steward might even dish out a tongue-lashing.

Indeed, if being 'off your face' was deemed acceptable in English cricket circles then the members areas would join in with the omnipresent Mexican waves in the final sessions of a Test Match rather than inducing the once-amusing, now-stale chorus of boos around arenas. In Australia for the 2006-7 Ashes Series, those who set the wheels of such a wave in motion were threatened with ejection from the ground so drinking to excess can hardly be seen as commonplace.

On the eve of the Twenty20 Cup Final in 2004, Amit Varna (Managing Editor of *Wisden Cricinfo* in India), wrote a blog asking whether the bat had started to dominate the ball in cricket to such an extent that the equilibrium would never be restored, thus constituting a crisis in the game. One of his respondents named '0 Drakes' offered the opinion that "... the real problem looks to me like the audience has changed. The new crop of spectators are into fast-paced, high action games such as soccer, baseball and American football. In many instances they are introduced to cricket well after they have experienced these games and thus their expectations of the professional game are already developed."

The summary was perfect. The regular folk who had been keeping watch whilst county matches were played in front of nothing but tumbleweed were still curious to see what happened in a three-hour cricket match. The only difference was that armies of sports fans who would perhaps fill the terraces across the Premiership and Football League grounds of England would also be interested. Like they could rarely do at a football ground, they could watch sport and enjoy a pint. A few beers down the road and yes, there would be chanting but could cricket really struggle to deal with a bit of noise? The same noise that would always rear up in dramatic matches even on the county circuit? Any sane person could be nothing but shocked if an MCC member started belting out a terrace chant in what would be the most extreme denoting of a revolution but then again, you wouldn't expect them to buy tickets for Girls Aloud or Atomic Kitten either.

It's impossible to bracket football fans as one lairy bunch whose very presence wreaks havoc and carnage at every turn but their imposition upon the Twenty20 format is undeniable. Whilst the players almost universally welcomed the added atmosphere and banter to the stands, there would be instances where a very un-cricket like crowd would be evident to the detriment of the short-form game in England. At Southgate in 2007, the Middlesex dressing room was ransacked by thieves who stole the personal belongings of players. The away team that evening, Hampshire, returned to the team bus to find windows smashed by missiles hurled from a nearby cemetery. Whilst that is not necessarily a reflection on the Twenty20 crowd, it acts as a welcome reminder that bigger gate receipts bring with them a broader prospect of trouble-making as an obvious side-effect. That isn't unique to Twenty20 though. It used to happen in the Sunday League and disorder rears itself wherever large gatherings of people are able to drink alcohol over long periods of time. That is a social issue rather than a sporting one.

Not withstanding that, can you imagine similar unruliness at Lord's, the home ground of Middlesex? The incidents are far from representative of either English sports crowds or Twenty20 supporters but they certainly mark a notable change from the days when I became a Lancashire junior member and would happily leave my baggage – often with plenty of valuable possessions – on my seat whilst I ambled off for a lap of the ground or a chat with a mate. Events at Southgate (later played down by Vinny Codrington, the Middlesex Chief Executive) illustrated the downside of the popularising of Twenty20 cricket, or indeed any other form of the game. A sport that had previously been unquestioning of it's public now had to be slightly more suspicious and perhaps a touch less gullible. But the big, football-style crowds had to co-exist for the long-term salvation of the game and the players loved it.

"If you went and played a game of Twenty20 in the parks and nobody watched it, I guess it wouldn't be a whole heap of fun", agrees Dagnall's captain for that Finals Day, Brad Hodge.

"But if you have thousands in with lights and playing in coloured clothing it can get quite special and that's what we had. There was a trophy up for grabs that day and you never really care which one it is, so long as you win it. We were the underdogs for the final against Surrey, no question but we got home which was amazing."

The bookies agreed with Hodge: Surrey had the names and the experience at the pressure-cooker level of international cricket so why shouldn't they have been the favourites but the target of 169 they set for Leicestershire was just short in the end, Hodge smashing 77 off just 53 balls to set up a famous win.

"I got another bite of playing in front of all those people", Dagnall adds, "and because everyone who didn't support Surrey seemed to hate them, we had about fifteen thousand fans! It was great to be at Edgbaston too because I knew plenty of people there from my time at Warwickshire and the PA announcer Rex, gave me a bit of a build-up when I came on. A lot of people in there must have seen the Notts game because I got a hell of a reception. People had seen who I was from the pool game and that wasn't a thing for me but for how popular the game was.

"It was a great game too. Ally Brown hit me for a six that I think is still travelling but it was a beautiful cricket shot. Then, Hodgey just paced his innings brilliantly. Snapey says he doesn't hit sixes but he hit one with twenty still needed to win off the last couple of overs. We knew it was over then and it didn't matter that Azhar [Mahmood] was coming on to bowl the last over. David Lloyd came to me and I've never been as nervous as that and excited too about what could happen. When it was over, we didn't know what was happening and just raced onto the field.

"To win it was immense and so stirring that it made all the days playing in front of ten men and a dog worthwhile."

That last comment from Dagnall gives the general impression that more youngsters would be compelled to take up playing cricket by Twenty20. Certainly it is feasible: after all, watching Premiership football in front of full houses must turn sportsmen into aspiring footballers, if not for the atmosphere than the money that it brings along as an obvious consequence. Martin Crowe had made the comment that Max Cricket had given cricketers in New Zealand the capacity to be paid properly for their profession but here was the glory reflected as well and that is something that can never be taken away from the Leicestershire Foxes' Cup winners of 2004.

In wrapping up the television broadcast from the Finals Day on Sky Sports, former England captain Nasser Hussain made a very perceptive comment when theorising that Finals Day is a day for the likes of Darren Maddy, Charlie Dagnall and Darren Stevens. They might not have been household names but thanks to their adaptability to the early Twenty20 competitions, they were now starting to become household faces.

Tradition And A Tart

"The Lord's crowd wasn't just big, it was broad: there were more Asians than usual, more women and more girls, more jeans and bare navels, more conversation and laughter. It was a cocktail party with a match attached."

Tim de Lisle,
The Times (17 July 2004)

DESPITE BEING A LANCASTRIAN and a Lancashire fan throughout my life, it was only in 2006 that I first visited the self-styled 'Home of Cricket'. I was covering the County Championship game between Middlesex and Lancashire for the BBC, rocked up early and sat with a newspaper in the Tavern Stand, taking in the atmosphere in an arena populated only by the cleaners and the gate staff. The aura of the place was quite overbearing.

The pavilion gazes eagerly down upon the 26,000 seats as an authoritarian headmaster might watch his pupils, almost threatening all who passed into the ground to maintain the status quo and the traditional things that had made the game so loved by so many. Going back to the point made by the former Lancashire all-rounder Ian Austin: could tradition really stack up beside this new crash-a-minute cricket of the video game era?

Lord's might be a reactionary place but it has come to tolerate many of the modern nuances of cricket in recent years. 24 years after the very first World Cup Final at the venue, Australia faced Pakistan in the 1999 edition showpiece in coloured clothing, an adaptation carried through to the domestic competition finals. It was hardly revolution but maybe a reluctant acceptance of the need to progress or be left behind, without stretching to the excesses of a Max Zone as touted by Crowe and his team in the nineties. The showcase finals of domestic cricket through that decade – the NatWest Trophy and Benson and Hedges Cup – were still played in white clothing and the playing conditions made allowances for a lunch and tea break; an anachronism even at that stage in limited overs cricket.

I was in NW8 for the final of the C & G Trophy in August 2006, thanks to Twenty20, the only Lord's Final of the summer these days. The prestige of the arena remained untarnished but the full house signs were barely up even though the competing teams were Sussex – a Southern county with a base an hour away from the capital – and Lancashire, with a strong tradition of healthy, vocal support. Two weeks had passed since Twenty20 Finals Day at Trent Bridge and this all seemed a case of 'After the Lord Mayor's Show'.

Despite the nervousness of the occasion and everything it evidently meant to the two sides competing (they were also neck and neck at the top of the County Championship standings at the time), there was something lacking in the whole day. A cliff-hanger of a final that saw Lancashire come up short in pursuit of 173 thanks to a sensational exhibition of new-ball bowling from James Kirtley deserved the old style trophy presentation and champers on the pavilion balcony. Instead, a hastily erected rostrum heavily branded by the logo of the lead sponsor ushered the victorious Sussex side onto the outfield for the official opening of the celebration party, another instance of modernism and traditionalism being uncomfortable and ill-suited bedfellows.

Despite that, and the fact that Lord's didn't even stage a Middlesex Twenty20 match in the Southern Group of the inaugural competition, the ECB would later admit that their original choice as the first host venue was Lord's, a position that with the dual benefits of both foresight and hindsight appears bonkers in the extreme.

The strength of early Twenty20 was in its accessibility: players became household names and their signing of autographs and posing for photos with new fans of the game, young and old, was part of it's appeal. Yet Lord's and the MCC is as exclusive as every club should be when it can be regarded as an institution in it's own right and far from easy to interact. On my first visit, I was shown up the pavilion stairs to wait outside the visitors' dressing room, awaiting an interview for the BBC after a day of play between Middlesex and Lancashire. My shirt was neatly pressed (I'm dreadful with an iron and as a result my appearance is far from smart on occasion) and tie present and correct. Innocently, I hadn't topped it with a jacket.

"Good evening," I cheerily addressed the steward guarding the door, to which the response was a glare of dissatisfaction.

"Nice blazer, sir," he cautioned before making it clear that he was allowing me in only against his better judgment.

I felt distinctly uncomfortable whenever I was carrying out my professional duties but as a keen admirer of just about everything within the confines of the cricket field, I could hack it and be happy just to be at Lord's. But would the same stand for the casual observer and the first time visitor to domestic cricket, or maybe even a cricket virgin full stop? It was hardly as welcoming as a Leicester, Worcester or Hove.

Eventually, the 2003 Finals Day went to Trent Bridge with the locals across Westminster City Council and St. John's Wood throwing in objections against the use of Lord's for floodlit cricket with concert performances, for which an entertainment licence would be needed and not granted.

"Around the country, I'm not too sure too many of the other counties would have been too impressed to see Lord's staging Finals Day", concedes Colin Maynard, the MCC's Assistant Secretary, "not when we get twice as much major cricket at this ground than at others. There's a lot of ancillary income generated these days that belongs to the ground authorities and it's quite a lucrative event. Besides, we can't have floodlights here." (Although a floodlit match would be staged at Lord's in the domestic 40-over competition in September 2007)

In spite of the negatives to Twenty20 at Lord's, the MCC applied for a licence to stage group phase matches for Middlesex in the 2004 season, keen to make sure they weren't left behind completely in a form of the game that had made great strides elsewhere. With the games scheduled to start at 5.30pm in the height of summer evenings, "the thorny question of floodlights" (in the words of Simon Briggs in the *Daily Telegraph*) was removed from the complex equation and no significant opposition was raised to the musical accompaniment that would be boomed from ubiquitous speakers whenever a wicket tumbled or a boundary hit. Indeed, as the music wasn't performed live, it wasn't considered necessary by Westminster City Council to have a licence at all.

Surrey provided the opposition and a nervy afternoon sidled into a thoroughly pleasurable evening. Rain teased and tantalised just after lunchtime before deciding not to arrange the most despised ticket in the house by ruining the show. Old Father Time was coming to the party and was welcomed, even if he seemed uncomfortable with the invite.

"There was something about the middle-aged dad trying to boogie at his teenage daughter's party about the whole exercise", opined David Lloyd (the journalist rather than the former England Coach) in the *London Evening Standard*. "But good on him for joining in and maybe next time he'll even take off his jacket."

As Twenty20 matches go, the game was far from a classic, Surrey winning by the comfortable margin of 37 runs to maintain their unbeaten record in the competition. But with 28 fours and 8 sixes, it was compelling and novel enough in terms of the cricket and the atmosphere to get the thumbs up from some of those who may have approached St. John's Wood with a fair degree of scepticism.

"We tried to splice some interviews through the public address system but we had to be very careful about that", reflects Maynard.

"We had [television broadcaster and presenter] Mark Duerden-Smith doing that for us and he knows a lot about both cricket and broadcasting but you always have to be a bit wary interviewing a guy who's just got out for nought. That didn't work too well but we had the music and that was a big novelty thing as well because we had never had that for anything else."

The music might have been celebrated but it had also been subject to close scrutiny and monitoring. The Evening Standard reported that the MCC had hired in a private firm to regulate the noise levels and ensure the local residents would have little to object to, even turning down the volume rather than pumping it up, as Twenty20 metaphorically demands.

That doesn't necessarily make the Lord's experience a negative thing. Any sport whether football, tennis or cricket, events need to be varied so as not to become the stagnant and predictable events that many claimed 50-over cricket was churning out in verbose volumes. Rather than the soccer-style dugouts that had become the staple diet of county grounds across the land in 2003, there would be refined benches by the ropes for the players at Lord's, both to give the crowd a chance to fully visualise the squads and also because it replicated something that keen cricketers in the stands would be used to in the more modest surroundings of the club game. Onlookers questioned whether it was a subtle rebuking of Americanisms at the Home of Cricket but it was undoubtedly in keeping with the surroundings: appropriate.

The one thing about the backdrop to this game that seemed distinctly at odds with English domestic cricket was the crowd: a whopping 27,509 making for the largest attendance at a non-major match at Lord's since the second day of Middlesex's duel with Sussex back in June 1949. Over twenty thousand of those paid in advance and 1,747 were full MCC members: the amount you might reasonably expect to show up for the fourth day of a Test Match against any side other than Australia. It would have been a reasonable assumption that the gents in the orange-yellow ties would be the ones to act as THE force of conservatism and to give Twenty20 the silent treatment but in the event, they were curious enough not to offer a wide berth. Perhaps 'turning down the volume' worked in keeping the MCC members interested in the same way that keeping Britney Spears' pop music off BBC Radio 3 maintains a stable listenership.

"We couldn't have got off to a better start", recalls Maynard, three years after the Surrey match kicked off the Lord's odyssey in evening cricket.

"Members could bring their nephews and younger members of their family and being a shorter game and with attention spans not as great as they used to be, perhaps it was a better game to introduce to them. In year two [at Lord's], we also tried to lay some things on for children like an indoor school so that kids could have a bat and a bowl but as things turned out it was quite unpopular and very few people actually left their seats during the games. For all other matches, there would be people wandering around all the time but in Twenty20, there would be a rush for the bars at the interval but after that, the fans were back in their places to watch the second innings."

The first one-day international to be played in colours at Lord's was less than six years before this low-attention span variant pushed itself to the fore so the famous turf was clearly being injected with some twenty-first century verve. I wanted to see it for myself.

In keeping with the rest of the Twenty20 Cup group phase in 2007, it rained at Lord's for the Middlesex and Surrey game, making the match something of a lottery. More important to me than happenings on the field though was the reaction of the MCC members to a three-hour contest.

After the interview with Colin Maynard for this chapter, he invited me to basically judge for myself how things were going with twenty-over cricket at Lord's, sending a few members' guests tickets — passes through the gates into the inner sanctum.

That inner sanctum was surprisingly cordial and welcoming. Despite the pressing gloom and feeling of an inevitably frustrating night of stoppages, the bar flanking the famous Long Room was vibrant and filled with snappy conversation. The very British subject of the weather dominated things: how it had fragmented the Wimbledon Championships, made garden work difficult, left plans for the weekend up in the depressing air. It's far from a scientific survey but the whole Twenty20 thing seemed alarmingly low on the popular agenda: acceptance.

The 5.30pm start time was marked with the creaking of the clouds overhead, rumbling with the weight of elasticity and dropping lumpy raindrops onto the outfield: the same storm that had curtailed play yet again in the tennis down at the All England Club. The captains made their way back towards the members. On the middle tier of the pavilion balcony, several dubious jacket and tie combinations, including my own, sought comfort indoors.

The rain delay helped the 22,000-strong crowd file in from their offices and schools and thanks to the umbrellas, ubiquitous nationwide, they weren't immediately presented with a shortened game. The early regulations of the Twenty20 Cup stated that a minimum of 5 overs constituted a game in the event of bad weather stoppages but such had been the ferocity of the summertime downpours that the England and Wales Cricket Board were forced to act to prevent counties losing the very money that was keeping them afloat — no pun intended. For evening games, a 30-minute period of extra-time could be added to maximise the chances of avoiding mass refunds. An hour could be tagged on to afternoon starts, a necessary amendment after a weekend game involving Kent in the Southern Group had been crazily brought to an end in bright sunshine shortly after 5pm using the Duckworth-Lewis method following mid-match rain. The punters hadn't been happy.

The buzz returned to the Grandstand at Lord's as an announcement came of a 19-over contest with the Surrey Brown Caps batting first. Yet something was missing.

Maybe something wasn't missing but after watching thirty or forty Twenty20 Cup matches in England, there was a substantial difference to this one. As Colin Maynard had pointed out, elements of traditionalism remained and they made for a compound cricket atmosphere that was at once difficult to analyse.

The major deviation from what had become the norm in the first four Twenty20 Cup campaigns away from Lord's was in the music. Time had been no healer in the three years since the first Middlesex-Surrey encounter and still, the loudspeakers dotted around the boundary edge acted as mere decoration. Every boundary and every wicket was serenaded by a snatch of popular music but the volume was so insignificant as to murmur beneath the natural atmosphere around the ground, quite like the tones you might stumble upon in a church in the immediate prelude to a wedding or a funeral: it happens but whether or not it makes a blind bit of difference to anyone is a bone of contention.

Not only was the volume minimised but the exposure around the ground varied to construct a kind of pick-and-mix atmosphere. The square boundaries were patrolled by small black boxes but the members were shielded from such an imposition with no speaker positioned in front of the Pavilion, Allen and Mound Stands. First impressions were that rather than the father making an effort at his teenage daughter's party, he was now just peering around the door to make sure the place wasn't being trashed. Peering out onto proceedings from the pavilion gave me the impression that I was watching a totally different episode to ninety per cent of the rest of the crowd.

It was surreal but it certainly wasn't an unpleasant experience. In fact, it was quite liberating to see a variation on such a standard theme. The tradition and the tart with the customers were living together quite happily.

The game was the same kind as you would find elsewhere. Surrey started with a blistering opening attack against the new ball and the medium-fast pace that was applied to it but having threatened to run away with matters, their opening pair of James Benning and Ally Brown were dismissed and the brakes forcibly applied. One good spell of bowling still transformed the course of proceedings and whilst this actually came from the first change bowling of South African Tyron Henderson before the spinners, the innings still slewed and swayed without direction like a drunken cyclist. Henderson's four-over spell returned a county-best economy of 2-11 and had the Brown Caps on the ropes at 85 for 5 when the latest storm swept the fascinated crowd towards the nearest shelter.

The MCC appeared to demand the new game to keep hold of some form of authenticity and similarities with the cricket that people knew and loved. Scorecards retained a traditional feel only the card for this game had a pink circumference, reflecting a theme for Middlesex in the Twenty20 competition in

2007 of playing in the colours associated with Breast Cancer charities, to whom a percentage of the merchandising sales would be donated. Pink has been stylishly associated with the Italian football side Juventus and the French rugby union side Stade Francais but for cricket it represented another step away from the archaic and towards the metropolitan.

Charities were at the heart of the matter in Australia at the start of 2007 when New South Wales invited a rugby league player to turn out in the "Big Bash" and whilst the pros and cons of that are explored elsewhere in this book, the whole issue would barely matter if a format of cricket didn't exist to draw the crowds in. Would it be worth Middlesex playing in pink shirts for an eight-game campaign if the stands were as sparsely populated as for four-day cricket? The very fact that cricket had the pulling power to bring about such innovation is worthy of plaudits, even from people who believe charity should always begin at home.

Not only were the players shrouded in pink but also the pavilion stewards, classily attired in white jackets and pink ties to further give the impression that something different, special was taking place. They smiled, bade good evening and farewell, enjoyed. They also had a game to watch which unravelled with spectacular haste after the cascading rains disappeared as quickly as they had made their impact. Middlesex – the Crusaders in one-day cricket – bludgeoned a comfortable path towards their 10 over target of 73, set them by a Duckworth-Lewis revision.

The fact that Surrey had been beaten was against the form book in itself but there was to be an even bigger usurping of tradition. It never seemed likely. The stroke play of both Ed Joyce and Jamie Dalrymple was of such high quality as to ensure the result wouldn't be in doubt from the fourth over of the chase onwards so a Mexican wave, that bizarre ritual of sporting self-entertainment, breezed around towards the Grandstand and made it's ominous way towards the Pavilion. There is a kind of members pact to refer to when dealing with these situations: your backside is riveted to the seat and you await the booing of the remainder of the crowd when the wave abruptly stops. I was under the vague impression that you were strung up beside Old Father Time looking out onto the St. John's Wood Road if you joined in. Imagine my surprise when the wave rippled through the pavilion with accompanying cheers from the guilty parties. This Twenty20 lark must be special. Either that or the crowd were really bored.

To refer back to Tim de Lisle's excellent colour piece in *The Times* after the first night of Lord's Twenty20 in 2004, there seems a change in policy when it comes to the wave, proof maybe that the crowds are keen to evolve with the sport.

"The brevity of the thing is catching," he enthused. "All the children liked the jingles. Everybody enjoyed the Mexican wave; yes, even me, which may mean a blackball from the Cricket Writers' Club. Seeing what happens to the wave when it reaches the pavilion is irresistible. The answer is always the same: nothing. That's what Lord's did for decades in the face of changing times. Why stop now?"

The wave is only dressing on the sporting salad but it's indicative of a bastion of English cricket and it's acceptance that a failure to progress will probably lead to progressive failure somewhere down the line.

It would be easy to make a quite utopian deduction from the night regardless of the rain and say that if Twenty20 worked at Lord's then it can work anywhere. I think it's a fair generalisation but there are perils and potential obstacles on the road ahead, one of which had been highlighted in a Middlesex home match against Hampshire just eight days before. The crowd had been less than two thousand at the Southgate out-ground and as well as Middlesex's dressing room being burgled and the Hampshire team bus coming under a hail of stones, Hampshire's stand-in skipper Nic Pothas complained of a torrent of personal abuse raining down on the fielding visitors. The Middlesex hierarchy went to great lengths to deny the claims but it wasn't the only place where a soccer crowd was reported and commented upon.

It was great to see Lord's moving with the times, if not solely because of Twenty20 dragging it along.

Hit And Global Giggle

""It might have a place in domestic cricket to increase crowds but it should never have a place in international cricket. I have told SKY Television in the UK that I don't want to commentate on Twenty20. I can't understand why New Zealand and other countries want to adopt it as a new competition. The idea is crap and it's all bullshit."

Michael Holding,
quoted in The Age (February 2005)

LORD'S ADOPTED THE COLOUR-CODED Branding of cricket a good twenty years after Kerry Packer's circus had forced the style upon a divided public. The fact that Twenty20 cricket was played under the gaze of Old Father Time just thirteen months after twenty-over contests were introduced to the English games goes some way towards cooling the view of the MCC as a reactionary body immovable amid the prospects for change.

The momentum of fast-food cricket was accelerating and whilst the counties were having a good time of it in England and the South African franchises were bubbling along nicely, it seemed only logical to play an international in the very near future – perhaps much sooner than some expected.

The guinea pigs were the ladies of England and New Zealand, who could hardly have locked horns in more quaint surroundings after pitching up at the sleepy seafront resort at Hove for an international in August 2004. *CricInfo's* Andrew Miller summarised it as having "an air of contented decrepitude" and also chronicled the event as having failed to capture the popular imagination, with a crowd estimated to be a long way short of four figures. But whilst Twenty20 might be about short cricket, this landmark match should not be judged by short-termism.

For starters, the women's game has some distance to go before emulating the levels of popularity and publicity of the men so even the residents of Hove might find a Chris Adams or a Luke Wright more instantly recognisable than a Charlotte Edwards or a Claire Connor. There's no real evidence to suggest that a standard one-day international between the same sides and at the same venue, would have been much more densely populated that day, neither that a Women's Test Match would have pushed more bums on seats. To broaden the point, for all the recent success of the male game across the county (Sussex won the first County Championship in their history the previous year), their Twenty20 play in the domestic cup competition hadn't been compelling enough, or perhaps successful enough, to implore fans to re-attend, certainly not on the same level as Leicestershire, Somerset and Surrey in any case.

With the benefit of three years of hindsight, the point of the match was as an ice-breaker and it was successful enough in that, aided by the useful coincidence that events on the field mirrored the trends that players, administrators and fans had enjoyed before and would do again in the future.

New Zealand batted first but they were barely able to exploit the music speakers employed to regale every boundary. In the very name of equality, the ropes were maintained at the distance that the men would expect them and on a big field and with the surface slow, the White Ferns managed to run the ball to the fence just twelve times in their allotted twenty overs, yielding them a highly competitive 131 for 8.

As Andrew Miller pointed out, "most of these musical interludes came when Rebecca Rolls was seeing off the seamers early in New Zealand's innings, and it was only when the pace was taken off the ball that England hauled themselves back into contention." As the likes of Jeremy Snape took no time to establish in Twenty20, the versatility of the spinner bowling well in the competition was to become the most prized and valued asset. The top three batswomen hit three boundaries apiece and then, with the softer ball and the seamers removed, only three were cobbled between the remainder. The main beneficiary was the gutsy off-break bowler Rosalie Birch.

"I have a lot of fond memories of it because I think I was player of the match on my home ground and in front of the television cameras," says Birch, "and I know it was the same for a lot of the other girls who were local as well. The wicket turned a bit and spin has often been the way at Hove anyway but at the end of the day, my catchers on the boundaries had to help me out a bit and they did it well: I suppose that they had to be in the right place! We've learned a bit now that 120 balls in an innings is a long time and I'm not quite sure we knew how to play it back then. It was all a bit frenetic whether you were bowling or batting but if you get into the mindset as a batting team that it's all a hurry, you can get out and commit the mortal sin of not batting out all of your innings."

New Zealand avoided that but subsided in a fit of confusion against the twirlers, caught between manipulating the strike, using the outfield or clearing it. Birch finished with figures of 4 for 27, emboldened by her decision to throw up the ball in temptation and the athletic support she received in the field.

The same could be said of New Zealand's left-armer Aimee Mason who cleaned up with 3/27 and was delightfully accompanied by the stingy Rebecca Steele. The spinners put the skids under England, who finished nine runs shy but as it went to the very last over, even the game itself as a spectacle can be seen as a success, even if fewer than 700 turned up to witness the historic event in person. More would be expected in 2009 if plans to run a Women's World Twenty20 parallel to the main event are approved.

Perhaps there's something in the perceived liberalism of New Zealand society that allowed for it but the first men's international in Twenty20 was scheduled for the following domestic summer in the southern hemisphere, when Australia would drift across the Tasman for a full tour and wedge a shortened game in on the way.

"I think New Zealand can be like that," says NZ all-rounder Craig McMillan by way of endorsement. "Unfortunately sometimes people are quite sceptical about new things but change can be good and things end up working out quite well. Already, it [Twenty20] is really popular and people are warming to it. In New Zealand people might start off by playing twenty over cricket and then move on to longer games, maybe even the Test Matches."

Five figure crowds might have just been apparent in Super Max Internationals but only twenty-six months after the last chapter of that mini-episode in cricket history, a full house jammed in to Auckland's Eden Park, the place where Martin Crowe's heroics had almost taken the Kiwis to the World Cup Final in the late summer of 1992. The man who step-fathered three hour cricket was present to witness yet another fresh start.

"I was commentating on the first Twenty20 international," recalls Crowe, "but by that time I'd already resigned myself to the fact that what I'd put together with SKY TV New Zealand was ahead of its time. There was no bitterness or anything like that from me and I had slowly worked away any frustrations."

The match came after only two editions of the competition domestically in England so much sooner than the first one-day international had followed the launching of that format. Crowe had railed against the fifty over game becoming boring in mid-innings and many an observer around the world had labelled a seven-hour sporting contest as an anachronism given the 'here and now' pace of modern life around the contemporary, leading cities. Maybe Twenty20 would come to have it's variant on the relatively dull periods too in time but as a newcomer on the scene, the patriotic party-goers to the maiden international mini-epic were all eyes and few looking to cast complaints.

"We probably had half the team who had never played it before and the rest who had played it in England," reflects Australia middle-order batsman Simon Katich, one of those present on the opening night of Twenty20 with the Hampshire Hawks side.

"Guys like Glenn McGrath had never played a game of Twenty20 so those of us who had offered a few thoughts up on how to go about it but there were really experienced internationals in that dressing room who had never played Twenty20. Thankfully, we got a big score on the board and blew New Zealand out of the water so that didn't really matter all that much.

"I think what was special about the night was that the Kiwi fans absolutely gave it to us – there's always a bit of humour when we play New Zealand and always a volatile crowd too. But the funniest thing was seeing some of the Kiwi guys in full eighties gear and I think Hamish Marshall had a big perm on and a few of the guys had handlebar moustaches too. I'm not sure how much we knew about it because our guys just rolled up and we would have had a bit of fun as well! I think Michael Kasprowicz might have tried to imitate Dennis Lillee at one point with the headband on and that's what the whole thing's about in Twenty20, entertaining people."

Constantly flicking through my research for this book, I was reminded of Stuart Robertson's words of warning after he unleashed the Twenty20 monster/juggernaut (delete depending on your point of view). He was keen to make sure that twenty-over matches weren't perceived as gimmick-ridden beer matches and a few of the more prissy pundits on either side of the Tasman Sea were mockingly critical afterwards along those very lines.

Yet how can that February evening at Eden Park be seen as anything other than solid sporting entertainment? Here were two of cricket's major rivals toughing it out in a format only seen before on soggy days in the international game, after which few people are ever in the carnival mood. They fielded the strongest of strong sides: Ricky Ponting lassoing 98 off just 55 balls, Katich himself finishing strongly with 30 off 25. Here were the crème de la crème, the Australians, as you've never seen them before: for one night only. The crux of the matter from a marketing perspective and a longer term one was that the 120-ball thrasharound adhered to all of cricket's principles. The only adultery committed on the laws of the game lay in the time allotted to play it.

McMillan takes up the story: "It was certainly very different! Of course we usually wear the black shirts but we had much tighter, beige kits, going back to the uniform of the mid eighties. There was a real retro feel to it and even though we were heading into the unknown, it was all about enjoyment and that's pretty much how it's been since. Of course, we were disappointed with the result because Australia were pretty dominant and Ricky Ponting had a great night but it was fun, even though we hadn't quite worked out how to play it."

Like Max, the relatively small nature of the outfields in New Zealand's international venues lent themselves to a successful party atmosphere. Although it's been refined in a number of ways since, cricket fans and newcomers to the game alike relished the initial suggestion that stumps would be flying everywhere and batsmen would swing from the hip in a manner that would qualify them for the Augusta Golf Masters, right from the word go.

They got their wish in Auckland if not the result. Australia racked up 214 for 5, twenty-four more runs than England had managed in the first ever one-day international at the Melbourne Cricket Ground 34 years previously, a game played over forty overs (of eight balls each as opposed to the modern six) rather than twenty. Openers Adam Gilchrist and Michael Clarke had both perished inside the first eleven balls but the Aussies, sporting retro canary yellow themselves in an ironic, if unintended, hark back to the days of Kerry Packer's World Series, already had 21 on the board by that time. Their pace would be unrelenting thanks to the incendiary Andrew Symonds and Ricky Ponting, the skipper stranded at the end unbeaten but two runs short of marking the landmark match with a ton.

Ponting landed five sixes (there were twelve maximums in all) and whilst the Kiwi bowlers might have cowered at the willow-wielding from 22 yards, it was certainly what was needed to kick off life on the global stage. Who knows what would have become of Twenty20 had it been born among sodden spectators in England with the party speakers cut away from the mains socket. Perhaps worse even than the parade being ruined on would have been a series of games going the distance but ending with one side winning comfortably chasing a low score. After all, every new idea in any walk of life needs a vitalising start to give it impetus and, to steal a theatrical phrase, keep people wanting more. Australia provided the pyrotechnics with the bat and even though the hosts were always behind the 8-ball in their pursuit, Scott Styris cannoned the ball to all parts to make sure the margin crept below the 50 mark.

The match ended with amusement as Glenn McGrath ambled to the wicket as if to bowl the final ball underarm to Kyle Mills in an echo of the famously controversial Trevor Chappell moment from 1981. The crowds got the joke and having reverted to a more orthodox delivery style, McGrath had a bit of a laugh too as their man Mills was caught five yards in from the boundary.

The moment was indicative of the whole, light-hearted night which started with a now famous photograph of Aussie captain Ponting tweaking the facial hair of his opposite number, Stephen Fleming.

But amidst that, the spirit of tough competition was hardly well disguised. So dominant a force are Australia in world cricket that fans of Twenty20 almost beseeched them to get off to a flyer in their first international so that the punters would take it seriously on either side of the Tasman. Their intent was spellbinding and the normality of their routine dismantling of New Zealand was such that few could doubt that whatever the format, the cream always rises to the top. Australians crave that competitive edge and even if many were yet to be sold on the idea of twenty-over cricket, the success of the introductory match couldn't have done any harm.

The New Zealand press were not immediately sold on the idea. In the *Herald*, Richard Boock scribed a piece headlined "it might not be real cricket, but it's fun," which at the time seemed like a sure thumbs-up but increasingly seems with every passing day since like a backhanded compliment.

Wrote Boock, "The Twenty20 concept, launched as the possible new face of popular cricket, was almost lost in the sea of dress-up and music, and it would be no surprise if it was finally reduced to Eleven11, then Seven7 and finally Zero0. The suggestion is that in time, the players could just come to the entrance of the tunnel, wave briefly to the cameras and then let the crowd get on with the real business of having a party."

It wasn't lost on Boock that with 29,317 teeming inside Eden Park, there was now at least a sufficient crowd to throw a decent bash.

So the fans needed to warm to it if they were to throw the big bucks through the turnstiles and in turn, convince broadcasters worldwide that fans would want to watch their 'product', as cold, calculating and uncricket-like as that phrase may be. However, both old and new spectators would find it tough going to give Twenty20 a chance if the players weren't getting wholeheartedly stuck in and the showmen past and present both appeared keen after the ice-breaking international.

Former New Zealand wicketkeeper Adam Parore was one of those to give the initial seal of approval but perhaps not for the prominent reasons that would become apparent further down the Twenty20 track. Basically, Parore was fond of what lessons could be learned to improve the flagging breed of the 50-over game.

"For years teams have dragged their 50 overs out for three and a half hours," lamented Parore in his *New Zealand Herald* column, "not because they need to but because they can. The ICC, who will have watched Australia's 44-run win over New Zealand with keen interest, should immediately drop the time limit per innings for 50-over internationals back to three hours.

"Ditch the drinks breaks and stop people running on the field every other over. What a difference that made to the speed at which the game moved along. If they're looking to jazz up the 50-over game, that's an easy first step. Get a game over and done with in six hours rather than eight."

Parore's argument would prove prophetic in the global domestic matches, although in the lead-up to the first Twenty20 World Championships in September 2007, no international team had played either regularly enough or often enough to get into the habit of rushing around between overs and hurrying to the crease as a new batsman at the fall of a wicket. The benchmark would be set in England but the trend would take three years to make a difference to 50-over cricket across the board. By 2006, the domestic one-day competition there saw teams get through their allocation of 50 overs regularly in three hours, even though thirty more minutes were scheduled. Fielders would be more alert to what their captain expects of them and where they need to stand for a certain batsman at different stages in the twenty over innings – that was carried over. Spinners worked their way through their spells quickly, confusing the batsman and cramping up his thought processes so that six balls will have passed before he's even realised who's stood where in the outfield. The Victorian Brad Hodge, renowned for his batting, admitted that he'd developed as a bowler by accelerating the game.

Parore also raised a point that might have seemed fairly hair-brained at the time but has been fully vindicated since: that the best cricket players in Twenty20 would be the ones who excelled at longer forms of the game. Ponting's 98 off 55 balls that night in Auckland was concrete proof, after all, he didn't throw the textbook out of the window and slog like a village batsman. Arguably though, he helped to redefine what a 'hittable' delivery might be. Where line and length used to provide the bowler's safe house, it just opened up a hitting zone to batsmen in Twenty20 who could then use strength to hit cleanly through the line of the ball. Phrased like that, there isn't too much of a disparity with the standard coaching manual and its illustration in the form of twenty-over cricket.

The batting repertoire was being extended by that good friend of experimentalism: necessity. With so little time to post a target, the leading players sought to score through peculiar areas and thus, the best bowlers were the ones who could vary their line, length and pace enough to make sure they wouldn't be clattered away. No surprise then that the Australian quick Brett Lee, one of the best pacemen in ODI cricket at the time, came to the fore that night in Auckland.

Of course, part of the reaction of both media and supporters to Twenty20 focused on what part it should play in international cricket in the coming years and on this, almost everyone willing to forward an opinion seemed unanimous: we couldn't have too much. Parore warned against killing the golden goose and along with many others ventured that the quality of cricket on show was actually "pretty ordinary" if entertaining. The Australian media were even less restrained in their appraisal despite victory.

"I'd see it as an ideal introduction to incoming tours each season," summarised Parore.

"England have the Duchess of Norfolk's XI at Arundel Castle, Australia like kicking off with a festival game at Lilac Hill outside Perth. Why not Twenty20 in Auckland and retain the beige? It would be a distinctly New Zealand way to welcome the visitors."

Parore's thoughts didn't fall on deaf ears. After their Trans-Tasman escapades the Aussies were shaping up for the defence of their Ashes urn, a trophy they had grasped comfortably since 1989. A traditionally heated rivalry would be stoked up further by a Twenty20 game against England at Hampshire's Rose Bowl.

* * *

LIKE THE NEW ZEALAND-AUSTRALIA affair, the 'Ashes Twenty20' was a win-win situation for all concerned. The players got a run out against top class opposition ahead of the one-day triangular series that was to act as forerunner itself to the five Test Matches. And both broadcasters and marketing chiefs alike were onto a winner by staging an Australia game at a new venue starved of international cricket at it's most popular format.

Excitement fizzed around homes across the nation: cricket had barely been this popular in England, certainly not in the era of Premiership football, and now there would be confidence in the national team as well, in good form since the Ashes were conceded Down Under in 2002-3.

The canny guidance of Duncan Fletcher, the captaincy of Michael Vaughan and a stable set of performers with both bat and ball led to a stunning home series with South Africa, an away mauling of West Indies and a winning streak of seven straight tests in the 2004 summer against New Zealand and the Windies again. The litmus test of course would be combat against the best side in the world. In all forms of cricket.

They could play Twenty20 too as they had shown in Auckland but if Plan A went wrong for Australia, you couldn't tell in the run up to the Rose Bowl whether they would have a plan B. Few were au fait with the game unless they had learned their trade in England (there was still no domestic competition in Australia by this time and when it did come, it came slap bang in the middle of the annual triangular series of one-day internationals across the country). Andrew Symonds had played a bit and been explosive at times with Kent, Simon Katich was there on the opening night at the very same ground but overall, experience was thin on the ground and that was just about the case in the England side, where most of the squad couldn't play for their county sides at the height of summer in the Twenty20 Cup because their ECB central contracts demanded their presence for the national team.

So with all that in mind, what came next was extraordinary. Not only were Australia forced onto the distinctly unfamiliar territory of the back foot but England's swagger that pervaded every aspect of their performance was so pressuring and their victory so comprehensive that some commentators were later to reflect upon it as the defining moment of England winning the Ashes three months later.

That itself is a matter for huge debate. Yes, the Twenty20 performance was good and the game itself was fun but in a summer of twists and turns, it hardly provided the point of no return for Ricky Ponting's side. The Aussies were blitzed at the start of the triangular tournament and even lost to minnows Bangladesh at Cardiff's Sophia Gardens thanks to an accomplished century from Mohammed Ashraful, yet still they maintained the composure and the class to share the series after a tied final at Lord's and then win a separate mini-series of one-day internationals against England. The Aussies strolled to victory in the First Test at Lord's after a first day wobble had seen them skittled for just 190. The series was turned on its head from the Birmingham Test onwards. Still, like the first Twenty20 international in New Zealand, the English authorities hoping it would become a long-term thing (and perhaps the Australian authorities desperately craving close competition from their rivals) needed a good first night. They got it.

"We just wanted to be very aggressive," says Marcus Trescothick. "Obviously it was the first game of what would potentially be the biggest series of our careers and it turned out to be that way as well. So we just wanted to be positive, vocal and in their faces really because here was an opportunity to stamp your mark on the rest of the summer."

England got the opportunity to set the pace when their captain Michael Vaughan won the toss and sent Trescothick and wicket-keeper Geraint Jones out to open the batting.

"Well you have to be positive and use the first six overs well when the restrictions are in place on the fielding team and that's partly why Geraint was up there, to take advantage of those. That sort of took the pressure of me a bit because I could then still set out to bat through the twenty overs."

Australia's side was as close as possible to their best available line-up with a one-day triangular series against the hosts and Bangladesh coming up and Brett Lee was generating a great deal of pace in his opening spell. Whilst his strike bowling proved expensive though, Glenn McGrath was the skinflint at the other end, conceding just two runs in his first over before getting rid of Jones in his next, an upper cut to Michael Kasprowicz at third man ending a dainty little knock of 19, mainly accumulated in a rapid spell of four boundaries.

It was the ebb and flow of most other sports and most other cricket types; England would nudge ahead in terms of momentum and then be hauled back in towards parity. Andrew Flintoff arrived at the crease at the fall of the first wicket and managed a run a ball whilst finding his feet but was undone lofting Kasprowicz in a bid to exploit those restrictions and holed out to Andrew Symonds at mid-wicket.

"I wouldn't have said that it helped us a great deal that Twenty20 had been played in England before that game because those of us with the central contracts didn't get to play too much in domestic leagues because of our international commitments. I'd only played two games of it I think before I played against Australia."

Trescothick used the Rose Bowl outfield to good effect too in finding the fences and also forcing good value from his strokes and the left-hander had the useful ability to drop anchor too if his partner was willing to take on the role of accelerating the rate. Joined by Kevin Pietersen, the five overs after Flintoff's dismissal yielded fifty runs but when Pietersen's cameo was ended by Michael Clarke's part-time spin, Trescothick for 41 and Michael Vaughan (golden duck) soon followed and equilibrium had been restored at 109-5 in the fourteenth over.

Equilibrium wasn't what the vocal Rose Bowl gathering were interested in though and their chanting and cheering was thrust up a few notches in volume by a fabulous partnership between Paul Collingwood and Andrew Strauss that laid a respectable platform for the home side. Strauss was canny whilst Collingwood started to carve himself as the natural 'finisher' for England in one-day cricket with manipulation and butchery in equal measure for an innings of 46 made at a rate of almost two-a-ball. Australia were left needing 180 after Collingwood was caught by Ricky Ponting off the bowling of McGrath from the final ball of the innings.

There was no hint of the ensuing carnage when Adam Gilchrist and Matthew Hayden eked out 23 of those runs from the first sixteen deliveries of the reply but suddenly, the green and golds were buried under an avalanche of pressure and under its momentum, they couldn't lift their head above the surface. Darren Gough opened up the rout by having Gilchrist caught at mid-on. Pietersen celebrated the catch and on the instruction of Vaughan, wandered around to mid-wicket for the next ball to Hayden, who picked him out to make it 23/2. Elation was unconfined.

"The atmosphere and the crowd was just amazing – you always get that from crowds in that part of the country – because it was like a football match, a goal being scored every five minutes. Everybody was buzzing. I'm not sure we could quite believe what was going on because it was just a special day. Everything went to the plan that we had and it really worked to our advantage because it just put us one step ahead before the Ashes."

Trescothick's words helped to push along the feeling that Twenty20 played third fiddle to the other forms of the game in the minds of the players that night. Australia would maintain that stance until the eve of the World Twenty20 in 2007. Yet with the all-conquering Aussies on the brink of meltdown, no Englishman in Southampton that night would want anything other than Australian blood – capitalise while the chance was there, the Test and ODI games may be very different.

The visitors hardly had chance to assess the damage done in their mini-slump before it worsened. Gloucestershire seamer Jon Lewis, on international debut, forced an edge from Clarke in his second over and soon Symonds was sent packing too too, a fourth wicket in seven balls.

The locals were now boisterous and the crowd felt confident that they could soon take the all too rare opportunity to gloat over their rivals, to do unto them what had been all too familiar in reverse on trips Down Under since Mike Gatting famously bellowed out the uncomplicated 'Barmy Army' anthem at the end of the 1986/7 Ashes. Those not wanting to jinx matters didn't take long to be persuaded because Australia were seven down by the time the fielding restrictions had been relaxed. Mike Hussey steered Gough to a wide slip, Ponting decided to go for broke and holed out to extra cover off Lewis who had four-for when Damien

Martyn was felled by Trescothick's assured catch in the cordon. 31 for 7. All of the wickets had tumbled for just eight runs in twenty balls and the game had been won, the power vacuum between the two nations sucked undeniably England's way.

Australia might have treated it all as a bit of fun but being bowled out for 79 to fall to a 100-run defeat really thudded into the proverbial box of a competitive nation, a nation that would soon find itself reluctantly embracing Twenty20 fever.

McCricket And Australia

""I'm sure that deep down, a lot of New South Wales players will have been frustrated too because at the end of the day whether you're playing cricket, snooker or lawn bowls, if you're a competitor, once you step onto the field you just want to win."

Brad Hodge,
Victoria

THE NUMBER ONE SPORTS GROUND in Newcastle raised possibly its biggest cheer of the day but the New South Wales team the fans had all wandered along to support were in a spot of bother. They needed to beat South Australia to have any hope of emulating their feat of twelve months before and making it to the final of the 'Big Bash', Australia's domestic Twenty20 Cup. 13 runs were required off the final seven balls and after the run out of Tim Lang, the new man wandering nervously to the middle was the unmistakable figure of Andrew Gary Johns, one of the best rugby league half-backs in the world: maybe ever. Just up the road from his NRL club, the Newcastle Knights, this was his crowd and they desperately wanted him to succeed.

In the year of the inaugural World Championship of Twenty20 it was almost inconceivable that such a marketing ploy could come to fruition. An Aussie dollar per ticket would go to Johns' preferred charity (Ronald McDonald House) and the marketing departments undeniably believed his presence would draw bigger crowds to the NSW Speedblitz Blues' two home games, the second of which would be against Tasmania at Telstra Stadium (the venue for the 2000 Olympic Games and the 2003 Rugby World Cup Final) three days later.

Australia had to embrace the concept of twenty-over cricket as the sport's most successful power of the era, or its global street-cred would plummet, especially in light of the sub-continental reluctance that we'll explore elsewhere in this book. Many commentators on the game Down Under were lukewarm at best though and the enlisting of a rugby league international to play for his state at the expense of players hoping to better themselves for the ultimate goal of playing for their country, did nothing to improve their mindset.

Part of the problem as far as the pundits were concerned was that not all of Australia would go out of their way to watch Andrew Johns play rugby league for his country and far fewer would tune into a domestic game in the NRL. The sport is heavily concentrated in New South Wales and Queensland, with only two franchises – the highly successful Melbourne Storm and the colourful New Zealand Warriors – hailing from outside those two states, meaning that rugby league doesn't share the same appeal as cricket, rugby union and Aussie rules, although the latter is dominated by Victorian interest. The national cricket team could even be said to unite the nation as far as sportsmen are concerned which goes a long way towards explaining why Adam Gilchrist, Michael Clarke, Brett Lee and Ricky Ponting seemed to appear on every second television commercial in Australia during the 2006-7 summer.

Now, "Joey" Johns was to try and wow the crowds with Simon Katich (still on the periphery of international selection himself) in a last wicket stand needing 13 runs at almost two-a-ball. The first delivery would be sent down by Dan Cullen, the 22-year old off spinner. Johns took a huge swing and missed: 13 off 6.

"It was scary with the game on the line," said Johns in the press conference after the match, "I suppose I didn't see the first ball, I don't know what he [Cullen] bowled. I didn't want to get down the other end, I didn't want to get out and I didn't want to get hurt," quite a statement given that Cullen's pace was somewhere around 50 mph (80 kph).

"I said 'look mate, whatever you do we aren't taking any singles,'" reflects Katich.

"We knew the quick was coming on at the other end. He was actually out stumped off that first ball and the umpire wasn't game enough to give him out and I know the South Australians were fuming because then we still had the chance to win the game with me on strike in the last over. Unfortunately, I hit the first few balls straight to the deep and told him we weren't running because I thought we'd get run out coming back for two. I hit a four but we couldn't win the game so the crowd weren't too happy with that but I tried to do the right thing for us. If he couldn't see the spinner bowling 80 kph, he wouldn't have seen Ryan Harris bowling fifty quicker and bowling well too."

A debate that had been pretty fiery from the outset now had its flames fanned. South Australia won the game by 8 runs with the boundary from Katich the only scoring stroke in the last over of a run chase.

"For 39 overs it was pretty entertaining," former Australian international Geoff Lawson told the press, "but the final over was hard to comprehend. It was very disappointing as a former NSW player to see NSW not trying to win. The last over was a farce. There was a bloke on the sidelines who's trying to get into the Australian one-day team."

Lawson unquestionably had a point but if anything could be a saving grace to the New South Wales officials, it was that their team had been pretty abject in away defeats to Western Australia and Queensland earlier in the tournament and virtually consigned themselves to an early exit irrespective of events in Newcastle. The other matter to factor into the equation was the fact that something similar had already happened 47 years earlier, long before even ODI cricket had been a glint in the administrator's eye.

Explains Johns' agent, John Fordham: "It came up over a long lunch I had with David Gilbert, NSW Cricket's CEO. I pointed out to David that back in 1960 the great rugby league player of that era Reg Gasnier played for a NSW XI against the touring Fiji team. Gasnier's team-mates included Richie Benaud, Jim Burke, Neil Harvey, Norman O'Neill, Alan Davidson and Keith Miller. Because the NSW Cricket Association (as it was then called) had sanctioned the game, a precedent had been established. Mark Taylor [a Cricket NSW board member] strongly supported Gilbert's recommendation at a subsequent board meeting."

The contrast in situation between the two instances were immense and in the modern era of busier lifestyles and the craving of intense competition that Twenty20 was ultimately invented to satiate, the Johns experiment was ill-judged despite the positives for charity. What it also did was to unearth the latent scepticism for Twenty20 among the Aussie press, pundits and some sections of the public.

"His call-up is only for a 20-over match and no accompanying stunt can be more puerile than the game itself," raged Andrew Ramsey in *The Australian*, adding that the formal recognition of the 'KFC Big Bash' from Cricket Australia meant spectators deserved better than a pro-celebrity match for their $15 entrance fee. In the same newspaper, Mike Coward felt the inclusion of Andrew Johns to be "an insult to the intelligence of cricket folk, not to mention those who have had the honour of playing for their state."

The exercise received plenty of publicity long before the start of the Australian domestic season, officials perhaps mindful that with the much-hyped Ashes series hitting their shores from early November, the second 'Big Bash' had the potential to be asphyxiated. Still, the quaint little ground in the West Sydney suburb of Newcastle had 10,652 souls wandering through the turnstiles for a glimpse of 'Joey the cricketer' rather than 'Joey the scrum-half'. Whether they would still have turned up with a genuine cricketer in Johns' place is unquantifiable but they were certainly not turned off at the prospect of the game being less competitive than usual.

Three days later 18,464 excitable fans welcomed Johns to Telstra Stadium, a venue he had graced so often in the deep blue of Newcastle and the sky blue of NSW in Origin Series rugby league but now he was far from his area of expertise.

"He's been a champion in his sport for a long time now," says Katich, "and a lot of the guys really idolised him because he's so highly regarded in Australia. A lot of the guys liked just sitting down and chatting to him and our game of touch footy in the warm-ups got a whole lot better with him in there! The guys got a lot from him and it was just good to see how he goes about his preparations for a game of cricket because he was out of his comfort zone, he was nervous and everyone could see that. He still managed to get out there and certainly didn't let himself down."

Johns looked a far better cricketer against Tasmania than he had proclaimed at the start of his whole cricketing adventure admitting his last experience to be "getting a scratchy 14 for Merewether fifths three years ago. It was nothing to write home about. It was on a concrete wicket and I think I'd had eight beers by that stage." Johns had bowled one over for nine runs against South Australia: expensive but certainly no disgrace in Twenty20. Against Tasmania, Johns appeared calmed by the no-win situation of the game. New South Wales needed 70 off 41 balls to win when Johns arrived at the crease, elevated to number nine in the order almost as a V-sign to the media who had criticised the whole exercise. He made 9 runs off 10 balls before becoming one of three victims for Daniel Marsh.

"It was a nerve-wracking thing [batting] and it was an experience," summarised Johns in a press conference at Telstra after NSW were beaten by Tasmania, a 37-run loss that left them with a one hundred per cent record of defeats in the competition.

"I've said before that I've found a new kind of respect facing these fast bowlers because you don't always know where it's going," continued Johns. "I wasn't too keen to get out there … I didn't know where I was batting and when the fast bowlers came on I was creeping towards the back of the stand! It's some-thing to say that I've faced a bowler of that standing [Tasmania quick Ben Hilfenhaus] but he looked after me too. He pitched it up and he told me when he was going to pitch it in short so I knew where it was going."

Johns must be admired for volunteering to wander away from his 'comfort zone' when there was nothing much for him to gain from it. His sporting reputa-tion was untarnished at that point in Australia (a drug-taking admission since has altered that slightly) and throughout the rugby league supporting world. Furthermore, the financial gain was zero as his appearances were in the name of charity. However, the admission of a softly softly approach towards him from opposition bowlers after the umpiring generosity reprieved him first ball in Newcastle virtually transforms NSW's two home games into benefit events: the kind of gimmick Stuart Robertson said the format couldn't afford when he teed up a domestic competition in England.

* * *

OFF THE BACK OF THE success in England of twenty-over cricket and the schedul-ing of Twenty20 internationals for Australia against New Zealand and England, a trial match of sorts was arranged at the WACA in January 2005. Sensationally for a friendly against Victoria, the arena was full to the brim.

"I played for Western Australia myself from 1977 to the late eighties," recalled Victoria coach Greg Shipperd, "and we could have ten or eleven Test players on show and the biggest crowd that I probably saw at the WACA was about

10,000 people. More than double that are turning up for this three-hour stuff and they're turning people away at the gate."

It was the biggest turnout for a game of cricket on the ground since Australia and West Indies met for a one-day international in 1981. Victoria made 141/8 in their 20 overs but even their favourite son Shane Warne was hammered in the reply, finishing with figures of 1 for 32 in 2.1 overs as the hosts strolled home with a massive 47 balls to spare. All that would be academic to the future of Twenty20 in Australia though. The people had shown the colour of their money and handed over their dollars. A national competition was now a formality.

By the time Ricky Ponting was smashing New Zealand's hapless bowlers around Eden Park the following month, state chiefs across Australia's six competing sides had already decided upon a blueprint for the first 'Big Bash' competition. In recent times it's been a priority of the Aussie administrators to minimise the amount of state cricket played so with that in mind, the six states were divided into two pools, meaning the less successful sides would play only two matches (Tasmania and Queensland only managed one each after their clash was abandoned without a ball bowled due to rain). Each state would feature in a round-robin competition with the phase winners then meeting in the one-off final.

Aussie sides adapted to the game pretty quickly, some of that an expression of natural talents and some of it using knowledge garnered from short spells with county sides in England. South Australia were hammered by Victoria at Melbourne's Junction Oval and the only real plus in their 8-wicket loss came from Darren Lehmann, so well versed in the hurrying of batsmen with the left-arm spin angling around the wicket into the right-handed batsmen. His experience with Yorkshire thundered to the fore: his was the only bowling in the innings not to yield more than a run a ball.

Innings totals were exorbitant down under, the average for a team batting first weighing in at 173 compared with 151 for the initial Twenty20 Cup in the 2003 English summer and the reasons for that are potentially endless. On the harder surface in Australia at the height of summer, surfaces can be truer for the batsman than the standard wickets in England (as if to exemplify that, the final of the first-class Pura Cup competition of four-day matches later that season saw Queensland rack up a stultifying 900 for 6 declared). Swing is often factored out of the equation to some degree too meaning that batsmen can get off to a more comfortable start. Allied to all that, the sheer physical superiority of the Aussie upper body ensured that six-hitting would be an even more regular pursuit than in England.

"I think that's all a case of the quality of cricketers we have over here," said ABC's respected commentator Jim Maxwell in January 2007, just days after Australia had slain England in a Twenty20 international at the SCG.

"We had a reminder of the difference in class didn't we with fourteen sixes to one! In everything especially the depth of cricket, Australians are gonna monster everybody in the coming months. I mean, they might lose the odd game but people like Cameron White weren't just clearing the ropes, they were hitting it way back into the stands."

Maxwell's rhetoric may have revealed more than a touch of national pride but the facts were indisputable. Whether in Auckland, Sydney or Leicester, Twenty20 cricket had proved in its embryonic phase that the best cricketers would shine through and achieve the best results whether the game is long or short. Now that a collection of players so talented were thrown together in one fifteen-day long competition, the potential was vast.

Victoria won through to a final berth alongside New South Wales at North Sydney Oval where another man empowered by his Twenty20 knowledge in England played one of the best innings in the early history of the game, Brad Hodge smashing NSW to all parts to crush them in their own back yard.

"I got hit on the head quite early in the innings I think and it just annoyed me," explains Hodge, in a rich vein of form during a season in which he marked his appearance on the Test scene with a double-century in Perth against the touring South Africans.

"I just thought 'I'll smash 'em' as I was planning to do anyway but I just got that bit of fire in the belly I think and it worked out perfectly on the day. That was an unbelievable innings – just to be able to strike the ball as cleanly as I did that day. It's an interesting part of sport that you don't look back on your own innings like that until a long time after they happen. I think Cameron White came in and smashed five sixes at the end or something like that and put people in hospital! It was a beautiful venue with over seven thousand in and it would have been twelve if it hadn't have been scheduled against something else that night."

Hodge bashed 106 off 54 balls interspersing power with manipulation, as if the ball was on the end of a piece of string rather than a flashing wooden blade. He was dismissed in the sixteenth over but still NSW weren't spared the punishment. White actually hammered six sixes in an unbeaten 46 off 16 balls as Victoria walloped 67 off the last 27 balls. Their 233/7 was so comfortably sufficient that the match was never a true contest from the midpoint – NSW were bowled out for 140 – but from the neutral perspective, the night provided scintillating entertainment.

Hodge's innings was a treat to the eyes of his coach Shipperd too but in the nation seen as a sporting utopia by so many, the impact of Twenty20 on the future of cricket across Australia perhaps comes as something of a surprise.

"The thing is that this [Victoria] is a football state and youngsters are more likely to be aspiring AFL footballers and want to experience a large crowd barracking for them," Shipperd summed up.

"Unless they're internationals, cricketers don't have that exposure to those kind of crowds so to have thirty odd thousand in [as in the Big Bash Final 2007 at the MCG] gives them the feeling that footballers have and that's something they'll always remember.

"Certainly the young people could start to see it as an exciting opportunity for them. They get an instant result in the game and there's a lot more crowd interaction than in a four-day game or even a fifty-over match. It's this type of cricket that will provide a pretty attractive option to our first class athletes because there are lots of incentives. Players will be well rewarded if the money comes through and we get the kind of dollars in to match other sports."

Victoria dominated in 2007 too. The authorities in Australia had been quick to recognise the popularity of Twenty20 and added matches to the schedule, broadening the competition to one group of all six states with every side playing once against each of the others, culminating in a one-off final between the top two.

It had to be an all-action brand of cricket just to get a look in from the Aussie press who were gripped in a jingoistic celebration of Pom-tonking when the Big Bash kicked off on New Year's Day. Having lost the Ashes in 2005, the "Dad's Army" of Glenn McGrath, Justin Langer, Shane Warne et al were busy dishing out retribution, 4-0 up after a three-day annihilation on Warne's home turf in Melbourne and heading to the New Year Test at the SCG hunting a first whitewash in the momentous series for 86 years. Five, six, seven pages a day in each newspaper were being devoted to the humiliation of the English upstarts. In Sydney, the *Daily Telegraph* dedicated a mere 150 words to the opening of the Big Bash, wedged uncomfortably between the racing form and a crossword. The *Morning*

Herald offered little over 20 words to NSW's defeat in Perth on the opening night. Whilst the second Aussie Twenty20 competition was getting underway in Perth, Adelaide and Toowoomba, Channel 9 were busy broadcasting a tribute to the international career of Warne, live from the Sydney Cricket Ground. Ashes fever was unrelenting.

"Chopper, Bomber, Krazy, Angry – one could be forgiven for thinking it's the start of the new World Wrestling Entertainment season," barked the *Morning Herald*.

"But Chopper is Western Australia's David Bandy, Bomber is David Hussey, the brother of Mr Cricket Mike Hussey, Krazy is New South Welshman Jason Krejza and Angry is Tasmanian Dane Anderson. They are all Australian cricket's latest brand of Twenty20 players."

A mood surrounded Big Bash cricket that it wasn't in the least bit serious and perhaps the nicknames on the back of the shirts helped peddle that along. Not serious in Australia tends to lead to disinterest among the paying punters but folk Down Under aren't all fun police by any stretch of the imagination and the average spectator seemed to take to the innovations well, certainly if the numbers through the gates can act as any guideline. 27,653 flocked in to the 'Gabba in Brisbane to see Queensland beat NSW by 9 runs (although many commentators believed there to be more people: the 'walk-up' to the ground on the day was such that some fans were reportedly shut out), over fifteen thousand rocked up at the MCG for Victoria's tussle with Queensland. Double that number wandered in to see the final.

Perhaps some of that spanned from cricket's dominance of the news agenda in Australia in mid-Ashes drubbing. Even on non-match days around the festive period in 2006-7, big things were happening. Arguably the best spinner the game has ever seen announced his retirement before the Melbourne Test, McGrath and Langer followed suit. Damien Martyn packed it all in before the third installment of the thrilling series in Perth. Cricket was everywhere.

With an incredible array of talent on show as well, expectations for the competition to be one of the best the world have seen shouldn't have been too far wide of the mark; indeed, quality levels were high. The only slight obstacle to overcome was the lack of ambiguity about the match outcomes with the apparent trend that the side batting first would win the game comfortably. It happened eleven times from twelve.

The scores were massive for a start so, as Tasmania captain Daniel Marsh was to admit after defeat to Victoria in the final, pressure became immense on the teams batting second to get off to a flawless start. Many teams started the chase demoralised by the flogging their bowlers had received less than twenty minutes before and faltered, maybe having lost the belief that they could prevail. Huge grounds multiplied by the upper body strength of the average player weighted an already batsman-friendly form of cricket further in his favour. Victoria chased down 202 to beat Western Australia and also racked up ten an over against South Australia. Tasmania also excelled.

For the neutral cricket fan of course, the inventive and productive swishing of the bat was all well and good but in such an abbreviated game the scarcity of tight finishes leaves a void. Victory margins of anything more than twenty runs in twenty-over cricket count as mini-hidings and twice in 2007, those margins were in the eighties. Even when Victoria chased down that monster 202 at the MCG, they did it with 11 balls to spare. One of the most tense and potentially nervy finishes in the competition came at Newcastle and ended in farce with a rugby league player waltzing to the crease at ninth drop.

The second final was at least a memorable contest.

"I love the Twenty20 format and I love the MCG," says Brad Hodge, captain of the Victoria Bushrangers against Tasmania with usual skipper Cameron White called up to the Australian ODI side. "Over here, there are little rivalries because there are all the counties within driving distance but in Australia, it's different so all the people flocked down to the G and it was an unbelievable atmosphere: just awesome. But having said that, to play there anyday whether there's 32,000 or 5,000 is special."

Victoria had still never lost a competitive Twenty20 game but that record was under threat when they slumped to 92 for 6 in the fourteenth over. There could hardly have been a more marked contrast to North Sydney's showpiece twelve months before. Hodge managed just 13 as opposed to his brilliant century against NSW and the din of regular wickets undermined the 'home' effort. Adam Crosthwaite then butchered a late half-century to restore an equilibrium. Like in 50-over cricket, the momentum towards the end of an innings counts for so much at the start of the chase. Still at 90/3 in the 11th over, Tasmania remained favourites until a familiar story was retold: spin changed the game.

Hodge adds: "Just the knowledge that I've had playing in England helped to know that the slow bowlers are pretty tough to get away when it came to the final. I suppose that's the lack of knowledge for them that because the game was new in Australia, they had probably all only played about four games and I've played 30-odd so it's a lot of experience to have so that's just something that we did at Leicester where as soon as the opportunity came up, we had the two spinners on.

"Honestly, what goes through batsmen's minds sometimes is amazing; just confusion and you just forget about the simple things. In that time in the final, that was just the perfect time to get myself and Dave [Hussey] on. All of a sudden, six overs go and the game's won. It was fourteen an over needed in the last four but if you're skilful enough as a bowling team, you can win the game, even though it's possible to chase that down."

For all talk of the twirlers changing the course of the final, it was the seamer Mick Lewis ripping through two middle-order wickets in as many balls that catalysed the Tasmanian demise. George Bailey subsided tamely to mid-wicket for 9 and when Adam Polkinghorne picked up a golden duck carving nonchalantly to third man, the scene was set for Hodge and Hussey to dominate by taking the pace off the ball and forcing the Tasmanian batsmen to work the gaps and apply the brute force themselves. Their application in the face of the challenge was found wanting.

"It's just a difficult game to always keep on top of the run-rate," Hodge would sum up in the press conference, "because you think that eight or nine an over isn't a lot but it is. Over here, we haven't yet grasped the concept of chasing successfully but over in England, the spinners are used quite often."

The evolution had gone further in England because of their three-season head-start on the Aussies domestically so what the counties were finding as consistent trends towards the end of the 2004 season, the Big Bash was still exploring, unearthing. As with anything new in sport the combatants with the bat found ways to elaborate their game and the bowlers were coming to terms with having to work harder to avoid becoming gobbled up in the hurly-burly of it all.

"It might be hit-and-fetch, a batsman's game and all that but bowlers come up with new tactics as they did in the fifty-over game," says Maxwell.

"I mean, who would have thought Shane Warne could be such a key player in the one day game? At the end of the day, the best way to slow down the run rates in any form of cricket is to take wickets and because of Warne, spinners became more important in other countries as well. I suspect that the same might happen in Twenty20."

Another similarity with the English evolution of Twenty20 was the fun element that seemed to be gradually giving way to a tangible desire to win throughout the second Big Bash. That was only undermined by the presence of a (pretty sensational) rugby league player with NSW: Andrew Johns. Whilst the Speedblitz Blues staff and supporters seemed to be all in favour, the view from the winners' enclosure was mixed.

"It was interesting but I didn't agree with it at all," offered the victorious captain Hodge.

"I don't think you need to play a player like that because people will come to watch the game anyway. They don't come to watch Andrew Johns play because they can watch him play rugby. If they want to see some kid from New South Wales hit the ball a long way it doesn't matter who he is but if he hits sixes, they love it. It was interesting as a marketing ploy but it probably didn't need it. Maybe people didn't know how successful it was gonna be or doubted that it would have the same effect in Australia as in England. But I reckon if you staged a Twenty20 international at the MCG at the moment, you'd get 100,000 people in."

Hodge was sceptical of that one move and if many were unflustered by the initial determination to draft in Johns, the revelations of spoon-feeding him the bowling would go down as well with the average cricket fan as putting coats down on the floor halfway down the wicket at Lord's to help a batsman get a run if he couldn't hit the ball too far. It all gave the misleading notion that players Down Under couldn't give a toss about the outcome of Twenty20 matches so long as they fulfilled their commitments to the schedulers: maybe those administrators would treat it as a fad and drop it when they realised it to be a silly idea.

But Australian players cared all right and were already starting to see Twenty20 as yet another way of showing superiority over rivals just like the Test and ODI scene. In fact, this was almost a new challenge because South African and English players had enjoyed a head start in this box fresh discipline.

Mid-Big Bash, and jammed between the one-sided Ashes and the Commonwealth Bank tri-lateral series of one-day internationals (also involving New Zealand), the Aussies took on England in a one-off Twenty20 international at the Sydney Cricket Ground. As was becoming vogue, players were miked up by the host broadcaster – in this instance Channel Nine – and Adam Gilchrist was keen to use the new medium for an all new form of sledging. Asked to perform a link to a commercial break at the end of an over, Gilchrist mischievously summarised: "Australia well on top here, and England in real trouble as they have been all summer, four for 60."

Gilchrist is an eloquent, honest sportsman. He holds the values of the game in high esteem to such an extent that he always 'walks' on nicking a ball through to the wicketkeeper without bringing the umpire into play. Undoubtedly, his opinions on the big debates in cricket are respected more than most. But despite his guarded public statements about abbreviated cricket, he wanted to win at twenty-over sport as much as he did in a Test or an ODI and the on-air taunting proved it. It might have been fast-food cricket but the Aussies were starting to shift the tectonics of it into their favour and under their control.

Allen Stanford

"In my opinion, for too long West Indian cricketers have been undervalued and underpaid. It is time for the WICB, the players and those of us in the private sector to step up to the plate and partner together to commit the financial resources necessary to bring about some much needed change in cricket."

Mr R. Allen Stanford

ENGLAND ARGUABLY PROVIDED THE breakthrough for Twenty20 cricket into the public conscience but the creation of a domestic competition in the Caribbean will undeniably be the one that has the most forceful impact on cricket and its soul. Whilst working with the established authorities – namely the West Indies Cricket Board – and securing their initial (if tentative) blessing, Mr R. Allen Stanford managed to financially reward players for their on-field work and simultaneously humiliate those same authorities who were burying themselves beneath the mounting rubble of debt whilst presiding over a talented yet ordinary international side. All of this came whilst the public were being wooed by possibly the most stimulating domestic tournament that West Indian cricket-lovers had ever witnessed: the Stanford 2020.

Allen Stanford is a Texan although since just before the turn of the century he was also granted citizenship in Antigua and Barbuda, where he and many of his business operations have been for two decades. He was left a monumental windfall of $300million after the death of his grandfather, who had kick-started an insurance company in the immediate upshot of the Great Depression that hit the United States after the Wall Street Crash of 1929. At the last count, Stanford was the chairman of over sixty companies and had used his inherited funds well to be worth a reported $35billion. Dealing with people wielding an abundance of wealth and helping them to manage it must have seemed the most ornate paradox to a dalliance with West Indian cricket but still, in October 2005, Stanford announced he was getting involved.

The time was ripe to inject something new into a brand and a culture of cricket that was nostalgically revered by many but was producing few world-beaters and even fewer positive results. The days of Viv Richards, Desmond Haynes and Gordon Greenidge had gone, Brian Lara was on the march towards the international exit door having divided the opinions of many and since the final curtain came down on Curtly Ambrose and Courtney Walsh, West Indian quicks of genuine quality had become an endangered species. Yet still the West Indies Cricket Board was haemorrhaging cash. In the financial year to September 2001, $7.5m was lost (£5.2m) making for an estimated $15m arrears in three years. Even with a World Cup around the corner in the Caribbean, something had to change pretty fundamentally.

That something would come from the private sector and from outside of the traditional game. Allen Stanford made his own competition with 19 teams drawn from the islands under the jurisdiction of the West Indies Cricket Board invited to take part. The Twenty20 competition would take place on his ground, the Stanford Oval, an excellent facility out to Antigua's eastern fringe near to the airport. The advantage that held over staging at the St. John's ground on the island, for example, was that Stanford was his own man that way and could not have his plans tinkered with by those who felt threatened by the emergence of a competition that wasn't their own. Remember Kerry Packer's biggest problem with his World Series Cricket at the end of the seventies? He had nowhere to play it originally. Stanford's self-funded stadium was purpose built for Twenty20 and it would stage every game of the tournament culminating in the glittering final.

As Mike Atherton commented in the *Sunday Telegraph* on 6 August 2006, "it is a one-man show: the cricket is played on his ground, the tournament is sponsored by his companies, the players wear his logo and they are flown to Antigua by his airlines."

It was a costly exercise for Stanford. The winners of the competition pocketed $1m, the man of the match in each game walked off with $25,000 with four times that the loot for the star of the final. To aid development in each territory, $280,000 was allocated to each. The overall cost arrowed up towards the $30m mark. Surely there was a better way for Stanford to promote the businesses he owned? Stanford explains:

"I have been part of the Caribbean community for over 20 years. During this time I have witnessed firsthand the power that the game of cricket wields over the people in this region. Cricket is an almost tangible force which can unify an entire country, an entire group of people, no matter the differences that exist off the field, in the houses of parliament or between nations. The energy, the pride, the passion that cricket has inspired in the people of the Caribbean is not only moving but also infectious.

"In recent years, however, I also observed the decay of these emotions, a slow erosion of faith in the sport which has given way to feelings of disillusionment and low expectations. I felt that I was able to offer a viable and innovative solution in the form of a 20/20 tournament.

"For a while now, I have been talking about the creation of a professional Super League where Caribbean cricketers can do what they do best, play cricket with their fellow countrymen and against their Caribbean counterparts and be rewarded for excellence. I believe that a lack of finance and professionalism is retarding the growth and development of cricket in the Caribbean and that we should follow the example of pro basketball and football in the U.S. and develop a professional, well-paid league in the West Indies which at the end of the season would culminate with the equivalent of the West Indies cricket Super Star Tournament.

"The Stanford 2020 tournament was borne out of this idea. It is from this pool of talent that we will pull the players who will play in this professional Super League.

"Cricket in the Caribbean is at a crossroads with a great opportunity to go forward. However, I believe a new approach must be taken for the sport to grow and prosper in the years ahead. We need to provide an environment for young, talented, up and coming players that will keep them motivated and interested in developing their careers in the sport of cricket and allow them to better themselves, not only in the sport but financially as well. The players must have the financial resources to devote the time and energy required to compete and fully develop into champions. In my opinion, for too long West Indian cricketers have been undervalued and underpaid. It is time for the WICB, the players, and those of us in the private sector to step up to the plate and partner together to commit the financial resources necessary to bring about some much needed change in cricket."

That was the motivation and at once shows the contrast and the similarities between Stanford and Kerry Packer, the Australian media mogul who polarised the cricketing fraternity with his oft-labelled circus from 1977.

The catalyst for Packer's elaborate and highly divisive broadside against the authorities came from the refusal of the Australian Cricket Board to grant exclusive screening rights to his Nine Network for Test Matches. The net result was that Packer, bemused as to how his bid could have been rejected, decided to put on the show himself and bought the services of the best Australian, West Indian and world stars to do just that. In his quite excellent book, *The Packer Affair*, the English writer and broadcaster Henry Blofeld acknowledged that while professing a love of the game and to have it's best interests at heart, profit was the driving force behind Packer's World Series.

Of course, maximising profit can't have been the senior motive behind Stanford's inauguration of a domestic twenty-over competition. In the *Wisden Cricketer*, Edward Craig put forward the assertion that Stanford didn't go into anything with his eyes closed and didn't believe in any investment without return: that much is obvious merely in the multiplication of his vast personal wealth over the years in his various business pursuits. Yet the hotel chains and airlines etc owned by Stanford could benefit immensely from elaborate promotion that would weigh in far cheaper than the $28million spent on the first year of Stanford 2020. The freelance journalist Vaneisa Baksh commented on Cricinfo that "gains may accrue through increased tourism, accomodation, transport or television rights but that would not diminish returns to the cricketers." But Stanford has also opened his chequebook to donate a seven-figure sum to help a modern library get up and running in Antigua so not all of his projects are driven by pure commercialism. Unlike Packer he had no television airwaves to fill either.

Albeit in different countries and eras, Packer and Stanford did share an understanding of the grievances felt by the players over their wages in the traditional system peddled by the national cricket authorities. Packer had to have his attention drawn to that matter by television comedians he had snaffled from the rival Seven Network but he acted upon it and made sure that world stars would perform at his show. With the destitute state of West Indian cricket, Stanford hardly needed a rocket scientist to figure out the same kind of thing for himself at the start of the twenty-first century. By upping the numbers hitting the personal accounts of players, Stanford could ensure the popular support of the players for his concept, from which point it would be a brave administrator to try and shelve the plans.

Of course, money talks and the current crop of players were always likely to be swayed by the dollars on offer from Stanford's initiative. Getting the recognised players from the historically strong West Indian sides would not only send out the message that this was a serious way of revitalising the game in the Caribbean but it would also be the seal of approval that would ultimately win over many of the doubters who perceived Stanford as a flash short-term resolution to the ills of 'calypso cricket' who would affect no improvement on the grassroots. It's exactly the course of action that Stanford took: incorporating a team of 'Legends' to over-see the development and preparation of each island and to simultaneously endorse the new tournament by association.

"I can throw all the money in the world into this programme," explains Stanford, "but these men understand the game on a level that I do not and for that reason alone, I need them. Their presence and participation definitely brought an increased level of credibility to the tournament."

Not one of these men enlisted by Stanford could escape the public attention across the islands. Wes Hall would look after Trinidad and Tobago, Sir Garfield Sobers: St. Lucia and Ian Bishop: the Cayman Islands. Other legends included Sir Viv Richards, Richie Richardson, Haynes, Walsh and Ambrose.

Continues Stanford: "Once I explained my vision for the tournament and for cricket in the Caribbean to each of them, all of the legends were keen to get involved. We all share a common goal: to revive cricket in the Caribbean, to reignite the passion for the game not just in the spectators but also the cricketers themselves, both current and prospective ones.

"These men all experienced the glory days of West Indian cricket; they know what it was like to win consistently, to be a force to be reckoned with, to have the entire region supporting and encouraging them as they crushed their opponents around the world. They want to see that again in the Caribbean, the profession-alism, the excitement, the fervour, the victories. Their depth of experience, wisdom and expertise is immeasurable. They want to be part of the solution and not just talk about the problems in Caribbean cricket. The Stanford 20/20 tournament is our contribution to the problem-solving effort."

The summary from Stanford about a 'contribution' as opposed to a control-ling stake is an important one. From many journalistic corners, the Texan was attacked for injecting his cash at the top of the domestic West Indian cricket pyramid rather than the base but why should a man risk his personal fortune doing the dirty work for the authorities of the game who have found such pacy development beyond them in recent years? Surely by raising the profile of the Caribbean game both regionally and internationally, Stanford was doing more than his share of boosting the game. In fact, in doing so in such a way, he was inviting the West Indies Cricket Board to hop on board and do their bit or risk running the gauntlet of public humiliation.

"The West Indies Cricket Board seemed shocked to some extent at the impact that Stanford 2020 had," says Mike Haysman, former professional crick-eter turned broadcaster who would patrol the boundary for television coverage of Stanford.

"I was having a chat over a beer to a guy from TWI [Trans World International] a few years ago and we said that the day they played cricket under floodlights in the Caribbean would be the day that cricket there would be turned on it's head and I think that's how it has turned out.

"So there's no doubt that the West Indies Cricket Board have to react now. They can not, with a capital N-O-T ignore what Mr. Stanford's been doing. If he's been prepared to invest that sort of money and that sort of interest, the passion and the excitement, then they have to sit up and take note. He has West Indies people and West Indies cricket at heart. It is the greatest product of the region and he quite rightly believes that when the psyche of the people is up because of the cricket, the whole place gets a lift. It seems as though relations are getting better though and that after meetings, there can be more synergy between the West Indies Cricket Board and Stanford and that's what everybody wants."

The major apparent stumbling block in the minds of the cynics appears to have been Stanford's role in the grander scheme of West Indian cricket with concerned onlookers counselling against handing over the reigns of the sovereign regional sport to one man – not to mention an American: what did they ever know about cricket? Was he looking to ease aside the existing structure with weight of cash alone and if he was, what would then happen to the whole sport if he got bored and walked away?

The year after the inaugural tournament pointed to most of the answers. Added dialogue between Stanford and the West Indies Cricket Board led to an amnesty of sorts between the two parties and any public uncertainty as to Stanford's motives would be washed away in another tidal wave of big bucks. In July 2007, the announcement that a further $100million would be pumped into the Antiguan cricket project over the following three years went a long way towards illustrating that Stanford wasn't going to get disinterested easily.

"I think many people were sceptical perhaps even suspicious about my motives," Stanford readily admits.

"This was understandable to some extent as many people view me as this Texan businessman who knows nothing about cricket. I think that many people were supportive of the vision but concerned about how it could coexist and mesh with the WICB's mandate for cricket development in the region. I think that we were able to successfully prove that we were not trying to diminish or minimise the role of the WICB, but rather to work in tandem with them for the greater good."

Such synchronicity wasn't always evident. A semi-permeable partition seemed to be drawn between Stanford and the West Indies Cricket Board, both seeming to plough on with their own individual projects whilst eyeing the other with suspicion. The living illustration of the division was personified by Clive Lloyd. Lloyd's 7,500 Test runs and captaincy of two World Cup winning sides quite rightly marked him out as one of the legends of West Indian cricket and he was asked by the Stanford contingent to help breathe life to the inaugural 20/20 competition by becoming the chairman of the organising board. Yet conflict brought about the end of his tenure.

As a director standing on the WICB, Lloyd felt that one position or other would be untenable if the respective plans of the two parties reached collision course. One bone of contention was believed to be the planned $5m match between the Stanford Superstars (a 20-man squad consisting of a kind of 'dream team' from the inaugural Stanford 20/20 competition) and South Africa in November 2006 impacted upon the official West Indian squad, set to be on tour in Pakistan at the same time.

Now there would be an iron test of who held the upper hand in what had the potential to become a power struggle of some substance. Stanford claimed he had sought, and gained, approval from the WICB the previous January when no clash of commitments had been apparent. Lloyd walked away with low-key mutterings about the importance of the national team coming first under any circumstances.

Both sides were of course correct in their statements but they slightly missed the point. From the outside it seemed like the WICB didn't want to get it, apprehensive about the longevity of Stanford's interest and openly curious as to what he hoped to achieve from it. For anyone au fait with the confetti currency of Premier League football in England, that in itself is commendable. Yet still, this man was looking to throw $5m into the game for forty overs of showmanship with a marketable South African team already on board and up for the challenge so surely his proposition deserved some recognition, especially in a year that had seen WICB auditors declare an overall debt approaching seven times that figure, as highly respected journalist Tony Cozier pointed out in his excellent *CricInfo* article of July 2006. As Cozier went on to ponder, perhaps the profligacy of the WICB had forced it "to close its academy, slash its first-class tournaments in half and ponder its future," thus creating the penniless environment in which a private financier such as Stanford could thrive.

Undeterred, Stanford sought to expand upon his untried theory anyway and announced a $20m mini-tournament after the second domestic competition, again pitting his SuperStars against the best of four competing ICC member sides, planned for June 2008.

"The cancellation of the Super Stars match did not tarnish the success of the first event at all," countered Stanford, "because I think the majority of people know and understand that the cancellation was NOT [Stanford's emphasis] our fault.

"We had all of our ducks in a row; we went through the proper channels and were promised something that ultimately wasn't delivered. We, meaning myself, the legends, the players and the fans, were all sorely disappointed at the turn of events that caused the cancellation but we were always secure in the knowledge that we did our part and that the blame did not fall to us. If anything, that entire debacle only served to strengthen our resolve so that next time around, the same problem will not recur."

In the middle of 2007, Ken Gordon stepped down as the President of the WICB and hardly indicated a conciliatory approach in handing over the reigns to Julian Hunte.

"We admire the Stanford initiative and we are happy to hear that Mr Stanford is having fun," patronised Gordon in a departing speech to his Board of Directors. "But however attractive the short-term benefits, these must fit into the overall plan for the rebuilding of West Indies cricket, not the other way round. Once this is understood and remains the common objective of us both, there is no reason whatsoever why a satisfactory formula should not be found."

Perhaps the most bizarre irony to be lost upon Mr. Gordon was the pious belief that the WICB should act as the sole arbiter of what would be good and bad for the whole game. Wasn't this the same organisation that had been forced to decimate the academies that would provide the next generation of high-class cricketer, all through lack of funds?

Many of the negotiations between the various parties were not just about finding the best course of action for the development of cricket in the West Indies. Television rights would become an issue for the international matches against the Stanford Super Stars, something that the International Cricket Council (ICC) were wary of. Just as concerning would be the effect those all-star games would have on the ICC cap on Twenty20 internationals. The governing body restricted each nation to a maximum of two short matches in each tour, three in every home season and seven in a calendar year, although this excluded any ICC Twenty20 competitions, in which a team can play as many as ten games. Stanford's proposals muddied the waters a fraction as to whether his matches in Antigua should be counted towards that quota. If not, they feared a dangerous precedent might be set for other independent enterprises.

Partially lost within this labyrinth of agendas and arguments would be the incredible show put on by Stanford at his Oval. This would be perhaps the most colourful Twenty20 competition in the world and would bring night-time cricket to the West Indies – the hub of flair and finesse in the sport. With the 'Legends' on board it would bring the Caribbean public back into the game, a far cry from the World Cup the following March-April which priced locals out of the market with exorbitant ticket prices and saw matches often played out in front of half-empty houses.

In establishing his competition, Stanford had to battle against the established powers of Caribbean cricket. The measure of success of the very first

Stanford Twenty20 would go a long way towards deciding whether it was a fight worth getting into.

Are You Ready?

Twenty20 (it's a new spin), are you ready?
(Let the battle begin) It's time to party.
It's a cricket evolution,
we can start the revolution tonight.

Stanford 2020 theme tune ,
(Beenie Man and Patrice Roberts)

THE SEASONS MESHED INTO ONE around the Stanford Oval where a balmy evening was interspersed with light lashings of rain and the occasional gust that would perturb the ground staff as they temporarily cloaked the square with tarpaulins. It was just an almost obligatory part to an already eclectic combination that bolted together the first Stanford 2020 final.

The floodlights were barely needed as both teams appeared to have got dressed after an explosion in a crayon factory. Guyana thrust forward their quest for 176 to land the loot in national 'pyjamas' that stretched the usual boundaries of patriotism: a luminous banana yellow flanking green and red on the chest and the trousers. The old wives tale holds that green and red are the mixed colours of fools and as the Guyanese innings staggered, jolted, stuttered and accelerated, many in the ground would have been forgiven for thinking the same applied. Trinidad and Tobago were more sober in their red and black.

The crowd could have majored on neutral folk but still they made an awful racket and seemed to just embrace good cricket: inter-island challenges weren't new but popular, supporter-friendly versions certainly were. The importance in cash and prestige to the players had filtered down beyond the boundary edge. On television, Mike Haysman interviewed an English fan who had flown straight to Antigua to witness history after being at Trent Bridge 24 hours earlier to watch the controversial English final. Having swapped his waterproof jacket for shorts and t-shirt, he just grinned inanely – the effects of jetlag.

The two Caribbean heavyweights exchanged exploratory punches either side of the first innings rain delay and T+T were dangling onto their hopes at 122/5 after 17. Then, international star Dinesh Ramdin opened his shoulders to make a game of it, manipulating the bowling as if he was landing it on a length himself to tag 53 runs onto a sluggish looking score off the final eighteen balls. Ramdin's impact lasted just fourteen balls but the 38 runs he contributed swapped the Trinidadian status from underdogs to favourites.

Allen Stanford would later say that a better finale couldn't have been scripted and his statements would carry no hyperbole. Guyana saw their top order suffer semi-paralysis courtesy of the experienced international Mervyn Dillon, who trapped Lennox Cush in the crease for 5 and then got rid of Esuan Crandon third ball for a duck later in the same over. The significance of the latter was heightened by Crandon's incendiary hitting earlier in the competition, making a name for himself with a quarter-final blitzkrieg against the highly-fancied Jamaicans which yielded a memorable and match-deciding 71 off 39 balls.

What was to follow proved that some cricketing clichés were made redundant by the inception of Twenty20, namely the one that wickets in hand is the key to a successful chase. Between the opener Travis Dowlin and West Indian Test starlet Ramnaresh Sarwan, the glue was applied for fourteen overs that took in 110 runs before back spasms for Dowlin added further complications to a pendulum that had done it's fair share of swinging. As Dowlin trudged off, his team still had eight wickets in the can but what use were they when his team needed to score at 14 runs an over to perform the ultimate highway robbery. Sarwan had been inclined to play Pythagoras and use his unnerving ability to steadily accumulate runs, playing second fiddle to Dowlin but now, the dynamic of the innings was irre-versibly changed with the minimum requirement being two to three boundaries per over for a successful chase. With 33 off 35 balls, it was doubtful whether Sarwan could make the rapid adjustment that was needed.

Still, the Guyanese cheered and the neutrals adopted them as the mountain in front of them gathered gradient. Sarwan gambled and won in the next over from

Ramjass, swatting him over long on and then onto the pavilion roof for maximums with another boundary wedged in between. Sarwan was a bystander for the penultimate over which saw Imran Khan lose his middle stump for 10 and then Mahendra Nagamootoo turned things back into the favour of the Guyanese with back-to-back boundaries. The initiative was promptly handed back when Nagamootoo angered himself by playing out a dot ball and smashed the final ball down long off's throat with fourteen runs still needed.

Leg-spinner Samuel Badree stepped up to bowl the final over which in old money, was the same as a centre-half offering to take the last, decisive penalty in a football shootout. Theo Cuffy, the former Trinidad and Tobago captain, would later praise Badree as one of the finds of the tournament but on a pitch that hadn't turned appreciably, his success would revolve around the ability of the batsmen to hold their nerve. It does with all spinners in limited overs cricket aside from the likes of Shane Warne, Saqlain Mushtaq, Mushtaq Ahmed and Muttiah Muralitharan who could turn a golf ball at right angles on a motorway. Badree held his nerve with the first ball of the over which bowled Neil McGarrell to leave Guyana 162/5: their wickets in hand had counted for absolutely nothing, nunca, rien, sod all.

The fans didn't care. Their squealing was now borne of nervousness but television cameras picked up a group of Trinidadians and Guyanese dancing and singing together in the final overs, their national colours locked together in the odd respectful hug and embrace, like snooker players wishing each other luck when their match goes down to the final frame. With fourteen needed, it was Trinidad's for the taking but classics don't end as simply as that so there was still another time for five spanners to be thrown into the works. Narsingh Deonarine cleverly kept his head to get down to the non-strikers end, allowing Sarwan to feast upon the length of Badree and slam his next ball over long on for six. Sarwan was shorn of emotion as everyone around him went bananas with each side now one productive ball from landing a million dollars.

That ball came for Guyana as Deonarine lunged onto one knee as the bowler tried to pre-empt the movement by dragging the ball down short of a good length. It sat up for Deonarine to crash it over wide mid-wicket for a maximum from just his second ball and the winning runs were met with scenes of delirium as the Guyanese tore around the field like men possessed and both fans came together to celebrate the dawn of a new era in Caribbean cricket to the tune of *Beenie Man,* the man whose tune had become an omnipresent anthem of Stanford 2020. The dream final hadn't even been a nightmare for Trinidad whose tears were soaked up by 500,000 US dollar notes, a substantial reward in a domestic system where finance had almost become a dirty word.

* * *

I HAD FIRST ENCOUNTERED the frenzied buzz of Stanford 2020 from the far less frenzied comfort of The Blind Busker pub on the main street in Hove. I had been covering the first day of a potentially title-deciding County Championship match between Sussex and Lancashire with my good friend and fellow cricket nut Graham Hardcastle and our pint at stumps was being interrupted by a surreal pub quiz called "truth or bollocks?" A few of the twenty-somethings were taking it far too seriously – perhaps they had been in training for this post-modern Trivial Pursuit – but most treated it as the fun diversion from everyday life that it was intended to be. In a moment that felt hallucinogenic, a colourful animated eagle was going nuts in the corner of my eye and for a split second I wondered if there was something surreal about the lager. The eagle disappeared and some cricket peered out from the small television screen.

The highlights were from a game the previous week when Guyana had booked their spot in the last eight against Jamaica with a routine win over Montserrat. I had to admit I knew nothing of any significance about Montserrat. A small amount of research revealed that it was part of the Lesser Antilles and boasted dimensions of only seven miles by ten. Tougher to discern was it's sporting achievements. The tag of Montserrat's greatest ever sportsman went to a right-handed bat by the name of Jim Allen who represented the World Series Cricket West Indians at the end of the seventies despite never having played a Test Match. A competent batsman (and referred to in many an article as "occasional wicketkeeper"), he managed to feature in just one of the 'Super Tests' against Australia and chiselled undistinguished innings of eight and twelve before drifting back into obscurity away from Montserratian shores. Allen's status as the national sporting icon has hardly been threatened not even by Tesfaye Bramble, a footballing centre-half once-capped at international level by Montserrat but last seen milling around the fourth tier of English football with Stockport County.

It was a quiet day by Stanford Oval standards and that serenity extended to the playing area as Montserrat gave the aura of a team with limited experience and technique to cope with their surroundings. The canny Guyanese throttled their progress from the off and Montserrat couldn't lay one of their eye-catching black bats on ball. The tearing up of the cricket aesthetics handbook was the thing that really made us sit up in The Blind Busker and ignore the hitherto amusing questions about celebrity libido. The black bats gave the initial impression that serious cricketers were playing with one of those Kwik Cricket sets you see kids using in the lunch interval of a Test Match in England but in reality, all it did was add to the colour and vibrancy of the spectacle.

Montserrat made 115 for 8 in their allotted time, stifled at the top and then squeezed at their core by the spinners who set up a comfortable win. Sarwan enjoyed nothing more testing than a light net in cruising to 22 before falling to the gentle off-break of 36 year-old Trevor Semper with Deonarine in a hurry to get things boxed off for Guyana with 21 balls in hand.

Hoarding lofty aspirations of trophy winning in the Stanford 2020 was not the style of Montserrat, neither that of the other minnows assembled in Coolidge. For them, rubbing shoulders with the heavyweight islands of West Indian cricket afforded a fun and engaging opportunity both for a day in the sun and also to develop the infrastructure of their game. Such was evident on the second night in 2006, when Cayman Islands beat British Virgin Islands in an all-rookie head-to-head. "Cayman was as prepared as the local conditions and facilities allowed," wrote Philip Hackett on *Cayman Net News*.

"There were regular practice matches and several hours of gruelling physical training under the guidance of Alvan Babb. Based on the spectator interest to this point and the intensity shown by the players on display, the Stanford 2020 has already started to revitalise cricket throughout the region. Those who continue to berate it have obviously missed the point. The Stanford 2020 has provided countries with funding to develop their cricket that would not have been available otherwise. The benefits can already be seen in the high quality of fielding by most of the teams. It has shown the advantages of having a regional league that will sustain our cricketers who will then be able to remain in the Caribbean and earn a decent living. I can think of no other avenue by which a team can earn close to $EC90,000 for part of a night's work as St. Lucia did, or $US25,000 hauled in by Cayman through the Man of the Match award won by [batsman Pearson] Best.

"The Stanford 2020 also has the potential to set the standards for administration, another aspect of our cricket in the region that has proven calamitous over the years."

Of course Montserrat and Cayman Islands weren't the sole rookies invited to this all-inclusive bash. St. Maarten and the US Virgin Islands competed in the opening match; Anguilla, Bermuda and Dominica also made fleeting appearances but appeared nevertheless. The event was laid out by seeding to some extent. Ten teams were paired together in a preliminary round in all but name, the breeding nations of West Indian teams in decades gone by turning up in the next phase to teach them all a lesson. Of course, the net result was that the standard of cricket would improve as the competition drifted on, leaving behind sceptics aplenty all bemoaning the lack of early quality.

"There've been spots in some of the teams where they seem to have lost the understanding of one-day cricket," said former West Indian opening batsman and Stanford Legend Gordon Greenidge in *SPIN World Cricket Monthly*. "I still feel that most of the time, whether it is in this 20/20 tournament or in the one-day tournament in the Caribbean, our players feel they have to go out there and hit every ball for four or six."

The brevity of the game lends itself to bursts of over-excitement and the natural exuberance of Caribbean cricketers means that they are liable to appear more foolish than most should their death or glory batting go wrong. Yet the most successful method of development comes from pitting the rookie teams against the best; people to emulate, class to aspire to.

The more insular supporters of big teams from the English Premier League can have an arrogant demeanour about them when it comes to the qualifying or early stages of the FA Cup. The likes of Chelsea, Manchester United, Arsenal and Liverpool only enter the competition at the third round stage in January, whilst preliminary rounds kick off when the floodlights are still barely needed in midweek games as the late summer sun makes a languid journey down. Yet that doesn't mean the non-league teams just shouldn't bother. The sceptre of the giant-killers not only energises the players lower down the pyramid but can occasionally drive them on to great things. The same happened in cricket circles when associate members of the ICC were able to compete in the fifty-over World Cup. Bangladesh beat Pakistan en route to full membership, West Indies were skittled for just 93 by Kenya in 1996.

Gradually, those teams have stepped up their skill levels and consistency and started to present more of a challenge to the established order which is just what the lower ranking nations in Stanford didn't have the opportunity to achieve. In the first edition, Montserrat had just thirty-six overs of cricket with which to prove their worth at the Stanford Oval: one-match wonders alongside the likes of St.Kitts and Bahamas. In January 2008, British Virgin Islands sagged to 73 all out against Dominica, giving their twenty20 batting life a span of just a hundred and four balls: hardly enough to perfect techniques. The smallest quirks of the team game would also be helped by Stanford's money, which couldn't be reasonably expected to make a major immediate impact, rather one that would steadily build over time.

In the run up to the second series, Ian Bishop would be assigned the role of 'Cayman Islands Stanford2020 Legend'. "Having arrived late Saturday he wasted no time," reported *Caymanian Compass*, "and spent Sunday at the Smith Road Oval observing players. He had an even closer look as an umpire during the first match. Trinidadian Bishop conducted two practice sessions at the Smith Road Oval on Monday and Tuesday." The effects of the fast bowling hero weren't evident at first glance, after which the Caymans had the compass out to chart their journey home, managing only 88/8 in 20 overs against St. Lucia in falling to a humbling and quite pitiful defeat. It provided incontrovertible evidence that whilst Stanford was putting on a special event, it needed to have a much broader range.

The 'Legends' should be afforded time to assist the kind of wholehearted change that will give Stanford 20/20 the quality to match such high-octane action. By the time all the youthful developers had stepped aside from the 2008 edition, not everyone was convinced that the former greats on the field were assisting similarly special strides from the sidelines.

"We are gaining entertainment from the ongoing Stanford series but we are not seeing quality cricket," uttered former West Indies opener and selector Joey Carew in an interview with CMC Sports.

"The standard of some of the lesser teams is very, very poor in my judgement and I think that the Legends who are attached to those teams must do a lot more with them in terms of development. I think that the Legends should be doing a lot more to assist the development and help the players realise their true potential … intense coaching from these guys months before the tournament begins will benefit and we would gradually see a rise in the quality of the cricket being played. This initiative is a good one and once used properly could rebound to the benefit of West Indies cricket."

The overlapping of the competition with the end of the West Indian tour of South Africa can barely have helped. There, West Indies had capitulated to a 5-0 humbling despite having been a good session or two away from winning the Test Match series between the two sides the previous month. Public mutterings about the quality of domestic cricket in the Caribbean would have been the norm whether the Stanford tournament existed or not but that doesn't invalidate the claims or weaken the arguments of the people who were unimpressed by the standard. Neither was it lost on those people that despite the success of the first Twenty20 competition in August 2006, the Windies still flopped alarmingly in the world event of 2007.

"There is precious little to suggest that the competition is contributing in any meaningful way to the improvement of standards in West Indies cricket," wrote Fazeer Mohammed on *CricInfo.* "That has been one of the claims of the organisers of this elaborate and very expensive exercise.

"Like the fashion runway, appearances are everything, from the bowler wiggling his hips to the singing, prancing, wining masses who seem to have more energy than many of the players. Money can buy almost everything, even credibility. But like the emperor with no clothes, the plain truth is there for all to see, at least to those who are not blinded by the bright lights and the dollar signs."

The cynical punter might argue that the gradual growth in dissent towards Allen Stanford's grand plan for Caribbean cricket is a mere sign that the honeymoon period is over but quality sport can only thrive with a constant competitive element and it simply didn't exist in the early stages of either of the first two editions of Stanford 20/20. For all the romance and idealism of Montserrat's entry to the competition, their predictable demise against Guyana in 2006 was only usurped in its ordinariness by their defeat to Nevis in the first round in February 2008 where they were bowled out for 111. They weren't the only strugglers with Dominica rattled out for 77 by Barbados, Bahamas managing a surreal 73/7 from 20 overs against Jamaica (they were chasing 192 for victory) and St. Lucia also scratching around to squeeze into three figures.

By far the most cataclysmic disaster-zone of the second competition were Bermuda, who featured in the 2007 ICC World Cup complete with their super-sized spinner Dwayne Leverock but less than twelve months later they could only show their inability to develop as a team in the same way as his waistline had done. Their first round match against Guyana was as close to a car crash as cricket gets for those who witnessed it, Bermuda posting 62/9 in their allotted time having set precisely no pulses racing inside the Stanford Oval with a pedestrian five runs from the final three overs. Only the ageing David Hemp managed to make it beyond eight in a total that had been gifted six runs by wide bowling. Thoughtfully, Guyana dragged out their 'chase' to the twelfth over but it surely held back the development of their twenty-over cricket to be playing against a team who were quite clearly not able to compete at such a level.

The fall out was well chronicled in the *Bermuda Sun*, whose online edition ran in words a post-mortem unheard of in cricket since the image of the burning ashes was posted on the front page of an English tabloid at the end of the nineties to herald their exit from the World Cup. "We should remind ourselves," implored columnist Tom Vesey, "when confronted with the teeming, bat-wielding millions from cricketing nations around the globe, that we have only 65,000 people. And most of them are busy doing other things." Size can only be used to defend so much though and whilst it would misread the context of Vesey's piece to say that he thinks only that the taking part counts for Bermuda, it's a plus for the future of Stanford that some of his punditry colleagues were happy to apportion blame and call for a change in approach.

Also in the *Bermuda Sun*, Stuart Hayward threw the culpability with Bermuda's size, location and crucially, the temperament of the islanders. "We tend to have an overblown image of ourselves," he would argue. "Another ego factor impedes our training and development of skills. I believe we have a cultural norm of not valuing teachers. We tend not to see the learning opportunities from devoting ourselves to those with expertise. This may be the flip side of our education troubles - an ego-based attitude against learning typified by the words 'Bye, you can't tell me anything.'"

Mitigating circumstances were not in short supply and most Bermudans made a noise about having to send a team to the Under-19 World Cup, something that they claim weakened their cause. But the cliché holds that nothing is ever won with kids and if the nucleus of Bermuda's international team couldn't even stage the brief pretence that they were competitive then how players barely out of school could shove them along to greater things is a question perhaps nobody can answer.

The quality from the quarter-finals onwards was so good as to be barely credible given the omnipresent weakness of the minnows. The presence of international incendiary Chris Gayle in Jamaica's last eight match against Guyana, alongside fringe player Wavell Hinds and the bowling duo of Jerome Taylor and Jermaine Lawson, bought class and credibility for the competition. Gayle hit 36 at the top of the innings as Jamaica posted 163 but despite an economical four overs with the ball during the chase including a wicket, Guyana were able to cruise to victory with six balls to spare. That highly-fancied Jamiaca could bow out so comfortably eased fears about the overall quality at the top end of the Caribbean spectrum but cruelly emphasised the difference between the 'haves' and the 'have-nots' in the region. The surge of popular curiosity and excitement at this novelty event papered over the smallest of these 'cracks' in Stanford over the first two editions but whether such momentum will be drawn out if the minnow nations are unable to keep pace with the big boys, is the biggest challenge facing Stanford and his Legends.

That isn't to say that Stanford 20/20 hasn't already achieved a great deal during its short existence. Aside from offering a source of invigoration and national pride to smaller islands whose respective infrastructures stood little chance of a cash injection, the early signs were that new internationals could be plucked from the dance floor of this Caribbean party. Keiron Pollard would be the most notable of them, smashing 83 off just 38 balls after coming in at number three for Trinidad and Tobago in their semi-final obliteration of Nevis. At the age of 19, the knock proved that he held an amazing temperament and forced a one-day international call-up the following April albeit an undistinguished one: an innings of 10 and bowling figures of 0/20 from three overs in a heavy defeat to South Africa. He would travel to the ICC World Twenty20 too and although he is still to make his mark on the biggest stage of all, the exposure and the pressure of Stanford 20/20 has at least propelled his name to the international selection table.

Crowds provide pressure and nothing below the elite tier of West Indian cricket could really help players like Pollard to progress before Stanford's innovation. The final of the first edition provided that and between Sarwan and Deonarine, Guyana scratched their way home. Stanford led the onlookers in being awestruck by it's success; Trinidad's faltering from a winning position barely seemed like a failure. Surely, there could be no failures in such an environment. So far there haven't been but all cogs in the Stanford wheel will have to face the same way or the juggernaut won't only become stoppable, it will reach a standstill and become a mere cash cow rather than a product capable of reviving and bettering West Indian cricket.

The Word Spreads

"Some people threw their stones and their glasses and some things like that so we decided to go back to the dressing rooms. Lots of the army were involved in that game and the security arrived around 11 or 12 o'clock so we finished very late."

Rana Naved ul-Hasan,
Sialkot Stallions and Pakistan all-rounder

TWENTY20 IN THE WEST INDIES had its moments of appearing as a cricketing utopia over the first two seasons: partying crowds, kaleidoscopic colour and simmering sporting passions. Yet despite being one of the most revolutionary inductions of three-hour cricket across the world, it had been beaten to it by most of the other nations bearing ICC full membership.

England got the show on the road in 2003 and South Africa were the next to get in on the act the following April.

"The Standard Bank pro20 series is going to launch a new era for professional cricket in South Africa," lauded Gerald Majola, the South African Cricket Board's Chief Executive.

"Everybody on the park has to go hell for leather from start to finish to win the game. We believe that the public is going to love it and an exhilarating stage will be set for the new season and a new era of cricket."

Perhaps the imitation of the Twenty20 Cup that had been such a roaring success in England was lost in South Africa amid the upheavals that saw the customary eleven-province cricket system chopped to six franchises – a move to strengthen domestic cricket to produce a higher quality nursery for the international outfit. The whole business generated debate. Top grade opportunities were cut meaning some cricketers lost their dreams and careers, even though the provinces remained and their matches retained first-class status despite now being played effectively by amateurs. There was a fear that some home talent would move abroad.

The South African hierarchy pulled out all of the stops to ensure the competition would be a roaring success, in spite of the backdrop. The Proteas backed out of a regular triangular tournament date in Dubai to try and showcase their strongest and most recognisable talent in front of the biggest crowds possible and fans certainly turned out in force despite the fact that the teams on show were man-made creations rather than the provincial bodies that almost commanded support and allegiance from those living inside the regional boundaries. Five-figure crowds were evident at many of the latter round-robin games and the semis whilst Centurion Park sold out more than a day in advance of the final, which rounded up the support of almost 18,000.

Those kind of figures are put into context by the unwanted greenery of South African Test Match venues where, England games aside, the empty green seats are king. It takes something special to compete with rugby in the Rainbow Nation (it will become even harder when the hype surrounding the 2010 FIFA World Cup of football kicks into gear) and whilst 'Pro20' wasn't quite on that scale, it had at least entered the market place to jostle with those sports for the attention of the young.

Such was the momentum of getting twenty-over cricket in South Africa that it seemed to many in retrospect to be its' creator or at the very least, a co-parent alongside the English. The responses elsewhere though remained mixed.

At the top of the cricketing tree, the conservative reactions of the Australian hierarchy could have been predicted. After all, wasn't it their insistence on not playing too much cricket that had installed them as world leaders in the first place? India's governing body looked down their noses at this perceived fast-food sport for political as well as sporting reasons, outlined in the next chapter. Yet like a curious brother, Pakistan found the temptation too much to resist.

With a committed financial backer in ABN Amro sponsoring the competition, Pakistan's leading sides took to the experiment in flamboyant style for the debut season in 2004-5. Even the names were sensational: the Dolphins and Zebras (Karachi), Leopards (Islamabad) and Stallions (Sialkot) to name but a select few.

Like in England, the first season provided a lot of fun and a glimpse toward the future as well. Moin Khan, the ex-international wicket-keeper who had helped his country over the line in that remarkable World Cup semi against Martin Crowe's New Zealand thirteen years before, bashed the first century in the domestic event with 112 at a rate of almost two runs a ball for the Dolphins against Lahore. His big-hitting and big match expertise was to come to nought though as Faisalabad Wolves were crowned champions of the inaugural edition and later, Twenty20 champions of the world (see chapter 20).

Faisalabad were in the second final too, a game that would display both the pros and cons of cricket's newfound popularity. Ultimately, they would go down to defeat against the Sialkot Stallions in the National Stadium, Karachi, where their 152/8 would be comfortably chased down but the match was made memorable for the unruliness of rioting supporters whose antics delayed the game by over two hours, starting with the throwing of bottles and stones onto the playing area.

"Karachi City Naib Nazim, Nasreen Jalil, who was chief guest on the occasion, called upon the crowd to calm down, but her calls remained unheeded," reported *The News*. "In the meantime, miscreants remained busy in breaking gates and chairs of the general enclosures while around fifty of them were seen running and jumping on the roof of the stadium."

"It was a pretty late night," says Sialkot all-rounder Rana Naved, whose three wickets allied to some forceful striking with the bat earned him the Man of the Match award.

"It didn't take us long to decide that we should go off the field but for a while, we didn't quite know what was happening. I'm not sure why it started and got so bad because we were just concentrating on the game. It was in the early hours of the morning when we finished the match but still, there was a massive crowd inside the ground."

The estimated attendance was a phenomenal 30,000 yet questions were asked from all quarters about the lax security around the final. Many wondered why the reaction times had been so slow when minor skirmishes had littered the championships.

At a basic level, the figures piling in to watch these events were unprecedented for top level, non-international cricket in the modern era but like in

England, it brought with it a reminder of what can happen at mass gatherings when passions are running high. It might only take a few idiots, "a minority" as many would like to term them but still, a minority of mindless thugs can still endanger a high volume of people. Onlookers would hope and pray that hooliganism would not seep into cricket from elements of various other sports.

In Twenty20 though, cash speaks far louder than violence could ever hope to and in Pakistan, it was coming through by the bucket load. Impressed with what they had seen on the field, the sponsors bumped up the loot for edition three so that the winning team would scoop an amazing Rs1,000,000, the runners-up Rs500,000 and the man-of-the-match in the final, Rs25,000. The figures were astronomical and made cricket seem worth playing, especially to those outside the international arena or with no genuine hopes of aiming so high.

Sri Lanka opened their Twenty20 for the first time just ahead of Pakistan and surprisingly, New Zealand, for so long at the forefront of innovations like these, waited until the next southern hemisphere summer along with the Australians. By that time though, there was still no inkling of the Indians being tempted to join in and even when the ICC announced a Twenty20 World Championship would take place in 2007, India were perilously close to being cut out of the loop.

One Outside The Circle

""If something be not done, something will do itself one day, and in a fashion that will please nobody."

Thomas Carlyle

THE SCOTTISH ESSAYIST THOMAS CARLYLE might have died almost a century and a quarter before the grand jamboree of Twenty20 made its explosive incursion onto the established cricket scene yet his sentiments can't be bettered in helping to summarise the way that the Indian hierarchy failed to embrace it and found themselves peering into short-form cricket from the outside. At first, they didn't want the child and then they wanted a litter of them.

History informs us – and with an air of authority – that burying heads in the sand is seldom a good idea for progress. For various reasons, the Western Allies stuck their fingers in their ears whenever Germany was mentioned in the mid-thirties but had to contend with Adolf Hitler anyway. The Soviets refused to publicly acknowledge the carnage wrought in the Chernobyl disaster until it was far too advanced to avert huge casualties and if you take the logic and apply it to cricket in it's most simplistic sense, it took the Kerry Packer affair for cricketers to get what they believed was enough of a fair deal from their employers.

For better or worse, richer or poorer, India were left behind and both the stakeholders within the game and the public seemed reasonably content with that whilst the rest of the world got into bed with Twenty20 cricket. Overall, there appeared to be no clamour for a different style of cricket when the existing brands were proving so fruitful. It wasn't broken, so why fix it? Yet an indifference that seemed to be an endemic national trait helped fuel a multi-million dollar private tournament launched little more than two months after India's coronation as the first ever World Twenty20 champions. The fissures between the governing bodies and established orders in the world game and anyone daring to join the group quickly tagged as "rebels" would widen almost irreparably as the Indian Cricket League (ICL) neared realisation in late 2007. Anyone with a reasonable comprehension of cricket's recent past will not be surprised by how it came about.

Indian cricket is a multi-billion dollar industry yet that same money has brought with it occasional rancour in some quarters. A revolt over pay made an unwanted appearance before a Test Match series against Pakistan and the lead-up to the 2003 World Cup was blighted by similar concerns. Moreover, contract negotiations with a dizzying number of zeroes over advertising revenues and commercial broadcast rights always seemed to hit so many headlines as to overshadow the actual action had we been talking of anywhere else other than India.

Indeed, there had been a danger that India wouldn't even send a team to the inaugural Twenty20 tournament and the administrators seemed to hold the new game in sufficient contempt to use it as a bartering tool in their wish to co-host the 2011 ICC World Cup. India presented a bid for the 50-over tournament to the governing body along with Pakistan, Sri Lanka and Bangladesh but presented it three weeks after the initial deadline and with more than double the venues than the guidelines for staging the competition dictates. India shared the hosting of the competition in 1996 but were incensed that some factions believed their late bid should be dismissed and lobbied furiously to get back in the frame. Australia and New Zealand had prepared a document believed to be pretty much in line with what the ICC were looking for, so they weren't stuck for options, but with suggestions rife that India would consider not sending a side to South Africa for the Twenty20 competition having gained an exemption, the deadline was shifted back by the best part of another month so that the sub-continent could have a second bite of the cherry. Negotiations done, India would send a side the following September and the rest would be history.

Unsurprisingly then, cash was at the core of the creation of the ICL and like the prelude to the Packer case, the main gripe was in the allocation of cricket rights in India. Zee TV had tendered a bid to screen Indian cricket and it was indeed believed to be the highest sum on the table. Yet the deal remained unsealed and Zee were denied the broadcast rights, the reasons given centring on their inexperience in screening live sports events although there appeared to be some internal concerns on shelling out well over $200m. In the end, they would sort it out in the same fashion as Packer had when his Nine Network had been inched out of the reckoning Down Under in the seventies. If they didn't have an invite to the cricket party, they would have to throw their own.

Again, it was a two-way street. For Zee TV and the Essel Group that owns them, a new private competition to hit back at the BCCI could not possibly see the light of day if it didn't have the top-class cricketers to make it entertaining and thus, a viable business plan.

Thus one of the major contradictions of Indian cricket was exposed, that whilst the elite rung of cricketers were richly-remunerated with enviable status, the aspiring players or those who had been on the international circuit already and awaited a second chance, were struggling to make ends meet. Not only that, some cricketers were missing out altogether.

"It is the stated aim of the ICL to source new talent," former England captain Tony Greig told *CricInfo Talk*. Greig was a key aide in bringing the ideas together and acting as an intermediary to bring the players. Also an accomplished broadcaster, Greig was 'in the know' on breakaway events too as a cohort in Packer's World Series where he skippered the Rest of the World side.

"There is a school of thought that there are talented people missing out and not getting through the system," he continued. "Zee are very committed to making it work and they also believe that there are a lot of opportunities around India where cricket isn't being catered for the way it should be." When the private enterprise came along flashing the colour of their rupees, you could hardly blame cricketers for wanting to jump on board and convert their abilities and potential into banknotes.

"The money involved is too much to ignore," an ex-India interntional anony-mously told the *Hindustan Times*. "What we earn now will stop once our first-class career is over. It would mean going back to ordinary middle-class living after that. Since many of us don't have the motivation to do well in the Ranji Trophy and win back our India place anymore, accepting the ICL offer would make sense. It's worth taking that risk."

Some spoke of central contracts worth around £250 with their clubs (ICL top-bracket players were rumoured to be scooping around £30-35,000 per year), others of sleeping on long overnight bus rides to and from matches with funds not available to book a hotel room instead. Disenfranchised players were not particularly hard to find across India although it is fair to suggest that many didn't vent their frustrations with the system until the figures promised by the ICL made it plainly obvious that they weren't earning as much as was possible from their stock trade. The same source in *The Hindustan Times* complained that once he had been contacted about signing an ICL contract, nobody from the existing cricket bodies sought to improve his deal or sound him out about steering clear of the Zee TV group.

Of course, big money backed the Indian Cricket League but like in Packer's day, it needed highly-respected personalities from the world of cricket to help set the wheels in motion not only in India but abroad. Tony Greig jumped on board and brought with him a working knowledge of circumventing the authorities from his active involvement in World Series Cricket whilst Stuart Law – the Australian who was to captain the Chennai Super Stars in the first edition of ICL – was recruited through Dean Jones, the former Australia batsmen. The biggest coup for the oft-labelled "rebels" was the leading role assumed by Kapil Dev, arguably India's greatest ever cricketer who was sacked as head of the National Academy after taking up a position on the ICL board.

For a long time, Shane Warne and Glenn McGrath were linked to ICL contracts as was Stephen Fleming, having recently been deposed from the captaincy of New Zealand. Whilst such grandstand names gave the fledgling competition added credibility at a time where it was little more to the casual punter than column inches, a place in one of the six regional teams didn't eventuate. Brian Lara would feature, the first man to put pen to paper on an agreement, as would Inzamam ul-Haq and the retired Kiwi trio of Chris Cairns, Chris Harris and Nathan Astle. Other reported approaches bordered on the surreal, none more so than Warwickshire's Neil Carter, an excellent all-round cricketer but nevertheless one who struggled to nail down a place in his county's Championship team for the most part of the 2007 summer.

The names being bandied about disturbed the BCCI hierarchy and their reactions to just about anything to do with the ICL intensified and strengthened with each passing day. Ultimately, they banned any Indian players who signed on from accruing any benefits whatsoever from BCCI events and with the national team coming under their umbrella, that means an effective suspension from Test and

ODI cricket. The whole thing raised a number of debates that will, in time, shape the modern politics of cricket. Again, we are left to ponder who exactly owns cricket whilst also accepting that in other walks of life you can't expect to freelance for too many rival enterprises at any one time. How many people have keys to the head offices of both Pepsi and Coca-Cola?

The major flashpoint of this political muscle-flexing came in the form of Kapil Dev, a hero of Indian cricket for multiple generations. In leading India to a World Cup win at Lord's over the mighty and all-conquering West Indians in 1983, he became revered for life in his homeland and he had first registered on my youthful, sporting radar seven years after that at the same venue when he clobbered Eddie Hemmings over the ropes from four successive balls to avoid the follow-on in the Test Match that will be eternally remembered for a triple-century from Graham Gooch. His experience had seen him ushered in as head of India's National Cricket Academy but his involvement with the ICL wasn't tolerated by the BCCI, who promptly sacked him, entirely in keeping with Kapil's expectations.

The Indian Cricket League had a number of stumbling blocks as it prepared for life out of nappies but had it not been for the politicking of the governing body and their reluctance to stage a Twenty20 competition of their own, then there would have been hardly any market at all for the Zee TV venture. After belatedly confirming their intention to play in the World Twenty20, a domestic tournament was hastily arranged for April 2007 – almost four years after England's big launch of the Twenty20 Cup, but the boost in popularity for the domestic game was barely replicated. Television rights were not sought with anything like the same verve and vigour and in heat well in excess of 40 degress centigrade at times, grounds were sparsely populated even though many of the India internationals were involved. The protagonists remained unconvinced.

"Look, let's be honest, I don't really see that happening here," reflects Dinesh Mongia, "In India people only go to the ground for international matches. Of course it would be brilliant if people came and supported their teams like it happens in England. It's a huge difference playing in that atmosphere. But here, even with international stars playing, whether it is in Ranji Trophy or Duleep, we can't seem to draw crowds for domestic cricket." Yet Mongia clearly wasn't unimpressed enough to give Twenty20 in India a completely wide berth, accepting an offer from to become a 'rebel' and swap the state crest of Punjab for the more fluorescent attire of the Chandigarh Lions.

His was hardly an endorsement of the Twenty20 brand but the Indian Cricket League would have different parameters. It would be played in December so as to have reasonable weather, the stars would be multi-national as well as local and no expense would be spared on entertainment, all of which would be beamed across India and the world via the Zee network.

However, the waters were to get ever muddier when the old order decided to stage their own competition as well. The Indian Premier League franchises would fight the corner of the reactionary forces in cricket and look to hold hands with other national associations to act as a bulwark against the threat posed by the ICL. Pakistan would have a Premier League too and they would all build up to a Twenty20 Champions League when the best in the business would get their heads together in India and squabble over megabucks. Now this was becoming brinkmanship of the highest order but whether such proliferation lies in the best interests of the game is anybody's guess. From the outside looking in, it didn't seem like many people cared about the greater good of the sport in India. So many people had their own individual agendas that Twenty20 had initially slipped off the radar completely. Now it was at the core of the grandstanding and the fissures were starting to widen.

One assignment for those associated with the ICL would be to try and find somewhere to play the games. The BCCI had already laid their cards on the table by showing that they wouldn't work again with collaborators – the same stumbling block hurdled by the Packer group – but after a protracted search, taking in minor enquiries in Hyderabad and on the outskirts of Mumbai, the ICL settled on the Tau Devi Lal Cricket Stadium, just outside the northern city of Chandigarh.

The open-plan arena in the town of Pachkula boasted a stately-looking pavilion but was flanked by low-rise spectator areas in places that gave the early impression of an archetypal rugby league stadium from the seventies. However, the boundless faith the ICL organisers had invested in their 'brand' meant that even in the early stages of planning, they were looking for a stadium with the possibility of further construction if the competition got off to a flyer. It would have the capacity to hold 7,000 in the first competition but by taking out a ten-year lease with the regional administration owning the land, they had laid down their own marker to the BCCI that the Indian Cricket League would carry on regardless.

Cricket as a pastime, sport or business has been such an acquiescent and respectful game that 'rebel' or 'breakaway' events like the ICL have been rare. At a function to celebrate a benefit awarded by his English county Lancashire in the summer of 2007, Stuart Law gave praise to Kerry Packer's initiatives of the 1970s that ultimately improved the cricketer's lot and it's only by pitting the two side-by-side that we can get a clear picture as to whether or not the Indian Cricket League is on the march to success or expensive failure. Packer was bent on acquiring the biggest and the best of everything and staging early episodes of his new cricket form at Melbourne's VFL Park could hardly have been conducive to looking like a slick and polished product. "A huge, soulless, concrete edifice with acres and acres of open concrete terracing," complained Henry Blofeld of the 77,000 stadium in his excellent tome *The Packer Affair*. Fewer than a thousand attended the first WSC match at times. By contrast, the ICL could hardly go wrong with the tinge of realism in a nation where anything but ODIs and Tests against Pakistan seemed certain to be played in front of the proverbial three men and a dog.

As with any of the Twenty20 tournaments across the world, no measure of hype can ever stand the scrutiny of even the most casual cricket fan if the quality of the cricket is poor and reservations about the standard of the Indian recruitments were emblazoned across the Indian press in the run-up to the wickets being pitched for the first time in late November 2007. From the original forty or so Indians to sign up, only fourteen played for their state teams although players of the quality of Deep Dasgupta were held in high enough esteem that their loss to the breakaway competition would help weaken Bengal in the Ranji Trophy, for example. Of the state sides, Hyderabad, Punjab and Tamil Nadu were particularly badly affected. If not boasting quality across the board, enough players signed up to discredit the BCCI's assertion that the only players signing up to the ICL were "retired players."

On the field would be the only way to settle the debate and even after the first tournament, whether you thought it was a high standard of sport or not would generally depend on which camp you were in in the first place. The opening match was inconclusive, Chandigarh Lions led by former New Zealand international Cairns inching out a Delhi team captained by Sri Lankan Marvin Atapattu and blitzed by the seam bowling of another Kiwi in Darryl Tuffey, whose 3 for 16 proved the difference in a low-scoring game.

The main difference was in the field. Indian cricket at the sub-international level had been left behind in the preceding four years whilst rival nations honed their athleticism in Twenty20 fields across the world, making the India success in the ICC World Twenty20 all the more remarkable. Now they had to play catch-up and were excelling, the run-out of Imran Farhat by 22 year-old Abhishek Sharma the embodiment of what would be a breakthrough competition for ground fielding.

Not everything was quite so slick and having publicly clothed their decision not to award Zee TV with 'official' broadcasting rights on the tag of 'inexperi-ence', the BCCI hierarchy might have worn a sage smile watching the second match of the series, when the Chennai SuperStars defeated the Kolkata Tigers. Commentators struggled to recognise players, especially those plucked from various levels of the Indian cricket pyramid, the denouement coming when Tony Greig was heard pleading with his broadcast team about the identity of a new batsman when he thought he was off-air. His embarrassment on learning it was Stuart Law, a veteran of 54 ODIs for Australia, was palpable. Yet with dance shows enlivening the action and also with heart-rate monitors attached to the players and their figures displayed on live television, the coverage did at least offer something fresh.

Law's case is an excellent one in showing how terrific cricketers can gain increased longevity through Twenty20 cricket if it is structured in an accommodat-ing way rather than one that favours a survival of the fittest. At 39 years of age, he had been made the captain of his county side in England and had just aver-aged 63.9 in a County Championship summer that had seen him rack up almost 1,300 runs. Whilst Twenty20 with Lancashire wouldn't rate among his top priori-ties because of the county ambitions at first-class level, there is no reason why a competition based exclusively on twenty-over cricket can't see him play on for two, three, maybe even four years depending on form. To a greater degree, the same can be said of players such as Cairns if the hunger persists. Signatories to ICL were constantly reminded in the media that many regarded them as selling cricket's soul but to servants such as these, surely the governing bodies owed the chance to maximise their earning power by playing as much as possible so long as broadcasters and supporters were paying money for the privilege.

"It was one of those things where we all turned up not really knowing what to expect," Law would reflect. "We found that these young Indian guys had given up everything. They were sponsored by their companies so as well as not being able to play cricket again, these guys had lost their jobs. So we went in there with the idea that we had to get our heads together and it turned out pretty well.

"I learnt a lot about the Indian way of life and they are very excitable people. If things went wrong for the team out there, they expected to be shouted at. With Michael Bevan [the former Australian international enlisted to coach the Chennai side], we tried to get across the message that it didn't work like that and if we lost or something like that then it was because we didn't follow our plans properly: it wasn't anybody's fault. As a group, they were so thirsty for knowledge but they had never had a team meeting before so things like that were completely new to them. We take it for granted that we sit down in the dressing room and have team meetings but here these guys were having them for the first time."

Law floated around the batting order and scored his runs at a strike rate of 110 per 100 balls but his experience in preparation would add a new, professional dimension to another strata of Indian cricket.

Not every big name proved to be as big a success on the field. Brian Lara flopped for the Mumbai Champs on the second day, leg-before to Azhar Mahmood for a golden duck in a dismal defeat to the Hyderabad Heroes. A run of 4, 3 and 9 followed before he dropped himself so far down the order that he didn't bat in the final group game against the Kolkata Tigers, by which time the Chumps (sic) were scraping the bottom of the pool and couldn't make the semi-finals. Lara's grappling for form was rather undignified, although his bank manager might argue to the contrary. Sporting greats not knowing when to call time on their careers is always a sad thing to witness: remember Nigel Mansell trying to wedge his expanded frame back into a Formula One car and Paul Gascoigne fighting the urge to prolong his footballing career as long as possible. Yet for each Lara, the Indian Cricket League would unveil to the public a star who otherwise might have been hidden from the glare of publicity forever.

A bald head and omnipresent grin greeted Lara when his side took on the Chennai Superstars and the man wearing both bears more than a passing resemblance to Dmitri Mascarenhas, the Hampshire mix-it-up artist. His name is Thirun 'Kenny' Kumaran, a 31-year old medium pacer with intelligent variety who was discarded by the India ODI set-up after eight matches at the turn of the millennium. This was his chance to remind everyone what they had been missing and on television too so the determination was a given yet the way in which he played the game seemed infectious, the jolly yet whole-hearted professional acting as the perfect antidote to the top-level experience enjoyed by most of the overseas recruits. Without ICL, his career would never have taken such a lucrative twist but even the loot will have seemed secondary when he sent Lara packing for 4 for his third wicket in seven balls, a sequence started off when he surprised Nathan Astle with one that dragged back to bowl him through the gate.

"I remember standing at the presentation at the end and he [Kumaran] was next to me with Dean Jones on one side and Lara on the other," recalls Law. "I tapped him on the shoulder and said 'how's it going mate?' and he just couldn't believe what was happening. He had played for his country on an Australian tour and then not been seen again and hadn't even played first-class cricket for five years and now he was having these experiences that he wouldn't have at any other stage of his sporting life. It was proof that the concept really worked. This was all happening live on Indian TV and people were starting to recognise these guys in the street before the tournament had finished."

The players must have been fairly distributed across the different teams because four of them had to be separated by net run rate of the six competing sides, all of them going through to the semi-finals. Despite the leadership of Inzamam (who had recently retired from international cricket with Pakistan) and the often-incendiary hitting of Abdul Razzaq, the Hyderabad Heroes sulked off to the fifth place play-off with just one win fewer.

Does anyone care? It seemed that no cricket fan would really take an interest in who won the Indian Cricket League, it would just become a detail of history. Supporters in India certainly couldn't identify with teams loaded with overseas players as well as local (ish) talent, in their garish uniforms. What they could do though was enjoy the spectacle and whilst India were playing Pakistan in a Test Series to lure away national attentions at the launch of ICL, the competition proved a rather good rival for channel-hoppers. India won the three-match affair and Sourav Ganguly excelled but two draws stultified a series that started as a battle of two decent cricket nations and turned into a batathon. "The cricket remained uninspiring throughout; often it was insipid," commented Sambit Bal on *CricInfo* in his series review, by which point the Zee Group might have been half-pleased that they didn't win the broadcast rights.

The finals weekend came after India-Pakistan viewers had arisen from their enforced slumbers but also before the hype about India's tour of Australia (starting with the First Test Match in Melbourne on Boxing Day) could really get into full swing so it filled a void.

Chennai crushed Kolkata in a surreal game that best summarised the unpre-dictability of Twenty20, charging up to 167 after first wasting the solid platform afforded them by the fearless striking of Ian Harvey and wicket-keeper Chris Read, the England reject cleverly brought in from Nottinghamshire. 104/6 became 167 mainly thanks to Raj Sathish and his lusty half-century. As was the fashion in the ICL, the chase faltered and Kolkata subsided for just 74 with no batsman managing to break into the twenties. Chennai would be joined by Chandigarh, the nominal home side staving off the challenge of the Delhi Jets. The final would show that all of this amounted to an event that the locals wanted to see, if only to satisfy their curiosity.

"We were shocked and surprised by how many people came," said Kapil Dev. "It is such a small city and to have fifteen days of cricket there was great but we were not equipped to bring so many people in. It was totally unbelievable but we were mixing cricket and entertainment because we had the games and then the girls who were coming and dancing too."

Chennai would edge a final with plenty of endeavour and hard graft but where some of the younger charges still looked a bit rusty and perhaps over-whelmed by their surroundings. The Superstars didn't quite "live up to their billing", in the words of the beautiful Zee TV anchor Mayanti Langer but they were dedicated enough to get home, Australians Ian Harvey and Stuart Law hitting thirties out of a total of 155/8 which was successfully defended thanks to a hat-trick from Pakistan's Shabbir Ahmed, who finished with 4/23. It was a tangible reward for the sixteen squad members involved for their bravery in defying the closed shop mentalities of the cricket authorities.

"Please tell me, what did we do wrong?," asked Kapil Dev, "we had Brian Lara and Inzamam playing and our young players will learn from that. If there were no opportunities and Lara will retire tomorrow, lots of ability goes into the ground. The ICL offers something back to the cricket community, it gives opportunities to cricketers."

Once the games commenced, it became clear that the longer the ICL per-sisted, the more hardened the resistance would be from the different strands of the BCCI and in turn, Shubash Chandra (Chairman of the Essel Group funding the competition) and the ICL top dogs would stand even firmer. The first post-competition flashpoint came shortly before Christmas when Darryl Tuffey of the Chandigarh Lions turned out for his state side Auckland in a first-class game against the touring Bangladeshis. The ever-protective BCCI detected a softer line on the 'rebels' from New Zealand Cricket and immediately registered their protests, wanting Tuffey to be ostracised and left to rot in grade cricket until he was no longer marketable to organisers of events like the Indian Cricket League. At least the overseas stars appeared to enjoy their month-long stay in India.

"The whole tournament was just brilliant to be involved in," reflects Law. "It was made very clear to us from the outset that it might not be a spectator sport and that it was for television and that's why we had the brightly coloured uniforms – they stand out more on TV. So they [the organisers] weren't catering for crowds but for the final, five thousand seats were sold two or three times over because they didn't expect people to turn up. So ten or fifteen thousand people were trying to get in and then they were turning people away as well.

"In future they want to build a bigger venue, maybe to hold forty thousand people so you can see how much it has all gathered momentum: it didn't take long to realise this is pretty serious stuff. At 39, I didn't feel as though I learnt a lot about cricket from it but I was batting in a different role than usual. At Lancashire I either opened in Twenty20 or batted at three but using the experience in the middle order was something I had to get used to. As it transpired, I didn't enjoy that as much but the whole event was great. It was one of my best physical work-outs in years."

The Indian Premier League (IPL) was the official response and at every mention, their aims and objectives heightened in trajectory. Eight teams would play on a franchise basis, again focusing on the major Indian cities, and at the media launch, the biggest stars were there by way of endorsement: Glenn McGrath, Sachin Tendulkar, Sourav Ganguly. The games could be played in a number of different stadia because of the official status of the competition and that was expected to be a popular move in a nation of twenty-plus Test and ODI venues, all of which would compete to stage as much international cricket as possible. Here, the biggest stars were coming to the biggest cities come what may.

They were heading into the tournament with mega-bucks stuffed into their cases too. Pakistan's Mohammed Yousuf was rewarded for turning his back on the ICL with a contract worth US$330,000, Muttiah Muralitharan would pocket a quarter of a million dollars and Justin Langer US$175,000, not bad at all considering the public song and dance the same officials had made about retired players taking the money of the rival Indian Cricket League.

One of the sticking points appeared to be over Langer's former international team-mates. Eleven centrally-contracted Australians had signed a pre-agreement that entitled them to play in the IPL and whilst Cricket Australia were happy with the principal of the tournament, Chief Executive James Sutherland was dismayed at not being consulted first. A tour of the West Indies was perched on the calendar perilously close to the first outing of IPL and Sutherland was insistent that nothing would come to impede Australia's world domination.

"The workload and the timing of when the Indian Premier League is," argued Sutherland, "in spite of perhaps players looking to sign contracts, it might be that Australian players are only able to play one out of the next three years."

Adam Gilchrist backed him up, saying albeit belatedly that the collective desire to pitch up in the IPL came second to the needs and demands of his country.

Money continued to pile in. ESPN-Star's TV network forked out a reported US$240m for the rights which offered the tournament some kind of public validity and with the Champions League concept offering another layer of clothing (for the best two Twenty20 sides from England, Australia, South Africa and the IPL in October 2008), the rival event was being written off as a failure by the more sycophantic media outlets, before it's inaugural series had even drawn to a close.

Of course, the ICL had a response with a press conference that acted as the prelude to the Chennai against Chandigarh final: they would not only be hosting more events in 2008 but they would be expanding into other forms of cricket too to get the most out of their investment in talent. The Indian players among the six squads would play a fifty-over competition, there would be a triangular Twenty20 tournament for select ICL teams from India, Asia and the Rest of the World and then an ICL Grand Championship, in which the original six teams would become eight.

"In five years time we will produce talent that will be fit to play for the country," said Kapil Dev, who would oversee the opening of ICL academies half-way through 2008. "I'll be very disappointed if they do not want to include that talent."

Even though there had been a domestic tournament in India for twenty20 before ICL, the 'rebel' event hit the stage at the right time, soon after the public conscience had become aware of short-form cricket and wanted more of it thanks to one of the most unlikely international successes since Kapil Dev's charges stormed Lord's in 1983.

Last Minute Party

"I see it in a similar way to the 1975 World Cup now in that it will set the benchmark for future events but we're going to have something new and that's how we see it being run."

Steve Elworthy,
ICC World Twenty20 Tournament Director 2007

WHEN THE ICC FIRST LAID ON THE cricketing dinner-party known as a World Cup in 1975, only eighteen one-day internationals had ever been played so the whole idea was construed as something of a gamble and a fad by some. It worked. Without any of the contemporary rule contrivances to crank up the entertainment – the power plays, fielding restrictions, pyjama clothing and floodlights – people paid to watch it and were entertained by the new international theory that a result could be achieved in a day, even if the sixty-over matches made those days bloody long ones. It still fitted into the needs of a population finding time to be increasingly of the essence.

32 years on and little had changed in the way that a new structure of cricket match would be landed upon the international community as an official tournament. Before the twelve competing teams had surfaced in South Africa in September 2007, sixteen Twenty20 bouts had been staged across the world in little over two and a half years. Of course, some nations had enjoyed more exposure to these contests than others. New Zealand – administrators perhaps softened up by Max Cricket not long before – had featured in five such shortened games,

quickly latching onto their marketability to become the first nation to host two matches at the start of an international series. Australia might have been sceptical towards various aspects of Twenty20 but on the quiet they were weighing in with some practice, playing 6 in the same space of time. India and Pakistan found themselves already committed to an array of one-day internationals in the seasons leading up to the first World Twenty20 competition and were far less acquainted with the whole idea.

Having proved themselves to be admirable hosts of multi-national sport, South Africa was selected as the inaugural venue for what was to be known as the ICC Twenty20, reflecting the success of the 50-over World Cup in the Rainbow Nation four years previously and also the confidence shown by FIFA, football's governing body, in awarding them the first World Cup to be held on the African continent in 2010.

"I think it's the domestic set-up with the Standard Bank pro20 that has been so successful as a whole to set this up," proclaimed the former Springbok allrounder Steve Elworthy, installed as the Tournament Director.

"It's given cricket some great exposure in South Africa and revitalised the domestic game. We've been selling out pro20 matches and that's a bit of a factor as well because we've learned how to put these matches on and in our presentation to the ICC, we could show that we've escalated the game. Our reputation for staging world class events now goes without saying after the 2003 World Cup so we have good stadium facilities and ticket services and the successful bid for the football World Cup shows that we're still going forward."

The challenge for Elworthy and his team was at once bigger and smaller than that of his predecessors in co-ordinating ICC major championships. In the eleven months leading up to the Twenty20 tournament, the much-maligned Champions Trophy (described in Wisden as "the unwanted stepchild of international cricket") had produced the dampest of squibs in India and the World Cup had produced little quality cricket of note and left a sour taste in the mouths of fans who were treated with disdain when they could have feasibly expected a carnival atmosphere for seven weeks.

The ICC World Twenty20 would last for just thirteen days and be played across just the three venues: Kingsmead in Durban, the picturesque Newlands in Cape Town and Wanderers in Johannesburg so logistical problems would be kept to a minimum, no small matter for the organisers with little more than eighteen months to cobble it all together. Another major help would be the fact that four of the minnows the ICC felt duty bound to hurl in among the big boys in the World Cup would be relieved of further embarrassment with Kenya and Scotland having to win the right to qualify. In essence, it would more of the actual matches competitive.

The competing nations would be divided into four pools of three sides with the draw seeded in accordance with the ICC world rankings of March 2007, six months before the competition. With the format still emerging and fighting for parity with other types of cricket, the seedings had to be figured out using form from fifty-over cricket but no true anomalies could really be spotted by anyone but the most alarming pedant after the eventual draw.

Old rivalries would be allowed to simmer in new surroundings: Australia would face up to England, India would tackle Pakistan and, as in the curtain-raiser for the ICC World Cup in South Africa, the hosts would open up against the West Indies. The top two sides in each group would progress to a 'Super Eight' stage.

However, the great paradox with the longer tournament in 2003 would be in the nature of the playing conditions each nation would encounter. Ever since the end of apartheid and the re-emergence of South Africa onto the world sporting stage, floodlit one-day cricket in the country appeared an idea of incredible folly. A team winning the toss in the mid-afternoon would invariably bat first, knowing that a steady if unspectacular performance would make it nigh impossible for a chasing side to win with the dew factor making sure the white ball bent around corners.

"We hold the games either between 2 and 5 in the afternoon or 6 and 9 at night," Elworthy emphasises, "so the idea is that you can come down and watch the cricket and then go out somewhere else and fit some other things into the day or night. Because the game is short, the conditions are less changeable too. So you might get some dew or colder conditions at night but they don't drastically change WITHIN a match – you could have a game all in the day or all under the floodlights."

Whatever Elworthy's pronouncements about the potential of the event in his homeland, rather like the global domestic competitions, it needed some serious competitors and their major entertainers to catch the popular imagination. That World Cup in 1975 had most of those and with a glittering final between West

Indies and Australia, just about managed to survive the ignominy of Sunil Gavaskar's rather ludicrous innings of 36 not out painstakingly acquired over 174 balls against England. The naming of the squads that the major nations would take to the ICC World Twenty20 would be the early indication of how seriously the respective nations were approaching the event.

The Australians are traditionally precious as to who pulls on the green and gold and when they became the first to show their hand, it was little surprise that only one change to the entire squad was evident from the one that had completed a hat-trick of World Cup wins in the Caribbean earlier in the year: Brett Lee fit again after injury and able to displace Glenn McGrath, who had retired on a high. Such has been the routine nature of just about everything the Aussie cricketing fraternity have done over the past decade or so that their announcements were made with barely audible fanfare. They believe their biggest talents represent their best cricketers in just about all forms of the game and they weren't about to tear that up over some twenty-over bashes.

Playing catch up with Australia perhaps led the peloton to mix and match their approach in an attempt to find rabbits in their collective hats. New Zealand made a public statement by dropping Stephen Fleming, the man who had been their influential captain for over a decade up until the end of the 2007 World Cup, despite an average of 22 and, perhaps more crucially, a strike-rate of 129.4 runs per 100 balls that hardly disgraced him over five matches. South Africa left out Jacques Kallis citing concerns about a high density of cricket over a short period of time (Kallis rubbished those claims and resigned the vice-captaincy in an immediate fit of pique) but the host nation had enjoyed some success in Twenty20 internationals by trusting a broader pool of players rather than simply their tried and trusted 'big names'. The Indian team had a youthful glow: Sourav Ganguly, Rahul Dravid and Sachin Tendulkar told to rest up ahead of a seven-match series of one-dayers against Australia on home turf and eighteen year-old leg-spinner Piyush Chawla among the rookies drafted in.

Just being there as a participant seemed to have been a result of sorts for India, as we have already established. Ahead of the tournament, it could also have been seen as a positive thing not to have been confused and weighed down by too many theories regarding Twenty20, having had so little exposure to it. Many of their rivals sat on the opposite side of the fence.

England for example had learnt very little from their dalliances on the international scene and by September 2007, memories of that thumping of the Aussies in Southampton two years previous were scant. The nucleus of the international side had been stripped bare: Jon Lewis flirting with the side but never nailing down a long relationship, Darren Gough deemed too old and ineffective despite still being one of the nation's best death bowlers, Marcus Trescothick, the lynchpin at the top of the order, was laid low by a stress-related illness that threatened his career on the world stage. Now it was back to the drawing board and that was where the debate really raged.

Test cricket has long been the priority in England and one-day internationals have often been seen as a kindergarten for prospective Test stars to see if they had the mettle to cut it under pressure. Such neglect of the one-day side fed down to the Twenty20 internationals and led to defeat when England took the field for two more in their domestic summer of 2006. The fans expected something positive to happen because the game was born in England, so why shouldn't they be the world-beaters at it too? It was all so depressingly similar to other sports.

Sri Lanka were first up in June, again at the Rose Bowl, in a game inched into the evening to avert a clash with England's group game with Trinidad and Tobago in football's World Cup in Germany. The place of Twenty20 in the pecking order for both sides was brought into immediate question with their respective team selections: England largely ignoring the Mal Loye, Darren Maddy kind of cricketer who had performed with admirable freedom in the domestic competitions and instead sticking in great measure to a group of talented and centrally-contracted stars whose suffocating schedule denied them the chance to perfect the art of Twenty20 with their counties. Sri Lanka omitted their two best bowlers in seamer Chaminda Vaas and the inimitable Muttiah Muralitharan ahead of a five-match series of 50-over games.

Had it been a one-day international then the Southampton crowd might have torn up their ticket stubs and gone bananas with so many big names missing. But the condensed nature of Twenty20 made for close ties anyway and a trend started to emerge of world-class performers proving marginally less important.

Sanath Jayasuriya and Upal Tharanga got the golf clubs out early and blazed away with an intoxicating mixture of power and indifference to their new surroundings. Their opening stand of 75 used up fewer than eight overs and sent international newcomers like Yorkshire's Tim Bresnan and Durham's Liam Plunkett back to graze in the deep with their tails between their legs. After the early fireworks had subsided, Sri Lanka fizzled too but they were able to defend their total of 163 despite the absence of Vaas and Murali.

The home crowd might have gone home unhappy with the result but they could hardly debate the entertainment value in the 2-run defeat. Trescothick's belligerence threatened to steer the home side to success but Geraint Jones and Bresnan fell short of the nine they needed at the start of the last over.

Familiar stories were played out across the globe as the major nations got to grips with Twenty20.

Pakistan were greeted by an under-strength South Africa with Kallis and wicket-keeper Mark Boucher omitted and neither Andre Nel nor Makhaya Ntini among the bowlers but they were hammered by 10 wickets in February 2007. The better team unit won, the bigger names meant relatively little because having failed to compete with basic cricket against a swinging ball in amassing 129/8 and having come up short with the bat, the visitors found twenty overs not to be enough time to fight back, ultimately picked off by Loots Bosman and Graeme Smith.

Fun cricket came in different ways. In a farewell lark of a game to say good-bye to Chris Cairns as an international all-rounder, New Zealand and West Indies finished with scores tied in Auckland in February 2006 and settled the game on a penalty bowl-out, a bizarre tie-breaker that has often been threatened to settle matches but seldom utilised down the years.

Almost 28,000 squeezed into Eden Park that night and by the time of the ICC World Twenty20, nearly every major nation in the game had experienced some drama or other. Little surprise then that there would be a clamour for tickets when the finals came around.

The paradox with the World Cup and Champions Trophy was the serious effort to include and incorporate cricket fans and local communities into the tournament and help to inject excitement and fervour. Some group stage tickets went on sale for just 20rand, approximately the price of half a pint in the UK, with some final tickets available for as little as £7.50.

"We have to ensure that every person is able to enjoy the event and that the stadia are full," issued Gerald Majola, the Cricket South Africa CEO as a mission statement of sorts.

"We looked at the previous two ICC tournaments and in my opinion, they were not successful. So we have looked at those pitfalls and will take care of those in South Africa. We understand what Pro20 has done for cricket in South Africa, we wanted to make it a truly national game, accessible to all," added Majola before waffling something about taking the sport to the masses that seemed to have been borrowed from Lenin's big book of rhetoric. Still, apart from an assertion that SA was the spiritual home of Twenty20 it was hard to disagree with most of his stance.

With twelve squads and people queuing up to get through the turnstiles, all that was needed was a memorable fortnight to leave it's mark on even the most cynical cricket fan.

Fail To Prepare, Prepare To Fail

*"I don't think there's really time to choke,
everything happens so quickly."*

*Shaun Pollock,
South Africa*

IT'S AWKWARD TURNING UP AT A party without knowing the etiquette. Dressing in jeans and a t-shirt when other teams of people are dolled up in tuxedos and classy nightgowns can make you a short-term social outcast. The reverse just makes you seem an idiot. Do you turn up early and become all self-conscious, waiting to mingle or arrive late and face scorned people who think you couldn't give a toss. When do you get onto the dance floor?

All of these questions would be asked of the leading competing nations in the ICC World Twenty20 as they peddled into the unknown for the start of the southern hemisphere summer at the start of September. It wasn't that national bodies had prioritised the competition in different ways for ulterior reasons, just that without any experience of these parties, how do you know what to take as a present?

As explained in the last chapter, England and India tried to turn up fashionably late after a longstanding agreement to play a seven-match series of limited overs internationals off the back of a Test series that was often ill-tempered, always entertaining but cut dreadfully short at just three games in length. Far from being the staid and predictable spectacle many had forecast, it had drama and quality cricket in equal quantity.

England introduced new faces and unlike those of the previous generation, susceptible to failure and imminent discarding, their temperaments made for performances that seemed almost Antipodean in class. Luke Wright was one who transferred his county form to the international scene, bashing a rapid half-century on debut. Dmitri Mascarenhas, touted as an England star by none other than his county captain Shane Warne, lassoed five sixes from the last over of one innings and earned a place in the ICC Twenty20 squad thanks to an injury to seam bowler Ryan Sidebottom. They won the series 4-3 but fielding improvements led by the Indian newcomers such as Robin Uthappa and the embroidering spin of Piyush Chawla left the impression that the resting of Ganguly, Dravid and Tendulkar would leave less of a void than first imagined.

Just three days before the ICC World Twenty20 would kick into top gear, the last throes of that series were being drawn out at Lord's whilst, in a different hemisphere, the other competing nations were all flexing their muscles in Twenty20 warm-up matches and developing their strategies for the fortnight ahead.

Pakistan were among that number too and they gave the competition a bit of real kudos and credibility by having their usual inter-tournament fall out just days before the games were about to begin in earnest. Their speedster Shoaib Akhtar would not be given the chance to flatter to deceive yet again in South Africa, sent home in disgrace for attacking team-mate Mohammed Asif.

"I apologised to Asif and he forgave me," said a semi-repentant Shoaib. "But another team-mate, Afridi, took the matter further and it forced the management to send me back. The incident began with a verbal spat between me and Afridi, who used foul language, and Asif intervened. In anger, I hit Asif with a bat. Afridi said things about my family which I could not tolerate. He made comments that cannot be called jokes."

Afridi responded by saying it was all rubbish and challenged Asif to tell the truth, something he could hardly be brought to do in public once the PCB had slapped a gagging order on its players in a hopeful, but not expectant, effort to get them to concentrate on winning the tournament. Asif did however tell the Urdu newspaper Express that "Afridi had nothing to do with the fight. Afridi was trying to make Shoaib understand that he needs to change his attitude with the junior players and communicate more with them. He told Shoaib that juniors were wary of him."

It was all rather a shame. In a form of cricket where the batsmen had become so dominant, players who could splatter stumps and bowl with fearsome pace added to the razzamatazz. That Brett Lee was fit again and Shane Bond had given injury the body-swerve were all ticks in the championship box but for all Shoaib's public pronouncements about playing for Pakistan meaning everything to him and that he had turned down an offer from the Indian Cricket League to go on representing his country, it was scarcely a surprise that it would be the Pakistan side that would be affected by this kind of incident.

The build-up to the ICC Champions Trophy in 2006 had been hurled into the shade by the expulsion of the often controversial yet eternally melodramatic Shoaib and his seam bowling partner Asif, both of whom had tested positive for the banned anabolic steroid Nandrolone in an internal drug test run by the Pakistan Cricket Board (PCB). A month or so after the tournament had ended in the usual fashion – with Australia winning comfortably – the two were acquitted on appeal. At the Cricket World Cup the following March, the usual controversy surrounding the Pakistan camp turned to tragedy, misery and conspiracy theories aplenty as their coach Bob Woolmer was found dead in his hotel room after a shocking and unexpected defeat to minnows Ireland, a reverse that spelt the end of the competition for the 1992 champions.

They were in South Africa nevertheless and in their now customary bickering state, started off their campaign with a handful of warm-up matches. Zimbabwe were vanquished at SuperSport Park thanks to an unbeaten knock of 64 off 37 balls from Shoaib Malik, which gave the regrouping rookies too much to do in pursuit of 182 to win. Sri Lanka were beaten with more than an over to spare as Pakistan then chased 163 the following day, Mohammed Hafeez and Salman Butt opening up with a stand of 94 that almost indicated that inter-squad batfights were good for morale.

So much of what would happen over the fortnight of the finals would be dictated by the Australians though and their preparations were thorough, if not without hitch. The centrally contracted players assembled for a pre-winter camp in the third week of August and pitched up in South Africa relatively early in comparison with their opponents. They did arrive without their skipper and talisman Ricky Ponting, who remained in Australia with his wife Rianna ill, but the rest of their squad was suitably familiar and knowledgeable of their roles within the squad to continue apace with their adjustments for Twenty20.

Despite their world domination though since the back end of the nineties, Australia gave few examples of their superiority in back-to-back friendlies over the weekend preceding the competition, played in the absence of Ponting and the bustling all-rounder Shane Watson who had picked up a hamstring strain in the Brisbane training camps. One thing they did retain is their ability not to panic in a potentially pivotal situation with little margin for error.

Against New Zealand they also found that the success of spin that many of their squad had witnessed in domestic competitions in their homeland and in England might make itself a fraction more scarce in South Africa. Hurried seamer Ben Hilfenhaus returned figures of 3-11 in his three overs as the Black Caps motored to 182/8 but left-arm spinner Brad Hogg didn't enjoy his day quite as much in Benoni, thumped for seventeen runs an over. The target looked unhealthily far away for the green-and-golds when they floundered at 15/3 in reply only to regroup in mid-innings and get home with ten balls to spare courtesy of a maximum from Brett Lee.

They wouldn't use the 'get out of jail free' card in time the following day as South Africa powered to 180 with just two wickets down and five balls in hand. Having been 21/3 in just the fourth over, it took Andrew Symonds and the left-arm seamer Mitchell Johnson to blast Australia up towards a competitive total only for Graeme Smith and AB de Villiers to dwarf it with an assured and continuous pounding. Again, the spinners copped it with Hogg and Brad Hodge joining forces for five overs that yielded 54 runs.

Having already omitted Jacques Kallis from their squad for the competition, the South African hierarchy seemed desperate to divert attention from the actual cricket in their approach to an event that, on home soil, seemed to suit many of their strengths and experiences. Opening batsman Loots Bosman, who had starred so prominently alongside Smith in the Twenty20 international win over Pakistan earlier in the year, found himself excluded from the Springboks' side with an injury and replaced by the pace bowler Andre Nel, among whose strengths is undoubtedly getting in the faces and up the noses of the opposition. Bosman was livid and like wicket-keeper Mark Boucher had done regarding the Kallis omission, the anger became public. Bosman argued that he was fine and his physiotherapist had backed up his assertion that a resting period for his injured back of a

Middlesex were one of many sides across the world to mix Twenty20 with fundraising, adopting a pink strip in 2007 to support Breakthrough Breast Cancer.

The "Finals Day" brand in England included animal tomfoolery in the form of the Mascot Derby – a popular reincarnation of Football's Grand National as cricket reached out to new audiences.

The MCC solidly resisted change in staging Twenty20 fixtures at Lord's, the benches replacing the standard dugout to better reflect the everyday conditions for the club cricketer. Despite the rain against Surrey in 2007, it looked much more classy too.

Three matches in a day
made Twenty20 Finals a
war of attrition. Here,
Kent and Gloucestershire
finished eleven hours
after the first semi had
started.

All of a sudden, county cricket was fetching in the punters again. Standing room only for

Sussex against Kent in Birmingham.

The proverbial 'jack of all trades' became even more important in twenty over games. Rana Naved, pictured here in his time at Sussex – was a hero of Sialkot's win in Pakistan.

Twenty20 became so important to county sides that stars were being recruited for one tournament only. Sri Lankan run machine Sanath Jayasuriya put pen to paper for Lancashire in 2007 and Warwickshire in 2008.

Cheap ticket prices in South Africa saw grounds fill up again after the lack of interest in the 50-over World Cup.

India and Pakistan observe the anthems ahead of the dream ICC World Twenty20 final at The Wanderers.

The dancing squads in South Africa added to the spectacle of the World Twenty20.

India come to terms with winning their nation's first major cricket trophy in 24 years.

The ICC World Twenty20 was so important to Sri Lanka that Muttiah Muralitharan – interviewed here by the author – was called up from his spell with Lancashire to play.

Through the mass of glitter and tickertape, India celebrate their victory in the Johannesburg final.

It might have been South Africa but it could have been the sub-continent as India fans crammed in to the Wanderers for the final against Pakistan.

Eager to show nothing but impartiality, the 32 dancers waved the flags of India and Pakistan in equal measure in their pre-final routine.

Pakistan fans leave the Bullring as their Indian counterparts celebrate their world champion status.

As the ICC unveil the new trophy before the World Twenty20, Chief Executive Malcolm Speed is blissfully unaware that an Indian would be lifting it at the end too. Virender Sehwag was to miss the final through injury. (Copyright: used with kind permission of the International Cricket Council)

month to six weeks was excessive. His coach Mickey Arthur countered against the assertion that he "tells too many lies" [the words attributed to Bosman in the newspaper Beeld] and rubbished Bosman's claims.

It all added up to a picture of mayhem and mini-factionalism in the South African camp described by Peter Roebuck in the *Sydney Morning Herald* as "the sort of internal rumblings usually reserved for a cowboy picnic." Some sides need it as a jump-start from an inactive winter, a distraction from the real business of chasing trophies. As the quote from Shaun Pollock shows at the start of this chapter, the Springboks were more than aware of their ability in the past of faltering under pressure. Maybe with that history in mind, the lowering of public expectations would work to their advantage. Roebuck would counter the arguments of many and say that far from depressing the gap in class between the world's strongest and weakest nations, "doubtless the best team will prevail. A five-over match could be arranged and still, the strongest would find a way to set themselves apart." South Africa would line-up among the best in the world and so, even with all the unscheduled theatre, they would still be expected to reach the semi-finals.

It wouldn't just be the teams that would prepare meticulously for a big two weeks. The lowered ticket prices would lure the punters but there was also an emphasis on them to produce a memorable event too. Musical instruments – banned at various stages of the previous winter's Ashes series in Australia – were encouraged. Cheerleaders were limbering up ahead of the big kick-off at the Wanderers in Johannesburg to illuminate the place between boundaries and perhaps, to titillate some members of the public too. The closer the event came to exchanging roles from pipedream to reality, the better the weather would become in the South African springtime. Still, ground staff at Newlands in Cape Town had to contend with 33mm of rain in ten days with the teams touching down in the country and according to The Australian, staff there had to ready the pitch beneath a tent with it being too late to use a back-up venue at Centurion.

"There are no rest days, so you can reach the point of no return," said Tournament Director Steve Elworthy, "it's in the hands of the Gods. We're backing the Union and the plans they've put in place. It's a matter of managing the amounts of water that gets onto the field and Newlands has those contingencies covered."

The only contingencies required for the groundbreaking opening match at the Wanderers in Johannesburg would be hard hats. Fireworks illuminated the early evening in the capital as the opening ceremony whipped up the locals into a frenzied buzz. Hype filled the stadium as it had the preamble in the media. The beats of several drums around the boundaries offered synchronicity with the musical accompaniment on the stage. With red shirts and combat trousers it was chilled and leant truth to the rumour that a world cricket tournament finally had a pulse. This one threatened to burst through it's own skin.

The festivities, the waving of inflatable stumps and national flags became increasingly feverish as South Africa and the West Indies neared blast-off. They would be entrusted with cutting the ribbon in the style of a showman rather than a safe man. As it happened, few inside the Wanderers would feel safe at all.

Ramnaresh Sarwan, the West Indian skipper with knowledge of success in twenty-over cricket from his Stanford win with Guyana, called heads and the tail gave Graeme Smith the first decision of the competition, opting to chase, reasoning that the strip looked good enough to last forty overs without deteriorating so why not bat with a target in mind rather than not knowing what a manageable total might be.

To back up the evidence of the warm-up matches, both teams were stuffed to the brim with medium-quick bowlers and seam-bowling all-rounders, only the lethargic Chris Gayle and Smith himself could have considered themselves realistic spin bowling options in limited-overs cricket from the two sides and given the respective selections, even that seemed to have been reserved for the last resort. South Africa might have rejected Kallis as he approached veteran status but Shaun Pollock would shore things up with experience, Makhaya Ntini would offer the pace whilst Johann van der Wath, Morne Morkel, Vernon Philander and Albie Morkel would back up with varying styles of bustling seam-up. For the hit-and-miss West Indies, Fidel Edwards and Daren Powell would look to Ravi Rampaul and Dwayne Bravo in particular for reinforcements.

The first ball of the tournament gave every indication of what was to come. Pollock approached the crease in his measured manner and offered a touch of width to Gayle who forced him through the off side for four, backward point laying a hand on the ball but only parrying it to the boundary for four. Hip-hop cheerleaders started to shake their booty on the edge and rather like Stuart Robertson on the opening night of the English domestic Twenty20 at the Rose Bowl in 2003,

I got the shiver of excitement that the world was about to cotton on to a form of cricket that was alive and breeding new life into the rest. Gayle punctured the infield again with an uppish drive for two to deep extra cover and as Pollock took his cap having conceded eight runs from the first over, his cursing would be drowned out by the sound of Everybody Scream, pumped out of the loud speakers. Twenty20 had become an education in music as well as cricket with expression.

Ntini took the new ball at the other end and launched quickly into his rhythmic action. Having singles taken from his opening two deliveries, he bounded in with the third to beat the bat for the first time in the match with Devon Smith pushing nervily outside off stump. In this so called 'game for batsmen', the dot ball got a bigger roar of approval than usual and Ntini followed it up with two more before dropping short from the final ball and being cuffed to the wide mid-wicket fence to ruin the over and finish it on 14/0.

That was serene judging by what was to come. Gayle nonchalantly picked the first ball of Pollock's next over off his legs and scattered the paying public with a maximum, then mid-wicket would be peppered again as the fence was found for four more. This was Gayle's game and the altitude at the Wanderers sent the ball crashing towards the stands as if it were stolen from a ping-pong tournament. His World Cup on home soil had been ineffective, his contributions sparse and as always when the results don't come for the gangly leftie, his body language came under question. He eternally wears the expression of a man who prefers the fun side of sport to the hard yards and here was his free ticket to do just that. In the fourth over, he tucked into another hitherto tidy over from Ntini in a major way by smashing a length-ball over the ropes for six and following it up with a cross-batted swipe over long-off that appeared to land five rows deeper.

This was serious now for the hosts. Four overs in and the West Indies were rocking the place on 42/0 and even the most partisan of South African fans inside the Wanderers could do little but applaud the brute force and sheer self-belief that Gayle was to exude. Smith changed the bowling to introduce van der Wath, who opened up tidily. Morne Morkel replaced Ntini and found himself subjected to the backswing of a professional golfer second ball as he came around the wicket and was nevertheless punished through extra cover for four to bring up the West Indian fifty, Gayle boasting 39 of them in just 17 balls. When van der Wath's next over disappeared for fourteen runs, the DJ blasted out Pink and *Get The Party Started*. Perhaps unbeknown to him, it had done so twenty minutes before.

South Africa looked perplexed and Smith was starting to wear a small grimace in the field albeit far away from his players. Morkel over-stepped to give Devon Smith a 'free hit' but the thrill of trying to swat the ball into orbit meant that it came to nothing and with a single out to the sweeper on the cover fence, Gayle raised his bat to acknowledge his fifty in just 26 balls. Neither was he finished. Having had a look at the relatively new face of Vernon Philander by playing out a dot ball, Gayle dragged his front foot to the leg-side and deposited him over wide mid-wicket for a massive six. The remainder of the over was milked until a desperate Philander, with Mark Boucher stood up to the stumps, hurled a quicker ball down the leg side at the cost of five wides. Albie Morkel fared no better and at the mid-point, West Indies were 109/0.

Still, the crowd had fun. Banter was widespread, the cameras got their whooping from the guys and their hollering from the girls. They were further endangered though by the introduction of spin to the championships in the twelfth over, Smith loping in for six deliveries after which there would be no more in the opening game. A snick through the vacant slip region off the first delivery sent Pollock hurtling towards the third man fence as the batsmen crossed for two and Gayle then carted Smith over extra cover to beat the sweeper. The cheerleaders were loose of limb and fully expressive by the time Gayle tucked into the next delivery and bashed it over long-on for six more. Smith looked suitably shell-shocked and didn't offer up much more than a grimace to the rampaging Gayle. It's quite tough to sledge when the opposition end the twelfth over on 131/0.

Already it was time to chime in with some 'death bowling', the popular cricketing terminology for the lines and lengths preferred by an attack to restrict free scoring batsmen at the end of an innings. I just feel the whole concept is a bit bizarre. If the 'blockhole delivery' – full and straight – is the best way to cut down scoring, why don't bowlers do it whilst the fielding restrictions are on as well? It seems odd but already Pollock was into that mode as he started the thirteenth in stereotypically miserly fashion. Just two runs came from the first four deliveries before Gayle got bored and launched a straight six followed by a sojourn to the leg side whereupon he lifted Pollock over mid-wicket to the top of the giant chute that doubles as an entrance for the players to the arena.

"I think we lost the first fifteen overs," admitted South Africa coach Mickey Arthur afterwards, "and that was due to a fantastic innings from Chris Gayle, he really played very, very well. But the last five overs of the innings was the turning point and I think our death bowling was very good because at one stage we were looking at 230-odd. Those overs just gave us more momentum and we took that into the chase."

As so often happens when teams pound the boundaries to get the best of starts, losing the key player who offered that impetus in the first place often allows the rest to crumble. There is an old cricketing proverb that one wicket brings two often used by a fielding team looking to break a partnership and fight back into a match. Not only does it ring true in Twenty20 as in other forms of the game but it can be said to be even more accurate than in a first-class or fifty-over match. A wicket lost in Twenty20 after a big stand leaves the remainder of the batting line-up to feel that they have the licence to slog with wickets in hand. Ultimately, they try to hit big without the timing and form earned only from time at the crease.

Devon Smith had an eye in but he was soon departing, looking to force a Vernon Philander ball from just short of a length off the back foot and nudging a catch to Boucher for 35. The opening stand of 145 was a record for Twenty20 internationals and powering through the nineties, Gayle was on the verge of setting another milestone. With a crisp yet reserved drive of a low full toss down the ground, he moved onto 99 before then picking out de Villiers again in the deep only for the brace of runs to bring Twenty20 cricket its maiden international century.

Gayle purred and grinned with delight but he had already lost another partner when Marlon Samuels holed out to de Villiers patrolling the ropes down the ground having connected with just the one scoring shot, a quite immense hook for six over deep backward square. Gayle looked to keep smattering away the most towering strokes but was felled on 117 attempting to swipe a short ball from van der Wath over the on-side, he nicked behind and wandered off to a roar of approval having faced just 57 balls, ten of which had been swatted off the playing area. The South African skipper led those who shook hands with Gayle in appreciation of his brutality, Justin Kemp followed and the batsman dragged his feet to soak up the ovation but partly in frustration at failing to see out the innings, the odd glance was cast toward his equipment on the way off. Without him, West Indies could muster just 38 runs from the final five overs and despite logging 205/6, they were muscled out of things from that point onwards.

Smith and Herschelle Gibbs looked to work and tease and stretch the bowling in the first two overs, which yielded only eight runs. In that time, the captain had been rapped on the gloves by Daren Powell, a painful blow but he soldiered on to tally 28 runs before being duped by Rampaul. Gibbs was in the wars too and needed a runner to deal with a hamstring injury but would still bludgeon the ball to all parts in a chase that was ultimately decided long before the tenth over, by which time the hosts had gobbled up half of the target. Shivnarine Chanderpaul and Dwayne Bravo had shelled chances to gift Gibbs a double-reprieve but even had he been dismissed, West Indies would have been hard pressed to maintain pressure when they were sending down a mixture of width and short stuff without backing the good bowling up with decent fielding. The Caribbean side soon looked disheartened.

"We didn't do ourselves any justice by dropping quite a few catches and bowling quite a few wides," uttered a disconsolate Sarwan afterwards, "I don't think you can blame the batters for their effort. I thought we should have gotten fifteen to twenty more runs but basically, it's the fielding that cost us."

Justin Kemp, in when de Villiers got out, was missed as well with Samuels the profligate one. He landed up with 46 unbeaten which along with the 90 not out from Gibbs, made the win look a comfortable one.

The tournament was off to an incredible start with over 400 runs on an opening night that involved so much cheerleading that you would expect the girls in question to wither away from excessive exercise after a fortnight and also a win for the home side to keep the locals dancing to the beats that would lurch from the stadium speakers with a consistent urgency.

Pundits would acclaim the era of crash, bang, wallop, the regeneration of Gayle and the progression of Gibbs in cricket's shorter circus but they had been granted the assistance of some rather amateur work in the field and with the ball. Bowlers may decry a game that they believe could assist their downfall from prominence in the game and turn them into fodder but with a reluctance to vary pace or use fuller length deliveries to cramp the hitting zones of the batsmen, what exactly did the bowler want? To be paddled around by batters to retain some kind of false equality between bat and ball? Fielders will always drop catches and they never intend to do it, it just happens. 23 wides in an innings should never happen, especially not in a Twenty20 International and that's what the West Indies would have to fight back from.

Groups And Regrouping

Day 2 - Wednesday 12 September 2007

THE OPENING NIGHT OF any show, if all goes smoothly and to plan, is always the hardest one to follow, to meet all the expectations head-on and deliver a series of fantastic performances. So it was the good fortune, or good planning, of the organisers that left three battles between major nations and downright novices to be played out on day two, before the dust had even settled on the first game in Johannesburg.

As with anything in sport, cricket reserved a right to shock with unexpected results and plenty of these had happened since the inauguration of the World Cup in 1975. In 1992, Zimbabwe had humbled England in Albury when chicken-farmer Eddo Brandes had been among the wickets and the mightier of the two sides on paper stuttered in search of 135 to win. Brian Lara's West Indies were humbled in 1996 by lowly Kenya who bowled them out for 93 only to trump their own achievements seven years later by reaching the semi-final, where they duly gave India a fright. India were upset good and proper in 2007 when a loss to Bangladesh sent them spiralling out in the group phase on the same day that Pakistan's reverse to minnows Ireland had them reaching for the suitcases.

These things happen but they are by no means frequent occurrences. For every one upset there are five or six absolute mismatches in which commentary boxes are filled with debate as to whether the emerging nation is deserving of a place in the competition. The first such upset in a World Cup though was arguably Zimbabwe's win over Australia at Trent Bridge in 1983.

The circumstances for a surprise on the second night hardly seemed to be in place. The Aussies hadn't played any competitive stuff since picking off their

World Cup opponents like irritating cat hairs the previous April but they still swaggered and sweated confidence. If self-doubt existed then they were damn good at hiding it. Their captain was back in the fold having missed the warm-up matches and he led into battle a squadron of clean strikers of a cricket ball: Adam Gilchrist and Matthew Hayden to fire the opening salvos at the top, Ponting himself at three with Andrew Symonds, Mike Hussey and Brad Hodge – the Twenty20 king at six. Even without the retired McGrath, Australia would certainly not capsize with the ball and they had learned from their warm-ups and left out the left-arm spinner Brad Hogg.

By contrast, Zimbabwean cricket had gone through the mill in the near quarter-century since Trent Bridge and been forced to regenerate itself as a result of political wrangling. Their ascent towards the World Twenty20 hadn't been the sharp incline hoped for by many with the lack of opportunities to play decent sides; Robert Mugabe's regime turning Zimbabwe into a pariah state. Still they had made peace with their former wicket-keeping prodigy Tatenda Taibu who had renounced his international retirement to come back as a batsman and with the dashing all-rounder Elton Chigumbura and Stuart Matsikenyeri in their team, they could at least give it a good go. One piece of good news for the African side would be the dank atmosphere at Cape Town's Newlands venue (caused by recent rainfall that had broken two decades worth of records), already conducive to lateral movement and therefore a low-scoring match. Australia opted to set the pace on it when Ponting won the toss.

After a short fit of drizzle over Newlands, Gilchrist and Hayden marched to the wicket in a gold shirt with rather garish grey sleeves looking like athletic members of the A-team – rather like what was to follow, there was something not quite right about it. Gilchrist was off the mark in patient manner by flicking a full ball from Chigumbura through the on-side for two. No room to really thrash the next ball either so Gilchrist opened the face and dabbed a single. Hayden now took guard and had an early opportunity to bully the Zimbabweans but it was to be a short one as Chigumbura found the outside edge for the perfect response after Hayden had swatted his first ball through mid-wicket to the fence. 7/1 after four balls made for a pretty eventful start. The fun wasn't to end there.

Gary Brent kept it tight in the second over, just doing enough to keep both batsmen honest as four runs came off the over. Ponting wasn't looking to open the shoulders early but then again, he hadn't had a competitive bat for over four months and might have offered a touch too much by way of respect as he looked to get his eye in. A square drive brought the captain his second single but Gilchrist mounted an attack having gained the strike and skied a horrible pull-shot to be comfortably taken by Matsikenyeri. It was 12/2 and the captain no longer had the freedom to give himself a light net to get into some touch.

Most of the 15,000 inside Newlands had seen this kind of thing before: Australia on the back foot but then pulling the game around from nowhere to stomp all over whichever upstarts happened to be providing the opposition. The next partnership always had the potential to be the game breaker. Ponting offered respect to Chigumbura with a couple of defensive shots that he was unable to manipulate into singles. In the end he got bored and launched an ugly shot towards cow corner where the slow outfield could only offer him a couple. Time to regroup.

Only there would be no time. Ponting – who despite Brad Hodge's assertions that he was coming round to it slowly, seemed to have a real downer on Twenty20 – played gloriously through the covers by dancing out of his crease but the boundary brought the wicketkeeper up to the stumps and Ponting didn't react well to the restricted freedom. A good old-fashioned slog was the end result, Brent sliced down to third man where Chigumbura steadied himself from the celebrations of his two wickets well enough to take a measured catch. Now it was game on at 19/3 but whose nerve would prove the stronger?

Whilst the neutral always seems to shout for the underdog, there was something truly special about this game. Zimbabwean citizens had been through a tumultuous and often tortuous existence in recent years with little sport to illuminate their lives but here on the biggest stage, their cricketers were competing with the all-conquering Australians, champions in both Test and One-day arenas, and making them struggle. For a moment, I thought back to a story of a couple of months before when Iraq's footballers, their homeland still in the controversial grip of coalition forces and murderously divided by what in many cases amounted to a civil war, had won the Asia Cup football tournament. Their subjects might not have believed it possible but it offered a delightful obstruction to the daily life that had become so grim.

Zimbabwe had won nothing yet though and pressed on regardless. Mike Hussey was the new batsman and whilst he's used to working with very little pace in fifty-over cricket, the margin for error in this situation was unusually slender. The irony would not be lost on the pre-tournament favourites that they had the chance to get a glimpse of the Zimbabweans with a three-match series of one-day games the previous month only for the mini-tour to be cancelled at the behest of the Australian government. In conjunction with Symonds though, Hussey was in the process of reassembling an innings that had threatened to become a wreckage before disaster struck in the tenth over. Hussey wanted to play tap and run to the off-side but was sent back by Symonds to leave the left-hander in limbo. "Mr Cricket" turned sharply in the realisation that his wicket was in danger only to be confronted by the leaping Visu Sibanda who threw the stumps down with just one to aim at and sent Hussey on his way after a brief referral to the television umpire.

The smiles were tangible on the faces of those in red and green and the approval from beyond the boundaries gathered momentum with every falling wicket. It takes neither a historian nor a rocket scientist to detect the intense rivalries between Australia and the South Africans and with a win at their backs already, the locals were enjoying the opportunity to barrack for their neighbours. The see-saw got another push; the Aussies scratching around safely for runs and then being undone by sterling groundwork, Symonds the next to fall over-balancing against the bowling of Hamilton Mazakadza and stumped in the fourteenth over for 33.

When the batting just doesn't function it's easy to suggest that the order was wrong, the plan was wrong and the approach was wrong but credit had to be given to Zimbabwe. Their fielding was their strong suit and they played it without fear or reservation. Yet their limitations were still occasionally exposed when Hodge was given room to smash the ball away and twice cleared the boundaries against medium-pace. Curiously though having started the seventeenth over on 23 not out, Hodge couldn't manage to get the strike back from his tail-end partners and added only ten runs to his personal tally as Australia closed on 138 for 9 after Nathan Bracken chipped Chigumbura to deep cover point off the final ball.

"Our top order has been diabolical, even in the practice games here," lamented Ponting, cutting the figure of a man who wanted to launch a scathing attack on his side's batting in the post-match interviews but remaining diplomatic nonetheless.

"You cannot afford to get off to those starts. It is a mental thing for us, we have to start respecting the game a bit more and thinking about what we have to do."

139 would still take some chasing but Zimbabwe seemed unflustered in their start which had yielded 31 runs by the time Sibanda had nicked Bracken behind for 23. Wicket-keeper batsman Brendan Taylor, at just 21, was the measure of composure and it would be his night just as the previous evening had belonged to Chris Gayle. The difference was that Taylor would land up on the winning side.

Chamu Chibhabha caught one high on the bat and propelled a firework straight up into the night sky for Gilchrist to come and take the catch. Taibu tested the will of his team-mates further when he got an edge on a rising ball from the left-armer Mitchell Johnson and departed without score. At 55/3, the underdogs needed 84 off 72 balls to turn the established cricket world upside down for a night and they soon lost Matsikenyeri too when he was caught at the wicket off the probing Stuart Clark.

The baton had been involuntarily passed to Taylor. He hadn't had a seismic proportion of the strike but he was still in good enough touch to tuck into the part-time bowling of Hodge when he entered the fray as the sixth bowler. The opener pierced the infield on the off-side and then went big to a low full toss down the ground. It all transformed the pretty delicate balance in the game when the players had drifted off at 74/4 with the rain coming down in the twelfth over. Ponting had been continually clutching his Duckworth-Lewis rain calculations on a scrunched up piece of paper in his right trouser pocket and when they alighted, it told him Australia would win by five runs if the game was halted there. It wasn't and Taylor's assault on the spinner would tip the scales back in favour of the African team.

"I never thought it was slipping away," insisted Taylor in the aftermath, "I just knew that batting through would be the main point. We do have good hitters down the order there so when the wickets were going down it was just a matter of ticking the scores over and letting the boundaries come and that made things a whole lot easier."

Brett Lee fired down a stingy penultimate over that rid Taylor of a fifth partner in Masakadza, who was pinned leg-before to an almost silent response from the Newlands crowd. That left 16 runs needed from the final nine balls, which turned into twelve off the final six which were to be bowled by Bracken. Eleven would guarantee Zimbabwe the lottery of a penalty bowl-out but from a position that few would expect them to excel, they had nothing to lose.

Bracken looked to the 'full and straight' virtues of death bowling and produced an off-stump yorker from over the wicket that Taylor somehow managed to wristily whip beyond short fine leg and to the boundary for four. The television cameras pried on the nervy giggles of the Zimbabwe bench as one by one, they realised just what they were on the threshold of achieving. Chigumbura was the latest partner for Taylor and he realised that deference was an early virtue as he picked up the strike with seven needed off the last four balls following Taylor's push to extra cover for a single. Ponting called a conference with his bowler but it made little impact as Chigumbura steeled himself for an attack down the ground, where he picked up an easy two. Just like with the batting, you expected Australia to halt the slide but they just found themselves powerless to do so, their grip on the match weakened and minor frailties exposed. Chigumbura forced Taylor back on strike and now the Zimbabwean bench were as one, arms linked in a unity that the nation had barely known in some respects outside of sport for a generation.

Another spice was added to the dish with the rain coming down but even as Bracken vigorously looked to dry the white ball with a cloth with two balls remaining, it would play no major role. Looking for a fuller length again to Taylor, Bracken erred to leg where he had little protection on the fine boundaries behind square and after a deflection off the pads, the ball just had enough legs to cross the foam and cement a major upset. After a few cursory glances around the arena to make absolutely certain it was over, the Zimbabwe squad piled onto the outfield in unison, hugged Taylor and Chigumbura and set out on their deserved lap of honour.

"To beat Australia in this form of the game is very special. It's the kind of thing that can happen in Twenty20," continued Taylor, having retained his composure. Already, his innings had ensured that the ICC World Twenty20 had produced more memorable cricket matches than it's bigger brother, the World Cup.

Those stories are so special and heart-rendering for their rarity though and events elsewhere on the second day of the tournament proved the gulf in class between the minnows and the established nations. New Zealand – four-time World Cup semi-finalists – pummelled Kenya in the morning game by bowling out the African side for just 73 which in itself was something of a recovery from 1-4 early in the piece. The whole debate about the merit of associate members competing in world events is for a different author and perhaps a different place as well but the confusion of the Kenyans was both predictable and evident given their lack of exposure to the fledgling game.

Scotland offered more in their opening game against Kenya and came close to justifying their inclusion in the tournament despite defeat against the maverick Pakistanis in Durban.

With the general uncertainty about how Pakistan would be mentally prepared as well as the unquantifiable effect of Shoaib Akhtar's histrionics, the Scots might have fancied their chances early on with the ball and they squeezed the top order tightly. Dewald Nel opened up with a seldom-seen maiden and the pressure assisted his opening partner John Blain at the other end with the first ball of the third over when Imran Nazir got his angles wrong hitting over the top and punted the ball right down Gavin Hamilton's throat: 9/1.

From there, the innings crawled without partnerships to glue and fortify it. Five batsmen were to get out between ten and twenty indicating a scarcity of knowledge on how to approach Twenty20 cricket and how to build an innings in it. Younis Khan was coming off the back of some fairly ordinary one-day form with English county side Yorkshire but still hung around enough for a brisk 41 and although he top-scored, the lingering memory of a stop-start innings was the brazen insolence of Shahid Afridi who wound his backlift up as if he were powering a chainsaw and blasted two maximums in his seven-ball stay of 22 runs which took all of five minutes to accumulate. Supporters have every right to feel short-changed when fieldsmen do the inevitable and take the catch to dismiss him. The unpopular villain of the peace this time was Majid Haq.

Needing eight and a half an over to win, the Scots could hardly have been in a more contrasting setting than their last competitive short game when they shocked Lancashire batting first despite not really appearing to know what they were doing when they pitched up for a 22-over contest. This time, Fraser Watts thrashed and weaved at the top of the order and even connected with a few against the new ball but Umar Gul's four wickets made light of Shoaib's absence and Pakistan emerged unscathed with a margin of 51 runs.

"I thought we bowled really well up front," said a disappointed but not disconsolate Scotland captain Ryan Watson, "and when we came off I thought we had done a really good job. But they came out and bowled really well. I thought their spinners did a great job and it proved too much."

Scotland might have been beaten but there was a much higher entertainment factor than there had been in the World Cup when they were summarily tonked by Australia, South Africa and even Netherlands. A posting on *The Scotsman* website indicated that not every Scottish breath was hanging on the fortunes of their cricket team. "Who gives a shit about this game," it read. Twenty20 would gather pace over the coming days whether the Scots were ready or not.

Day 3 - Thursday 13 September 2007

CAPE TOWN AND DURBAN had been thrashed by the rains at the start of the South African spring so it was something of a surprise that the Wanderers was unfit for play at the scheduled start of the West Indies game against Bangladesh because of over-exuberance from the ground staff in watering the playing area. The breakthrough of the sun enabled the game to be played in full and it was underway just an hour behind schedule. Facing a must-win game, the West Indies had the chance to set the pace after being inserted by Mohammed Ashraful.

"This is a very young side and a very talented side, all the fifteen players are talented and we knew that if we can keep West Indies to 160, 170, then we can go out and chase that," Ashraful was to reflect and it certainly rang true on the day for the Bangladesh captain, "this is a very confident team and it was confidence that pulled us through that game."

Confidence it might have been but for Bangladesh, a cricketing nation showing all of the same credentials as Sri Lanka had done the best part of two decades previously before emerging as a truly great side in their own right, a great deal of hard work had been done that Ashraful initially undersold. The squad had gone through a commando school in the months preceding the tournament and worked on their mental strength too. Their warm-up matches had been plentiful in Kenya as well as South Africa and now they were a pretty well-oiled machine, ready to fire.

Ashraful looks and sounds hurt at the very insinuation that his team may be minnows, rookies or even underdogs in tournaments such as these, so it would have been a big tonic to see the back of Chris Gayle just three balls into the match when South Africa just couldn't get rid of him less than two days before. The WIndies barely recovered and it took a couple of crusades from Marlon Samuels and Dwayne Smith to force them up to a par score of 164/8.

Bangladesh were bashful, experimental, happy-go-lucky. Despite the early wicket of Gayle, Ashraful chanced his arm on opening with the spinner at the other end, hoping to throw a blanket of confusion over the batsmen by using Razzak. His first over was launched for twelve runs that gave the West Indian innings lift-off but Ashraful had the presence of mind to be flexible and change his plans. The clichéd 'young man's game' was turning out not to be that at all but to be one for top quality cricketers and Ashraful would certainly parade himself as one of those over the course of the chase.

Flicking the ball daintily over the on-side and then to fuller deliveries, pounding through the covers, Ashraful orchestrated a pursuit that was at once harmonious and vicious. Whilst the medium-pacers and quicks gave him far too much leverage to do hoist and bludgeon the bowling around, the Bangladesh captain seemed so intent on doing damage to the ball with hands of dextrous concrete that the casual observer would wonder whether he would go back to Test and ODI cricket and try the same.

Twenty20 is many things beyond pure entertainment but still as the West Indies were finding out courtesy of not only Ashraful but also Aftab Ahmed (62 not out), the basics of any pyjama cricket applied. Solid partnerships changed games, bowlers' shoulders sagged and drooped further towards the ground with each boundary, body language changed. Yet on occasion, the first few days of the ICC World Twenty20 would show so many of the world's finest cricketers and most regular performers to be trying to hit the ball too hard, dispelling the virtues of timing and instead producing displays of batting that whilst occasionally effective, would be ugly to behold. This is what the purists were afraid of. Still, it mattered not to Bangladesh who with several swishes of Ashraful's wand, dumped West Indies out of the World Twenty20 and would progress themselves along with the hosts irrespective of the result between the two sides.

As soon as the action in Johannesburg had given way to the relative sense and serenity of the post-match presentation, the teams were already lining up beneath the gaze of Table Mountain at Newlands and Zimbabwe had the opportunity to become the second rookie nation through to the Super Eights with a match against England, starting just seventeen hours after their lap of the ground had started in celebration of the win against Australia. The smiles still radiated among the Zimbabweans throughout the warm-up and at the toss a mood that became ever more giddy with England 20/2 batting first.

The English approach was quite a new and refreshing one coming off the back of that series against India in which they had proved to an incredulous nation that they could adapt to short cricket. They had skipped the practice matches due to lack of time and arrived in South Africa with plenty of new facets to their squad. Wicket-keeper Matt Prior would be given another opportunity to cement himself as England's premier gloveman as well as holding the responsibility of getting the side off to some screaming starts with the bat but ultimately, his confidence had taken a battering from intense media criticism and some ordinary performances towards the back end of the India tour and it was a mercy of fate when a broken thumb ended his participation in the competition less than a week later.

Of course, no nation bar the Australians really knew their best batting line-up but England were even experimenting with being experimental and were still working on trial and error heading into their first match. Darren Maddy is the "Mr Twenty20" of domestic cricket but pushing up to open with Prior would be a major challenge whilst Prior's county colleague Luke Wright shuffled up to number three to take advantage of the fielding restrictions even though Kevin Pietersen wore more experience and could arguably strike a bigger ball.

What England would find arguably more than some of the other leading nations at the ICC World Twenty20 was the chasm in quality between domestic and international cricket and how much that would change a match. Spin had proved fruitful in England, Australia and to some degree the Caribbean in the respective domestic series but in South Africa, Chris Schofield and Jeremy Snape would be lined up as fodder no matter what kind of bowling they sent down, surely?

Schofield's was a remarkable story that Twenty20 barely seemed made for. A leggie who had been played as a specialist batsman by Lancashire at times after his England debut because his bowling was creating new pitch maps rather than hitting existing ones, he left the North-West in discordant circumstances and ventured around the Minor Counties for a while, even sleeping in the back of his car at one stage before resurrecting his first-class career at Surrey following a couple of failed trials. Seventeen wickets for Schofield in the English domestic Twenty20 had parachuted him back into the international fold and although his statistics will testify figures of 2-15 in his four overs in the Zimbabwe game, the ordinary analyses over the remainder of the matches was hardly justice given the dropped catches against his name. "Just think of it as any game at Littleborough," soothed team-mate and former county colleague Andrew Flintoff as England walked out to the middle at the Wanderers.

The major strike bowlers in world cricket would also feature more within the first six overs than just getting the binoculars out at the end of their follow-through to gauge how far they had been hit. The likes of Shane Bond, Brett Lee, Chaminda Vaas and Dilhara Fernando would be a good yardstick for England's 'bowlers of the future' as international cricketers rather than just players who could make up the numbers for the crash, bang and wallop.

More pertinently, the perception that England had been among the breeding grounds for Twenty20 and so would steal a march on their opponents was misguided at best. Few of England's leading players had ever had the chance to hone their skills at the short game because the domestic competition invariably takes place in the middle of a packed international calendar in the northern hemisphere.

No matter what exposure to twenty-over cricket the Collingwoods and the Pietersens of the England team had enjoyed in the past, they would have backed themselves to use their international prowess to stave off the threat of Zimbabwe and their ability would tell. The dismissals of Maddy and Prior might have given rise to more smiles among the Africans but it wouldn't be long before Pietersen and Collingwood got stuck into a century partnership collected in just nine overs that rocketed England to a fifty-run win, the favourites refusing to panic when Brendan Taylor was launching their bowling to all quarters at the head of the chase.

Day 4 - Friday 14 September 2007

WHETHER IN TEST CRICKET or one-day internationals, there is seldom any better experience in world sport than that of India and Pakistan playing each other, paradoxical communities joined hipbone to hipbone, cheering every dot ball boundary and wicket as if it were a winning run in the World Cup Final with the unfurling of a national flag and the chaotic sounding of klaxons. After years of disharmony, Twenty20 at least gave the two nations some common ground as they shared a suspicion of the new game and where it was headed, albeit to different degrees. After India's match against Scotland at Kingsmead had been abandoned, Pakistan now held it in their powers to eliminate their neighbours and major rivals from the competition.

The match staged in Durban would be a utopian setting for the colour, desire and atmosphere that such a match demands. Indians are the second largest ethnic group living in the city. They had emptied the Indian community and filled the ground instead. This would be a game to remember.

If India were diffident in their stance on Twenty20 then their batting would do little to swing that pendulum towards optimism. Their start against the moving ball fractured opinion between irresponsible and aloof, little respect offered to the bowling of Mohammed Asif who as a result, ripped out four of India's top five batsmen to leave the crowd favourites 36/4. Lateral movement was treated as a momentary aberration rather than a scientific product of favourable conditions and high-class bowling. It could have been either indifference or just inexperience in the Twenty20 form or just a rather typically ordinary display by an India side outside the relative safety of their own borders.

"I think that when we started the innings, we were very nervous," explains Mahendra Singh Dhoni, the trialling India captain during the tournament who scarcely needed a defeat to the bitter rivals if he had realistic hopes of succeeding Rahul Dravid as the full-time skipper.

"We didn't have a 160 or a 180 to defend so we were quite dependant on the bowlers really and they did their job. We knew we had to win and get through to the next round because we didn't have a good World Cup."

Gambhir appeared uncertain from the off and was outfoxed by Asif until the third strike when he advanced down the track looking to swat the seamer over the infield and could only present a sharp but neatly-taken caught-and-bowled. With the score on nine, Virender Sehwag came up with a flat-footed cover drive that took the inside edge and occasioned a violent ricochet onto the stumps. Asif persisted with the fuller lengths and Yuvraj obliged him by squirting tamely to mid-off where Shoaib Malik mopped up the catch. In the seventh over, Dinesh Karthik's stumps were disturbed after the ball had cannoned into his elbow. The spectacle so many had hoped for seemed ruined.

The difference between Twenty20 and longer forms of one-day cricket is that early innings collapses don't always lead to resounding defeats whereas if a team is 36/4 in a fifty-over contest, it can invariably lead to a slow death. Early casualties would be the most consistent feature of Pakistan's fortnight yet they battled out of the proverbial trench so often that they crafted it into an art form. As the Lancashire captain Mark Chilton once told me, "you are never out of the game in Twenty20." The sub-continental battle in Durban would prove his theory.

Robin Uthappa was the man who capitalised on the ensuing chaos to register a measured half-century and give India something to bowl at. Sohail Tanvir brought about his downfall with his quite unnerving action, delivering the ball off the wrong foot. The left-armer swung around his angle of approach to Uthappa and got one to move away in the moist air, taking the edge and clutched by a jubilant Kamran Akmal behind the stumps. The batsman hung his head and with a number of rain breaks punctuating the passage of play, concentration wasn't easy, especially when the emphasis is so heavily-laden on the clean striking of the ball with little time to waste. Irfan Pathan weighed in with 20 but was out soon after an unscheduled drizzle break to Shahid Afridi allowing Dhoni to rattle through 33 and set Pakistan 142 to win. What's more, if India surrendered those runs inside 14.4 overs, India would be eliminated and Scotland would progress to the Super Eights instead on a superior net run-rate.

"Before our openers went to the crease, I didn't tell them to go bang, bang, bang, I just wanted to win," says Shaoib Malik, "If we had a good opening, a good start, we might have gone for it."

That good start never made it beyond the planning stage and if Shoaib had uttered words of caution and safety-first sentiments to his openers, they both needed their ears cleaning. Imran Nazir swung as if trying to fell a cumbersome tree with the line and length casually ignored and certainly not respected and RP Singh pegged back the leg pole. Salman Butt also went at the ball with hard hands and was restricted in a scoring rate that staggered around the six mark despite Kamran Akmal's persistence as pinch-hitter. Both were out within an over of each other though and Younis Khan was bowled by Irfan Pathan as India resurrected their cause. They had been short with the bat but now they could sense a comeback and slammed hard on the brakes. Pakistan were left needing 42 off the last three overs.

When Afridi perished, the ask was 39 off fourteen balls — a gargantuan task left in the hands of the relative newcomer in 33 year-old Misbah ul-Haq and Yasir Arafat. The batsmen had crossed whilst Afridi's all too frequent mis-hit was swirling in the moist skies so Misbah had the strike and launched a do-or-die mission against the spinner Harbhajan, depositing him first over long-on and then picking out the mid-wicket boundary for four leaving 29 needed off the last two overs and a feel-good factor about the Pakistan chase in spite of the dismissal of their most volatile batsman.

Agit Agarkar would bowl the penultimate over but although Dhoni looked unperturbed at it's start, his bowler picked a shocking time to lose control of his length. His first ball was short and bashed to the mid-wicket fence, his second too full and driven by Arafat for two runs. Once again a game that threatened to be one-sided at the end had reached equilibrium right at crunch time. Arafat changed his approach to keep the bowler guessing and Agarkar was found wanting, a length delivery crunched down the ground before Misbah was brought onto strike by a miscued single down to third man: eighteen needed off the last eight. Misbah decided to gamble and took a leaf from the book of Bruce Grobbelaar, the eccentric Liverpool goalkeeper famous for his shuffling about on the goal-line in the middle of a penalty shootout. Misbah lunged to the off side and lifted a decent ball over short fine leg to the boundary. Twelve needed.

Sreesanth had the responsibility of salvaging the game for India, a match they might have thought they had already won twenty minutes before. Arafat punched the first delivery down the ground for one but Misbah was less restrained with the reigns, biffing through the covers and beyond mid-off for fours that tied the scores along with a couple of runs brought courtesy of a half-fumble in the deep. Pakistan couldn't lose and India had found the brake pads faulty just when they needed to slam on. Sreesanth came around the wicket and banged in a short ball, Misbah beaten trying to slash over point.

The field crept in and Sreesanth looked far edgier than he had for the previous ball. The Indian fans dared to believe a dot ball was still possible and started to mumble a few shouts of encouragement. Sreesanth hit the pitch hard and Misbah couldn't force the ball off the square and found himself yards short as Yuvraj bounded in from cover to run him out. India celebrated like they had just won a major Test series when in fact all they had achieved was a tie.

In the World Twenty20 though, a tie wouldn't be the end of the matter, instead they would be decided on penalties, just like that crude and rather cruel way of separating teams in knockout football. Neither team appeared to know the rules and had them spelt out by the umpires and team of back-up officials brandishing textbooks of instruction on the outfield. The novelty added drama and excitement but it seemed the ultimate bastardisation of what some believed to be a bastardised form of the sport that an oft-called 'batsman's game' would be settled by the bowlers and nobody else.

Both sides would nominate five players from their starting eleven to bowl one ball each at a normal set of three stumps with the wicket-keeper positioned a few steps beyond the timber as a virtual ball-boy. Rather like penalty competitions in football, the most hits after one ball each would be deemed the winner and a sudden-death situation would act as a tie-breaker if those scores were level too. It was all rather surreal. Players in both blue and green joked, relaxed and floated down a few practice deliveries on the outfield by way of a warm-up whilst the details of this novel decider were thrashed out.

Part-time spinner Sehwag gave the impression that the whole affair was a rather jovial one by approaching the crease for the first ball in his cap but he struck the top of middle and leg to give India the perfect start after Shoaib Malik had won the toss. Sehwag limbered in from his mark with his well versed action and didn't seek to change it to improve his accuracy but Pakistan did and the outcome could hardly have been worse. Yasir Arafat sauntered in off a shortened run-up and careered a high full toss wide of the off-stump to give India the advantage. Graham Gooch, the former England captain providing some much needed insight into the ESPN Star coverage from the commentary box, struggled to comprehend the wisdom in changing a bowling action that had got players selected for international duty in the first place.

Harbhajan got grip from the pitch but didn't need it to spin as he crashed into the top of the stumps to give the rather surreal cricketing scoreline of two-nil. Umar Gul worsened the crisis for Pakistan when he abbreviated his approach too and missed the off stump as well. Occasional slow bowler Uthappa doffed his cap in celebration and performed a small dance on turning the screw by hitting with India's third and when Shahid fired a full ball down the leg-side, India had made history by winning the first bowl-out in competitive international Twenty20 (New Zealand had prevailed in one such tie-breaker against the West Indies but that was a friendly international) by three hits to zero.

"I just told my bowlers to go out there and hit those wickets. Don't take any pressure and they tried but they weren't successful," reflected Shoaib Malik.

"Whenever you play against India and you lose, it hurts but we will get a lesson from this. We gave a hundred per cent and played quite well but we didn't lose in the ground, we lost in a bowl-out. I'm quite satisfied."

His opposite number was understandably amused by the surreal finish. "I'm very happy to win a cricket match three-nil because it doesn't happen every time," beamed Dhoni before adding a note of caution. "In future, I wouldn't really like to go through the bowl-outs though because we work so hard on the field that it would be good to decide on the field whether we win or lose."

Before the fortnight was up, Pakistan would have chance to forcefully ram home their revenge.

* * *

CLASSIC INDIA AGAINST PAKISTAN matches were ten-a-penny in modern cricket parlance, partly devalued by the irregularity of meetings over the previous decade. However, the acceleration of intensity in the Future Tours Programme in the years leading up to the explosion in Twenty20 cricket meant that some things in the game were becoming staid and almost clichéd. Proverbs were trotted out with such frequency that it seemed the commentators and pundits responsible could say them in their sleep, if they ever found the time for any. A popular refrain was that 'wickets in hand' was 'the key' to a run chase or to setting a testing target for any team batting second, a mantra that would more often than not prove to be at loggerheads with the reality of twenty-over cricket. If not making this crystal clear to all and sundry in the thirteen-day event, the World Twenty20 would certainly dissolve some traditional mindsets and allow for some revisionism over the weeks and months that followed.

As India and Pakistan thrashed out their sub-continental domestic affair in Durban, England and Australia were just cooling off after an event in Cape Town that would prove one of the big disappointments of the tournament. The picture was all too familiar. The Australians had lost one battle and non-Aussies world-wide had giddied themselves at the potential for world champion blood. The problem was that I'd seen this before. The previous winter, I'd splashed out almost two grand in all on a trip of a lifetime to Oz in the dreamy belief that the series would be flourishing by the time of the Boxing Day Ashes Test in Melbourne. England had downed their eldest cricketing enemies with the bat and ball equivalent of a left-right combination after the first test of the 2005 series and won it 2-1. Some of the squad had celebrated with the all-nighter to render every subsequent one pointless and rocked up at the open top bus tour with a bleary-eyed stagger. Yet in the return series, 'Dads Army' stuck their steel toe-capped boots onto the throats of the English and clobbered them out of sight with the assistance of comical moments such as Steve Harmison's series-opening wide. I arrived Down Under just in time to witness Australia reclaim the urn on Channel Nine rather than Sky TV.

The last two tests reinforced the Aussie hatred of being second best so with adrenalin haemorrhaging through every pore, it would have taken something quite remarkable from England, or docile from those in the gold-sleeveless-silver-swank tops, for the fifty-over champs to slum it against the Poms and slink away on the first available Qantas. Instead, the two nations reverted to type, England getting away to an unspectacular start in their scrabble for competitiveness and losing wickets through nerves and self-induced pressure rather than as a by-product of anything the Australians were doing from twenty-two yards. Mitchell Johnson forced a quicker one through to the under-pressure Prior who top edged to Bracken. Luke Wright found the accelerated introduction to the higher level just too tough and nicked behind and Darren Maddy, trapped in a venomous triangle of consolidation and construction, eked out just twenty at a run-a-ball.

England made 135, all out when Bracken bowled Stuart Broad with the last ball of the innings but there was never a thought that it could have been sufficient. As Brad Hodge admitted the Australians had been world leaders in amassing huge scores over a day of Test cricket and now they were part of the bashing rather than bashful Twenty20 gang, whose main aims included scoring off every single ball. With the likes of Matthew Hayden, Adam Gilchrist and Ricky Ponting in their top order, the likelihood was that some of those scoring strokes would reach the ropes, Gilchrist and Hayden wandered through the first 50 runs of the chase in just 32 balls and after the humbling experience against Zimbabwe, world order had been restored: Australia won by eight wickets with 31 balls to spare and had qualified for the Super Eights.

"We had a bit more intensity about our cricket today and I thought we were excellent," Ponting uttered rather ominously at the end, "we used our skills a little bit better and against a team who have been playing a lot of cricket and have a lot more experience than us at this form of the game, we came out with a comprehensive win so I'm really happy with that."

It was understated from Ponting but still with an element of self-protection in his words, indirectly warning the public not to expect too much from Australia.

The group had worked out just about perfectly from the viewpoint of the administrators though. Zimbabwe's performance had shown that the tournament had value rather than being a politically-motivated way of throwing sub-standard sides to the lions, the crowds were inebriated on excitement and continued to vote with their feet yet the fact that Australia and England had made it through as the top two sides (in that order too) offered proof that Twenty20 wasn't upsetting the cricketing applecart too much. The best teams made it through by and large and whilst the West Indies had bowed out from Pool A, losing to Bangladesh was hardly a major upset given the scalps they had pocketed in the two years previous.

Bangladesh were stepping straight out of a mauling against Sri Lanka in just about every cricketing facet so that the latter were in the mood for demolition in the group phase should have been a shock to nobody. Against Kenya in the morning game in Group C, the 1996 World Champions racked up a daunting 260-6 in their 120 balls, "minnow-bashing at its best" recorded Kanishkaa Balachandran on CricInfo. Kenya had frightened West Indies – and beaten them – in the 1996 World Cup on the sub-continent by persisting with the area of line and length that had made Angus Fraser an innocuous-looking annoyance during his international career. But in the modern currency, line and length meant dollars to the likes of Sanath Jayasuriya and he cashed in his chips with 88 made at a strike rate of precisely 200.

"I think that we can win the competition with the players that we have," the little master Jayasuriya soothed in the middle of the English summer, when he turned out in a Lancashire Twenty20 campaign heavily burdened by biblical rain.

"We have Mahela [Jayawardene] and Kumar who are very experienced and then Murali and Chaminda [Vaas] with the ball so we have the ingredients to do something special.

"I enjoy playing Twenty20 too. When I made the fifty in New Zealand [then, the fastest ever in international T20], there was nothing special about the way I went about things, I just tried to play normally and positively and it worked. I hadn't had too many games in Sri Lanka but we played quite well in that game."

What Jayasuriya omitted to mention was the potential for Jehan Mubarak to wantonly blitz the bowling around for multiples of four and six but that's what he did in an incredible assault that left Kenya wondering why they bothered to win the

ICC tournament that doubled as a qualifier for World Twenty20. Sixteen balls of the innings remained when Mubarek scooted to the middle with licence to have a bit of a giggle at Kenya's expense with the towering scoreboard at The Wanderers dwarfing the Africans at 212-5.

Two early singles barely gave credence and credibility to what would come next as Mubarek waited until the departure of Tillekeratne Dilshan before opening the shoulders in the nineteenth over, Lameck Ngoche pasted away for three sixes over the arc between mid-wicket and long-on before a more cultured cover-driven boundary gave way to more aerial mayhem.

Kenya would surely have preferred the fence to have been found off the final ball as it would at least have taken Mubarak off strike but a single meant that he would test the stamina of umpire Harper as well as Nigel Llong in the final over, when the scoring sequence read 4,4,6,1,1,0. Mubarek had biffed 46 off 13 balls to aid the complete mental disintegration of the Kenyans who were rolled over for 88 with half of the side out for just 50 in the eleventh over. Those people who believed the skill levels would concertina and bring the minnow nations closer to the title challengers were given a hell of a counter-argument.

"The whole squad is really disappointed because when you come up against Jayawardene and Jayasuriya you have to be on the money and we weren't," trotted out a bemused Steve Tikolo, the Kenya captain only forgiven for his stating of the bleeding obvious by the state of shock he seemed to be enduring. He even managed to trump that with his next line. "We let them get too many runs," was the observant claim.

Even in a fifty-over match, or even a first-class game, defeat by 172 runs would be an extreme, some would say a hammering. Everyone is due a bad day though and it was a shame that it came for Kenya on the biggest stage. Tikolo insisted that by doing the basics of cricket well, his side could have competed with the major players but it served only to hammer another nail of realisation home to his youngsters who had also faltered against New Zealand.

How exactly the players at the table were supposed to raise the stakes from the events of the previous day seemed crazy to even aspire to. I imagine it would be like still having chips riding on a hand of poker only to discover an opponent has already bagged a royal flush and is about to make the efforts of all others seem pitiful. Perhaps the burden was as strong as an aspiring Swiss tennis player being billed "the next Roger Federer" or as suffocating as for the next manager of Manchester United knowing that comparisons with Sir Alex Ferguson are almost the only yardstick once the great man hangs up his chewing gum.

The ICC World Twenty20 bounced along at a pace not wholly in keeping with the traditions of cricket full stop. Whilst that was the point, it allowed no time to reflect on, absorb and delight in an astounding day of cricket totalling one tied match, a world record and the small matter of an Australia-England match-up. Whether through anticipation and hope or rare expectation, those games don't tend to be too dull. Cricket was reflecting the society in which it now found itself. Everyone needs to be everywhere and yesterday so why not lay on a sport that does just that? But classics though they might have been, the matches on day three of the championships had underlined just how important Test Matches are as a game that can be lived, breathed and enjoyed without pressing engagements around the corners of our packed-out lives squeezing out the nuances of the game because we have better things to do than think of them.

Collisions And Decisions

"It is galling enough for England's rugby players to lose to South Africa at rugby; it is even more infuriating when England's cricketers lose to South Africa at rugby as well."

David Hopps,
The Guardian (Monday 17 September 2007)

THERE IS NO LOVE LOST BETWEEN Kevin Pietersen and cricket crowds in the land of his birth. But the crowing that had started with his explosion onto the international scene in South Africa in 2004-5 became at once more acerbic and gleeful with his dismissal in the Super Eight stage of the ICC Twenty20 at Newlands, Cape Town.

Having awkwardly paddled a delivery from Shaun Pollock down to short fine leg and called for a single, Pietersen laboured and dawdled before realising he was in some strife. England were chasing 155 to win and had found themselves in some early trouble so they could barely afford to lose arguably their best swordsman and 'KP' understood that well. As the shy arrowed towards the bowler's end, Pollock reached out and saw Pietersen's frame stumble into him and lose control as the ball clattered into the stumps. Inadvertently stricken and airborne, he was run out.

"The umpires Tony Hill and Asad Rauf could have called dead ball," wrote David Hopps in the *Guardian*, "had they judged that Pollock's obstruction was 'wilful' and that would be a brave call in the hurly burly of Twenty20. But there was no logical reason for Pollock to run towards Ntini's throw other than to force Pietersen to change direction."

The blame or absolution of it is not of the greatest relevance but the incident itself offers a great metaphor to the whole tournament as well as the brand of cricket on show. The previous evening, the hosts had been sweeping aside Bangladesh to finish off their group stage and less than a day after its conclusion, they were imbibing a contest so frenetic that it bore the occasional hallmarks of the faster sports such as rugby that Twenty20 was set up to compete with.

Much like Pietersen, the match itself had swerved and dipped like a drunkard. South Africa were staggering at 94/6 in the sixteenth over but then found a surprise extra gear installed by Justin Kemp, who was dropped twice in as many balls at one stage, and Albie Morkel, who cleared a hundred metres to climb onto the theoretical leaderboard for the 'biggest sixes of the tournament.' 154/8 was a staggering achievement given the two-paced start offered by the top order and England landed nineteen short after Pietersen's hurtling demise allied to that of his captain Paul Collingwood proved the point of no return.

* * *

THE ICC WORLD CUP had also boasted a Super Eight but a mixture of tournament fatigue, tragedy and lack of sporting quality had made sure the stage would be nothing to write home about. Even without the death of Bob Woolmer to unfocus minds from the pitch, the idea was ill-conceived and had an extra spanner thrown into the works when Ireland and Bangladesh qualified instead of Pakistan and India. That turned a 'Super Eight' into a 'Super Six' or a 'Super Five' if you discount an England side who only flirted with a competitive streak in most of their matches against top class opposition. Worse still as it turned out, teams carried through points gained in the group stage to the Super Eight ladder, so major nations with a poor start to the competition were effectively dealt a slow and painful exit unless they found some remarkable upturn in form.

The Twenty20 equivalent was much more open and fun. No points would be carried over and the eight teams would be re-divided into two sections, from which two each would progress to the semi-finals. It reduced the risk of verbose lists of permutations and endless matches with no meaning towards the end of the phase.

With all teams starting from scratch, it felt like a three knockout matches each, if you can pardon the contradiction. The pressure seldom eased.

India kicked off the second stage unburdened by expectation anyway. Their doting public had hardly been introduced to this renegade cricket anyway so not winning a competition in which they were still playing catch up to their rivals was no disgrace. Conversely, if it transpired that folk back home did like Twenty20 and India excelled, they would be afforded even more hero worship than usual. Rather like the Cricket Max series in New Zealand at the turn of the century, many — me included — were surprised by the natural aptitude the Indians had shown for short-form cricket, ridiculous given the inspired and often improvised way in which they played their many ODIs. Ironically then, their next taste of freedom would be against New Zealand in Johannesburg where The Wanderers witnessed arguably the tournament's greatest match.

Having taken over from Stephen Fleming as captain of the Black Caps for the competition, Daniel Vettori remained reserved about Twenty20 as a concept (for which Kevin Mitchell in The Wisden Cricketer labelled him "an intelligent young man talking like an old fart" and claimed it was a "coded rejection inspired by failure.") yet there was no sign of inhibition in the performance against the eventual champions. Indeed, Vettori would be the architect of the victory: a nerveless display in the field hinting at a promising future as a Test captain and some beautifully crafted spin reigning in the masters of that art after their volatile start to the chase.

As with many captains, Vettori started to warm up as soon as his field were allowed to scatter at the relaxing of the fielding restrictions. By that time though, the first twenty-six overs had yielded almost ten runs apiece and India were 76/1 chasing 191 for victory. Virender Sehwag had his authority entrenched in the boundary boards at The Wanderers having peppered or cleared them eight times in his brief stay at the crease. Jacob Oram affected his removal though and Vettori was able to give a rare master class of spin taking control as it had in Australian and English domestic competitions.

With his third delivery, Robin Uthappa was caught and bowled and the Delhi rookie Gautam Gambhir followed in his third over when he scooped a hopelessly miscued pull into the arms of wicket-keeper Brendan McCullum, the victim of expert slow bowling with Vettori having held back with an even slower ball. In the context of the match, Gambhir's 51 off 33 balls wasn't quite enough and the middle order found sustaining a rate of ten an over with the field spread too tall an order. Vettori finished with 4-20 and New Zealand had a winning start, over the line by ten runs.

Like New Zealand, Australia were now almost into their stride, although a routing of Bangladesh in Group F slightly papered over their rustiness. The Tigers were caught in a confusing tactical dilemma. Against West Indies in the group stage, their batsmen had tried to smash everything out of the park and had enjoyed a good day but their recklessness had granted South Africa a virtual bye through the second match, forcing Bangladesh toward Plan B. The Aussies did what they do best and added to the confusion with high-aggression, high-quality cricket, epitomised by a hat-trick from Brett Lee.

Meanwhile, Pakistan were embellishing their claims to the status of tournament dark horses with a mauling of Sri Lanka. Arguably, the power-hitting of Sanath Jayasuriya in one-day internationals of the mid-nineties (especially the ICC World Cup of 1996, which 66-1 outsiders Sri Lanka won) had shown what could be achieved over a short game but he received an unpalatable taste of his own medicine in Johannesburg, butchered for sixteen runs an over from his flat left-arm spin to leave him with world's worst figures in Twenty20 internationals: 4-0-64-0. Shoaib Malik (57) and Younis Khan (51) allowed Pakistan to amass 189 without the assistance of the maverick Shahid Afridi, who failed to produce an innings of substance over the fortnight but still proved useful in the spin department.

Drastic extremes of hit and miss are what Pakistan do best in cricketing terms but their team looked almost ideal for Twenty20. Inzamam ul-Haq was missing and would be out of international cricket altogether by the end of the calendar year whilst the classic stroke play of Mohammed Yousuf was a more surprising omission. Afridi would be a roaming threat, Younis Khan had the ability to win any game whilst Shoaib assumed the captaincy and both Umar Gul and Yasir Arafat had the capability of putting six deliveries on a sixpence to assert control with the ball. The theory proved compelling and seemingly liberated by the expectations of Twenty20, the reality followed a similar pattern.

Less than a day after destroying Sri Lanka, Pakistan were back at The Wanderers to confront Australia. Ricky Ponting's team appeared to have elbowed aside their problems with twenty-over cricket but still their fluency was missing. Shane Warne had left the fold after the Ashes annihilation of England and now

Glenn McGrath had gone too following the World Cup, there appeared to be no miracle worker to turn to if opposition batsmen got on top. Zimbabwe had initially exposed that and once England and Bangladesh were eased aside, it was easy to dismiss the opening loss as being down to lack of game time alone. The stack of quality opposition ahead would either back that up or blow the theory out of the water once and for all.

Pakistan chose to field first and might have harboured semi-regrets when Australia reached the 80 mark in the ninth over. Then, Andrew Symonds thrashed a slog-sweep at a quicker one from Shahid Afridi and lost his middle pole for 29 off 18 balls. It was one of a number of cameos with unfulfilled potential but still, the Aussies managed a 'par' score of 164, which they were well on course to defend as Pakistan stuttered to 46/4 in the seventh over of the reply.

Enter Misbah ul-Haq. We already know of his handywork from the devastation he caused in forcing India to a penalty thrash-out in Durban during the group phase but his determination to prove that was no fluke reaped further dividend. In partnership with his captain Shoaib Malik, the two contrived, nurdled and occasionally bludgeoned runs to reach the victory target with five balls and six wickets in hand.

Against arguably the greatest cricket side on the planet, Misbah's form would, over time, help dispel two myths about Twenty20 cricket. The first is that it's a game for youngsters. Misbah was midway through his 34th year when he got the nod to replace Mohammed Yousuf in the Pakistan set-up. In the English competition, Mushtaq Ahmed churned out results at every outing in Twenty20 in his late thirties, Stuart Law's batsmanship remained tough to beat whether with Lancashire or the Chennai Superstars in ICL and Mark Ramprakash of Surrey was also flourishing in the twilight of his career. So Misbah was not alone: quality cricketers would still excel in Twenty20 whatever their age.

Misbah was no "Twenty20 specialist" either, to steal the term given to those who had been quickest to adapt to the three-hour game. He had enjoyed a moderate and brief Test career in the distant past but his success in South Africa afforded him a return and he would average 78.7 in Pakistan's five Test Matches before the turn of the year including two spectacular unbeaten hundreds against India, in Kolkata and Bangalore. Many professionals espoused the view that 'the best players are the best players irrespective of the format' and Misbah was the living proof.

Two wins from two piggy-backed Pakistan to the head of the standings and they could even afford the luxury of a shambolic display against Bangladesh in Cape Town and still record a one hundred per cent record to make the last four. Again, Bangladesh found themselves to be formidable opponents at Newlands, enmeshed in the hurly-burly of Twenty20 to toss aside yet another promising start. This time 79/1 transmogrified into 140 all down for the 'Tigers,' 19 year-old Junaid Siddique smashing 71 off 49 balls but ultimately, in vain.

Pakistan were entertaining but it was the overall value for money of the tournament that moved Malcolm Speed, the Chief Executive of the ICC, to shower the event with glittering, if uncharacteristic praise in an interview for www.worldtwenty20.com, the official website of the tournament.

"The South Africans have taken to Twenty20 very positively and I've been a bit surprised that there have been big crowds. The one that really surprised me was back in Cape Town there [during the Super Eights] when it was cold and the match was on television but people still came out to sit in the grounds instead of settling by the fire at home so that's great.

"I think there'll be people out there who criticise it [Twenty20] and will continue to find reasons for criticising it but that isn't surprising: it's human nature. I certainly don't mind that: if people say they prefer a different form of cricket, that's great too. What we are seeing here is new people coming to cricket. I've heard a number of stories here about how a person has come to cricket or their family has and how much they've enjoyed it so much that they'll come back to Twenty20 and they'll come to watch fifty-over games and also Test cricket, so that's great."

The quality remained high in the other Super Eight group. New Zealand battled back from 31/4 against England, winched to 164 by Craig McMillan's intelligent and forceful 57. England's leading bowlers had done their job but their so-called 'specialists' in Twenty20 had shown themselves too raw and inexperienced in international cricket to compete. Unlike Misbah, the likes of Mascarenhas struggled among the world's elite and the Hampshire man saw his four overs disappear for 43 runs at a time when England should have been squeezing the life from the Kiwi middle order. Another man selected for his twenty-over prowess, Darren Maddy, got England off to a flyer with a half-century but the opening stand of 62 he shared with Vikram Solanki was to be wasted when no significant contributions were found at the core of the reply and the dismissal of rookie Luke Wright in the penultimate over was to effectively signal the early end of more England hopes: they had lost by five runs.

As Speed had signalled, the fortunes of South Africa hadn't necessarily had a massive bearing on the overall success of the tournament but few could deny the boost the local profile of World Twenty20 would receive if the Springboks made it through to the last four or even further.

From the emphatic nature of the chase against West Indies in the opening match to their willingness to 'mix it' with England in an often fractious Super Eight game, South Africa appeared to have all the ingredients for a successful squad. Shaun Pollock had even said that the game was too short for any team to lose their nerve and choke. Craig McMillan was in terrific touch again for New Zealand as they chalked up 153 against the hosts only for Justin Kemp to render the total insignificant with some savage hitting in an undefeated knock of 89.

Pollock's words were to return to haunt the South Africans in the final game against India though as a combination of big-match nerves and a slicker opposition moulded to dump the home team out by a grand total of ten runs.

Mahendra Singh Dhoni won the toss and decided to bat first - a decision that was never really vindicated until the chase. Pollock and Makhaya Ntini made inroads into the top order to leave India 33/3 in the sixth over, forcing Dhoni himself (45) and Rohit Sharma (50 not out) to post a defendable score, settled at 153/5. Even under the full beam of the floodlights in Durban, the task was not beyond Graeme Smith's side.

"We knew that batting under lights out there with a green tinge on the strip was going to be difficult," the captain would admit in the aftermath. "I think we bowled well for ten overs and then weren't clinical enough so 150-odd was always going to be a tough total to chase. They batted very well."

India's confident style at the crease transferred effortlessly to their bowling as RP Singh first unhinged and then left the Springbok top order in a complete mess. In the space of nine balls, Singh found late swing to have Herschelle Gibbs leg-before, Dinesh Karthik pulled out a scarcely believable catch to snaffle Smith in the slips and Sreesanth defeated AB de Villiers for pace and had him lbw for just one. Still with just two fieldsmen outside the ring, South Africa were five down and crushed. Needing 126 to eliminate New Zealand and sneak through on run rate, Albie Morkel had his stumps splattered by RP Singh and the game was up. The unchokable had choked and limped to 116/9.

"I guess the thing is that we do find ways to get out of these tournaments," Smith would lament. "We've only lost one game in the whole tournament and then we're out of the tournament. In this form of the game, the young guys are playing exciting and gutsy cricket and if they carry on doing that then the future is very good for them but at the end of the day when you lose you can't make excuses. You have to just try and come back as better people. In the big pressure games, maybe the experience was missing a bit. They handled the more intense and bigger moments better than us and bowled and fielded superbly."

Australia crushed Sri Lanka to make the last four but the basics of cricket had seen another South African challenge curtailed and seen India sail serenely through. But progression wasn't the only thing Mahendra Singh Dhoni's side were celebrating in the Super Eights.

Six Sixes

"England are having a conference meeting, they're in bits."

**David Lloyd,
commentating on ESPN Sports**

MODERN SPORTING HUDDLES ANNOY ME. They all emit a type of phoney sentiment best described as mock Americanness, but this one was different. On September 19th, I walked into a room where a group of cricketers were clustered together, absorbed in Yuvraj Singh's assault on England in the Super Eights, which was being beamed from a small television perched anxiously on a wall bracket. For the next two minutes or so, that television set would be the target for plenty of informed advice.

The information graphic at the foot of the screen read: 6 6 6, denoting Yuvraj's achievement in clearing the ropes from the first three deliveries of Stuart Broad's over. "Bring out the slower one," implored one voice from the huddle, "he'll be waiting for that, get it up around his chin," chimed another. The rookie wore a wry grin and was licking his lips pensively at the top of his mark and no doubt had all of the same questions racing through his own head.

England had underperformed yet again at a major championship and their hopes had, for some hours, clung on various mathematical improbabilities so the match against India at Kingsmead was more of an exercise in damage limitation than glory for them. However, the damage appeared to know no bounds and it was Broad who was bearing most of the collateral.

With the tall seamer conceding just twenty-four runs from his first three overs (more than sane by the crazy parameters of modern Twenty20), there was no indication of the carnage to come other than the score of 171/3 that gave a fair indication that Yuvraj and Mahendra Singh Dhoni might get a bit agricultural. The first ball sought variety to throw Yuvraj off the scent but the left-hander picked it and walloped it over wide mid-wicket for a maximum. "I think this is one of the biggest," exploded David Lloyd from the commentary box, "into orbit!" The television graphics agreed that it was a fair hump of over a hundred metres.

Yuvraj and Dhoni punched gloves and shared the briefest of smiles. They were having fun and another couple of similar blows would see England forced to hare down something in the region of 200. Yuvraj had his sights set higher.

How high exactly was exemplified with Broad's second delivery of the nineteenth over, again looking for the blockhole. Yuvraj sprung back early and inched his backlift upwards so it temporarily mirrored that of a baseball player, making the next piece of action all the more amazing as the full ball was wristily caressed into the stands at backward square leg. Yuvraj had somehow stuck 26 runs on his personal abacus in the space of just eight balls. Lloyd pondered with his viewers what might happen when he "had his eye in."

Already, Broad looked lost. He might have heard international cricket was something of a step up but this was vastly different to anything he experienced in the series of one-dayers against the same opposition the previous month in England. In that contest at The Oval, Yuvraj himself had been crunched for five maximums in the final over by Dmitri Mascarenhas and now looked bent on revenge. Like a soccer player instructed to re-take a penalty, he changed tactics next up and accelerated the mind games with Broad, getting his front leg out of the way after nudging his body to the leg side and clubbing the bowler over the top of extra cover for six more. The scoreboard started to spew out fireworks, the Indians in the crowd uncontrollable in unfurling the Dharma Chakra and illuminating the scene with their national flag.

The huddles in front of the television were firing their suggestions at the set back in London. They clearly empathised with Broad, whose dilemma now was to discover where to bowl to a man who already had 32 runs from nine balls. His instant reaction was to change the angle and come around the wicket, knowing that it's pretty hard to swipe a long way across the line and equally tough to smash sixes over the off side, even though Yuvraj had just achieved it with the third ball of the over. Looking composed from the top of his approach to the crease, the bowler suddenly lost control on delivery and sent down a horribly wide and loose full toss outside off stump which the batsman could flail at with virtual immunity. He did, carving over backward point and well beyond the boundary.

"After the fourth one, I thought it was possible," Yuvraj was to later admit, "and I had to go for the next two."

Armed with the grenade of self-confidence, the all-rounder set about throwing it into the England dressing room, ironically just about the only place the ball hadn't been deposited. Broad wished he was still there and in a state of epic confusion, switched from around the wicket back to over and after a small shimmy, stuck with the original plan. It made little difference as Yuvraj wound up back to the leg-side and smashed a length ball like a golfer through the arc to wide mid-wicket: a long, long way back. The fifth six brought up the 200 but the significance appeared to be lost among the euphoric Kingsmead crowd. England captain Paul Collingwood had already indulged in a lengthy discussion with his bowler after the fourth ball and now, television cameras closed in on him stroking his chin and silent out on the ropes. His words had changed nothing. Worse, Yuvraj was to jokingly claim afterwards that the fifth shot was a mis-hit.

"I knew after the fifth one that I had nothing to lose," added a fatigued-sounding Yuvraj afterwards, "I was using the crease really well and I knew that if I used it even better then I had a really good chance of hitting one more."

The voices huddled in front of the television now grew louder and more animated. All had different advice, from slower ball to under-arm delivery to off-cutter or bumper. Whether it is your own team or not, the chance to witness history drives any sportsman or sports fan to the borders of excitement and overs yielding 36 were few and far between in history. Sir Garfield Sobers had been the first to achieve it in Swansea almost four decades before and Herschelle Gibbs had panned poor Daan van Bunge for 36 in one of the few high spots of the turgid World Cup in the Caribbean just six months earlier. In between times, Ravi Shastri had achieved it for Bombay and by some bizarre twist of irony, he now stood behind the mic and ready to explain this attempt to the world.

The pictures told it all. Yuvraj dipped onto one knee and was fortunate enough to receive a leg-stump half-volley that was scythed over the on side. The cameraman could have slept through the blow and still, the raucous volume through the television speakers was enough to denote the sixth six. Durban exploded.

"For me it's a great feeling and thank God for it," admitted a relieved Yuvraj, "because after the five sixes, I had so many phone calls and when I get a hundred, I don't get so many, they were making fun of me. I thought God this isn't right. I wanted to give it back! I think he [Broad] was looking for a yorker but I was using the crease so well that I thought I could turn those into half-volleys and hit them cleanly."

Not only was Yuvraj cashing in metaphorically but also literally. As well as his share in a mega-bonus from the BCCI worth around US$2m for less than a fortnight's work, he was awarded almost a quarter of a million dollars as well as a brand new Porsche.

One of the faces by the television set had paid testimony to the smaller-than-most scale of the outfield in Durban but still, questions were raised about the direction cricket was taking in the aftermath of the six maximums. In the *Guardian*, Mike Selvey questioned whether technology should be marginalised to put an abrupt end to what he called a "slogathon."

"All too often, though, the boundary is being cleared by those barely making contact," complained Selvey. "Deceptive bowling is being deprived of the reward it deserves. A solution I've suggested before is to insist on a minimum pressing to bats, or a maximum thickness and weight." Nine days into the ICC World Twenty20 when that was written, Selvey would have been watching cricket as a virtual highlight package with six following six but as many of his respondents were to claim in comments to the online version of the above piece (No harm in big hits but the game's becoming a slogathon – http://blogs.guardian.co.uk), that is the whole point of there being a clear difference between Twenty20 "sportainment" and the more measured first-class game. Selvey's tone is reasoned. He is not a man given to kneejerk reactions to anything and his analysis as both writer and broadcaster is insightful. Yet on the metaphorical pundits' circuit, the wealth of forceful hitting from Yuvraj bred a feeling that Twenty20 had taken cricket down a one-way path to making bowlers extinct. It was a way for many of saying "we told you so."

It would have taken a brave, and perhaps foolish, person to label Sir Garfield Sobers a slogger in 1968 or to demean his feat by claiming that taking 36 off a Malcolm Nash over was proof of the sports' ruination. Such was the outcry at the inception of Twenty20 though that to some, any achievement was not only proof of the strength of short-form cricket but more importantly, a threat to the old order and a massive tick in the column marked 'negatives'.

Nash would be best remembered for having his bowling propelled onto the streets of Swansea by Sobers but 21 year-old Broad seemed to have a more pragmatic approach as he sought not to go the same way.

"He is never going to get rid of the tag of the six sixes unfortunately," came the candid admission of his captain Collingwood. "He realises that and he's a proud man. This will hurt him and it is up to all of us to get behind him. But he has the character to bounce back."

What might have pained the bowler more would be the ultimate knowledge that his costly six deliveries ultimately proved decisive in the match as India only won the game by eighteen runs. It is to the credit of Twenty20 as a brand though that it had never been achieved before in professional twenty-over cricket and it has never even looked likely since. Were it happening every week then the criticism would be more barbed and probably, more warranted. As it was, Yuvraj had made a match memorable when it had bore all the hallmarks of becoming just another "slogathon."

Turning Four Into Two

"We'll realise that this format is probably going to have a big impact on world cricket so there will be things that we can analyse and put some thought into now that perhaps we didn't before coming here."

Adam Gilchrist,
Australia vice-captain, after the semi-final,

"IT'S HARD TO PINPOINT ... we were a lot more relaxed than previous semi-finals and we'll have to go back to the drawing board and take a look at it. Unfortunately we are labelled as not being able to get to the finals. We have to find a solution to get over the line. I don't have the magic answer but I know we'll be ready next time when the chance comes."

The words of captain Graeme Smith explaining away the absence of South Africa from the semi-finals? No. Actually it was the so near yet so far reflections of Daniel Vettori, who, like his predecessor as leader of his cricketing nation, Stephen Fleming, found New Zealand's hard luck stories difficult to explain.

Kiwi disappointment had floated along unchecked since the very first World Cup in 1975 when Bernard Julien tore through them with four wickets for the West Indies at The Oval. Whilst that was an era of Caribbean dominance, the growth of New Zealand cricket since made it something of a surprise that they settled for bridesmaid status with such regularity: NZ would head home one stage early four more times in just eight World Cups.

The Twenty20 event proved that whilst some things in life change, others are immovable buffers of both past and future. New Zealanders may have been huddled by television sets whilst South Africa and India determined their fate at the business end of the Super Eights and their start to the knockout round confirmed that they still felt like passive participants.

Pakistan were asked to field first and from the green light, the intensity of their game was tangible. Mohammed Asif bristled with energy in his fluid approach to the wicket and immediately hurried Lou Vincent for time and space, hitting the opener on the thigh pad. Seam movement was more pronounced with the second and Vincent couldn't force the ball through the leg side. Sensing that the 'dot balls' were acting as the building blocks of pressure, Shoaib Malik tempted Vincent and his partner Brendan McCullum by commandeering fine leg into the circle and the tentative start could yield only a pair of singles from the first over. The same came from the second and the highly unusual scoreboard of 4/0 sparkled from the main Newlands scoreboard after the first two overs.

Asif continued to nip the ball back in the third over and he found both openers impatient. Two quiet overs is all well and good in fifty-over business but now it represented a tenth of the entire innings and set a concerning tone for the Black Caps. To the third delivery of the over, Vincent looked to whisk a ball from off to leg and despite his unnecessary aggression, escaped to the non-strikers end with a single beside his name, his nerves calmed when McCullum thrashed to the fence either side of the wicket to take the score to 15/0 at the end of the over.

With Tanvir carted for fourteen off the next over, New Zealand were implanting some impetus into their cricket and by the time the field could be relaxed, they had picked up 41 runs with the opening partnership still unbroken. The winds were ruffling and the clouds threatened, dropping enough in the seventh over to force a mini rain stoppage. The game wouldn't be shortened but perhaps the Vincent-McCullum axis was interrupted by the stoppage, shortly after which Vincent (28) was athletically caught and bowled by Fawad Alam driving uppishly down the ground. Introducing the 21 year-old Alam into the attack proved Shoaib Malik was a canny operator in the field: spin at both ends doing the trick with Shahid Afridi wheeling away as soon as the sixth over was complete.

Scott Styris had been bumped up the order to 'first drop' and soon found the ropes by chopping Afridi down through backward point for a well-struck boundary. Still, New Zealand looked to be teetering between genius and disaster and they fell off the balance beam when six wickets fell for 33 runs in just 35 balls. The last to fall in that sequence had been the very definition of panic as Vettori refused a second run to mid-wicket and became entangled in running chaos with Ross Taylor, the end result being the run out of the captain when he nobly wandered out of his crease to make sure the senior batsman survived.

"We put ourselves in a bit of a mire in terms of runs," a crestfallen Vettori would admit in the post-match press conference. "We thought we had to catch them up and that's when wickets start falling. We couldn't actually get any momentum going and after a start that was a good start – perhaps not as good as we would have liked but Lou [Vincent] and Brendan [McCullum] did well early on. I think we just allowed the Pakistan team to dictate to us and they bowled really well."

Shoaib's policy of drafting in the spinners so early allowed Umar Gul to spear in his arsenal of variation late on and again he was first called upon in the twelfth over, which would yield a miserly sum of three runs. With the opening delivery of his next, the dangerous Styris mis-timed a lofted cover drive and holed out. Two balls later, Peter Fulton chipped to cover and Gul then out-thought the big-hitting Jacob Oram by going around the wicket and having him caught behind. It was a marvellous piece of strategy that shows the virtues of thinking cricket in a pacy environment. Whatever the outcome of the competition, Shoaib Malik had unquestionably been the captain of the finals.

New Zealand were 107/7 at Vettori's departure. Their challenge had one recognised batsman to uphold it and Ross Taylor didn't have time to mope around, soon hoisting Mohammed Hafeez to the on-side for a maximum and finding the fence off the first three balls of the final over, bowled by the paceman Asif. Taylor finished unbeaten on 37 off 23 balls and received the kind of acclaim from the Cape Town crowd usually reserved for a Test centurion. They, like both teams, were aware that without his intervention there would be no contest. Pakistan needed 144 to win.

The chase was to be a controversial one, centring around an injury to Imran Nazir, the Pakistan opener. With six runs taken from the first over from Shane Bond, Nazir decided to chance his arm against Mark Gillespie at the other end and got lucky. The first of his three boundaries in the over came with an edge beyond the wicketkeeper. Point saw the ball as a blur as the next ball was slashed away and the arms were whirling again for the fifth ball, which obediently hurtled past gully to the fence. There had been little movement of the feet, less still need to run between the wickets. But at the end of the over, Nazir called for a runner. His captain responded to the call.

"He was struggling with his groin injury and he couldn't run at that time," explained Shoaib afterwards although New Zealand felt aggrieved and Vettori was forthright in his view that Pakistan had not played within the spirit of the game having watched the batsman rush onto the field to celebrate the eventual victory.

It would barely matter soon because New Zealand's flood defences were being routed from all angles. The usually dependable Bond dropped short from the next two balls and Hafeez cashed in to take the score to 29/0 after three overs. It was 54/0 after six with Hafeez lumping Bond over mid-wicket and Gillespie back over his head, both for maximums, to burst the Kiwi bubble which was now just counting down the balls to the flight home.

Whether or not the game was up, Vettori's mood was worsened when he brought himself up as the field dropped back. Second ball, Nazir used his feet and then swung his front pad out of the way to heave the spinner over wide mid-wicket for six. Styris dismissed Hafeez soon after but the game was almost up and even when Nazir (for a bizarre 59 that included five sixes) and Younis Khan departed in back-to-back overs, Pakistan needed only forty from the last six and a half overs. Misbah ul-Haq and Shoaib finished the job when they each cleared the ropes in the penultimate over. Umar Gul's stingy spell of 3/15 in four overs earned him the Man of the Match award.

The all too familiar exit of New Zealand ruined any prospect of a Trans-Tasman final at The Wanderers but India-Pakistan, arguably the mother of all international battles that so nearly graced a World Cup Final in 1987, was still on. First though, that meant India beating the four-time one-day world champions Australia.

On the face of it that was no problem but despite their aberration against Zimbabwe, the Aussies had been far more aesthetic than their kit, losing only to Pakistan since.

"Probably losing to Zimbabwe was the best tonic we can hope for," said Tim Nielsen, the successor to John Buchanan as Australia coach. "We now feel we can meet the challenges much better. The more work we've done the more comfortable the boys have been with where they're at ... we'll hit the semi-final in as good a shape as we can be."

Strength-wise, Nielsen's outlook was debatable. Ricky Ponting had missed the whipping of the Sri Lanka at the rear end of the Super Eights with a hamstring strain that would rule him out of the remainder of the series, so Adam Gilchrist would deputise. Meanwhile, the Shane Watson gamble backfired with the Queensland all-rounder shunted home for more rehabilitation on a weak hamstring. Conversely, Yuvraj Singh (tendonitis) and captain Dhoni (back) did come through fitness tests to feature.

Despite Australia's tendency to hammer even their closest rivals in the massive games, India enjoyed something of an advantage heading into the match. Not only did they have their big-game players available but also the plus of playing the match in Durban, with its large and very boisterous Indian population.

"It's the best dressing room environment I've seen in recent times," Dhoni told Ravi Shastri in the interview at the toss. "The Australians are the people who set the standards but we are here to play good, entertaining cricket, no matter what the outcome is."

His counterpart Gilchrist brushed aside concerns about not having played either under lights or in Durban with the same regularity, explaining that videos of other teams and their games had been studied at length by the assiduous Australians. But their suffocating detail was errant in the first six overs, despite the fact that India regularly moved from neutral gear to fifth and then back again in that time, scoring at a mere run a ball. Gambhir was granted width by Brett Lee and punished him over backward point. Nathan Bracken couldn't learn the lesson and was milked through the same area before the vacant slip region was peppered for four more. The dependable Stuart Clark was the next to be harrumphed from just back of a length — a boundary that unleashed euphoric yelping and high-pitched fervour from the stands. The delirium was muted when a flat-footed Virender Sehwag top edged a cut into the gloves of Gilchrist for a laboured innings of 9. The R&B bopping of the dancing girls and boys around the perimeter edge seemed out of place as the Aussies celebrated: they seemed to have the Indians in their pockets. Was this to be another New Zealand?

Whereas NZ were in a hole from which they never recovered, India counter-attacked. Robin Uthappa had a huge tranche of fortune when he produced a carbon copy of Sehwag's dismissal against the bowling of Clark but connected far better, Michael Clarke spilling the chance at backward point. Still, Clark conceded just ten runs from his first two overs and when Mitchell Johnson sent back Gambhir soon after (owing to a superb catch by Brad Hodge riding the boundary), India were stuttering at 41/2 with eight overs already drained away.

Every genuinely superb tournament has its classic contests though and this would be no different. Yuvraj puffed out the chest and admired his bat as he strode to the crease to face Clark. Perhaps in acknowledgement of his heroics against England, the New South Welshman welcomed the left-hander to the middle with a well directed short ball that induced no stroke. Sadly for the Aussies, it was the only sighter he needed and the next short ball was clouted into the crowd at square leg, Yuvraj swiftly shuffling his feet to treat Clark with disdain. The battle simmered but even with a quite astonishing flick off middle stump that planted Lee around a hundred metres away to deep backward square leg, India had only managed 60 runs and were two wickets down at the half-way point.

Conventional wisdom from domestic Twenty20 would offer poor tidings to India. In the early days of the game, teams generally found it difficult to double the scores in the second half of the innings with the ball getting softer and the spinners applying the squeeze. Furthermore, with middle orders getting less and less exposure to the game, they had been perhaps too uptight in applying themselves at the crease and gifted away their wickets as a consequence. International cricketers had proved cannier operators and add that to the South African conditions that didn't favour spin and the Indians were far from out of the match.

Perhaps the forty-five minutes that followed would actually breathe new life into longer forms of cricket because it would go on to prove that Australia were far from impregnable. Lee's full, fast and straight ball that yielded six runs to Yuvraj would be an occasional ticket to devastation for a batsman facing the same delivery in Test matches or all bar the last three or four overs of a standard one-day innings. That was the problem with Australia from ten overs onwards: they reverted to the basics of fifty-over cricket that got them to the top of the world leader board but bowling on a good length just gave any batsman an enormous hitting zone. The more 'length' Australia sent down, the more Yuvraj smashed it.

Uthappa wisely turned over the strike with a single at the start of the eleventh over, which arrived in the form of some medium pace from Andrew Symonds. It seemed the perfect variation to keep the buffers on the Indians but the margin for error was critically small when "Roy" over-pitched and Yuvraj picked him off the pads for four. The heart never seemed to skip a beat. This was Yuvraj in the groove. As if to emphasise the point, Symonds amended the length to drop shorter off the final ball, allowing Yuvraj to perform a neat pirouette and clobber an almighty blow onto the roof at midwicket. "There are no fielders on the ground anymore! Why do we have boundaries here?" the commentators screeched out through the television set. The personal haul for Yuvraj read 27 off just 10 balls.

At 92/2 with seven overs left, the ball was still in Australia's court as even conceding nine runs an over to the end would leave them with a gettable target of around 155. Gilchrist knew that with wickets in hand, India would have to choose a time to launch a 'death or glory' attack on the bowling and to heap on further pressure, he brought back Clark who was arguably at this point the seamer of the tournament alongside Umar Gul.

Yuvraj laid down a marker by digging an attempted yorker up and over Brad Haddin at cover and to the fence, causing Clark to temporarily lose his faith in the fuller ball. Instead, he opted to go slower and shorter and conceded a wide. Six runs came from the next three experimental deliveries and then a short and wide one outside the off stump was pulled into the crowd for six more. The bowler winced and hastened back towards the top of his mark whilst Yuvraj gathered the hero worship for a half-century off 21 balls. Compared to the assault on England earlier in the week, it was pedestrian but Kingsmead rocked to the tune of *Let Me Entertain You*. Robbie Williams could never have been so accurate.

The full house was frenzied and before the end of the over, Yuvraj would supply more for them to feast upon. Clark's "good areas" that had propelled him to international status in the first place were thoroughly screwed up and not knowing where to bowl, he came up with the worst possible ball. The full toss outside off stump was sent careering between point and deep cover for four more. Clark's over had gone for 21 runs and the momentum was now against his team and almost irreversibly so.

By the end of 2007, Yuvraj had transferred this abundant self-confidence into the Test arena where a spectacular century against Pakistan in Bangalore played a significant role in his team's series win. His place in the side would become so important that by the time of the Boxing Day Test Match against Australia in Melbourne, Rahul Dravid had been shunted up to open the innings just to accommodate Yuvraj in the middle order.

It had all started as a 20 year-old at Lord's in 2002, where an innings of 69 had helped transform near-certain defeat against England in the final of the NatWest Series to a thrilling and hardly credible win. Then, he had worked in alliance with Mohammad Kaif and the two appeared to egg each other on to hit higher, further and more often. Uthappa was now taking the lead of his more experienced partner and set about climbing into Johnson. He didn't start the assault with a half-measure either, confronting the left-armer with an impudent stride down the track before smashing him down the ground. The next ball was pulled over midwicket for six but the problem with big hitting is that it takes the practice away from running between the wickets. Confusion reigned as the next ball reached cover, Uthappa committed himself and watched in horror as Symonds ran him out with a direct hit.

The celebrations were low key and that was because Dhoni was striding out at number five. With Symonds back in the attack, Dhoni produced a piece of wrist-work that resembled the firing up of a chainsaw to dispatch him down the ground for the first of three boundaries in the over, the other two the inevitable result of the bowler not being allowed to settle. 81 runs had come from the last six overs and already, India had a competitive total.

Lee remained relatively economical but Gilchrist had been forced to use up his preferred options for the closing overs so he gambled and brought in Michael Clarke for the eighteenth over with his left arm spin. It cost six runs as Yuvraj perched on one knee to slog-sweep into the grandstand but with almost his first false stroke, he cue-ended to wide midwicket where Michael Hussey took a smart catch. The seventy runs had taken up just thirty balls and in the space of 38 minutes, the whole course of the semi-final had been altered. Dhoni finished off the job before being run out for a two-a-ball 36 and India had chalked up 188/5.

The magnitude of the asking rate (almost 9.5 per over at the start of the reply) could never affect campaigners as well versed as Gilchrist and Matthew Hayden and their strategy appeared to be ticking over the scoreboard around a minimum of one boundary per over. That criteria was satisfied from the first two overs and then a leg stump half-volley from RP Singh disappeared for Gilchrist's first six in the third over. Despite that blow, the serenity of Australian progress was such that Sreesanth could even bowl a rare maiden over in the fourth to leave the score 19/0, forcing the acceleration pedal to be crunched in the next over, which yielded seventeen.

This mini-battle was almost as compelling as Yuvraj against Clark had been but this time the batsman didn't win. Sreesanth blustered the ball into the slot to invite the drive but Gilchrist was trapped in critical indecision between front foot and back, ultimately doing neither. The smallest of gates between bat and pad was exposed and the stand-in skipper was on his way back to the dugout with his middle pole vaulting away from the scene.

Hayden took on the challenge almost as a personal crusade but was unable to pick the gaps with the kind of regularity that had become expected of him. At the half-way point, he had 33 off 32 balls and although Australia were seventeen runs ahead on the comparison, it was testimony to the belligerence of Yuvraj earlier in the day that they still needed to score at a rate of above eleven runs an over to secure a finals berth. By that time he had lost a partner too with Hodge pinballing a long hop from Irfan Pathan to the grateful hands of Joginder at short fine leg.

Whilst the broad-shouldered Queensland duo of Symonds and Hayden were facing the bowling, nothing was beyond the Aussies. Sehwag was smashed twice out of sight as Hayden passed fifty and then one of Harbhajan's flat arrows got the treatment with a pure slog from Symonds, dragging across the line to cow corner. The required rate dipped back below ten but Harbhajan hauled back the initiative by leaking just three runs from the next five balls. The battle was akin to a tennis tie-breaker with the mini-breaks tossed around like confetti.

The comeback ended before the end of the seventeenth over. Hayden (62) saw his furniture was disturbed by a full and quick one from the fantastic Sreesanth, Hussey's fluency nosedived thanks to a hamstring injury and then Pathan swung one back to Symonds as he looked to cut and clipped the top of off stump.

"I thought Sreesanth was the difference in the game," admitted Gilchrist afterwards. "I felt pretty comfortable chasing that total. The pressure's always on but I felt like we were in control particularly with Matty and Simmo there but Sreesanth, I think his spell of bowling with the three overs up front and then that big over there, getting Matty out, just turned the tables back their way and they played the better cricket over the last five overs probably."

India scored 61 runs from the sixteenth over to the end of their innings whilst Australia managed just 38. The difference between the two sides landed up as fifteen runs: who said the opening overs were the important ones in Twenty20?

"I know it is the biggest match and it is the biggest stage to have an India against Pakistan match but taking on additional pressure will not help you perform, it will only take away your confidence," said Dhoni, the rookie captain with the scarce commodity of carrying no expectation around with him as he led an India team. Less than forty hours away was the dream final for the neutral and he was in it without Sourav Ganguly, Dravid and Sachin Tendulkar: the other cricketing megastars for the nation.

After a titillating round of semi-finals, neither the arch-creators of Twenty20 nor the world champions would stick around until Monday's final. Instead, it would be Pakistan against their neighbours who nearly didn't turn up in South Africa at all.

The Springbok
Sub-Continent

"Let the doubters and critics now shut up."

Stuart Hess,
The Star (25 September 2007)

THE FINAL DAY OF THE County Championship season in England: 2007. Sussex, defenders of the title, had wrapped up an innings victory over Worcestershire inside a session on the final day to move to the top of the tree and then headed to the sanctuary of the dressing room to pace and wait. They listened through the internet and watched intermittent television coverage from The Oval, where rivals Surrey had set Lancashire an unlikely 489 to win.

The fact that it had gone to the wire at all was part-blessing, part-boot between the legs for this reporter, whose planned pilgrimage to the Twenty20 had been jilted at a twenty-two yard altar. In my second season of reporting on Lancashire for the BBC, my understanding bosses had given me permission to waive the last match and swap South London for South Africa. At the end of July, the Red Rose title hopes (significant because of the absence of that trophy from the Old Trafford trophy shelves in seventy-three years) were just about wilting as they crumbled against Sussex inside three days at Liverpool so I took the liberty of booking the flights to Cape Town and gambled. Ultimately, the punt reaped the same dividend as Nasser Hussain's decision to field first on winning the toss in Brisbane almost five years before.

For just about every run Australia made in that first innings, I shelled out a pound for a late replacement flight to the Rainbow Nation, figuring that the chance to witness India take on Pakistan in landmark, yet surreal, conditions was too good to pass up. The heroism and grafting Lancashire effort to make history in the face of a massive target at The Oval (they landed up just twenty-five runs short of the title) meant that I had left it too late for a direct flight but I fancied my own shot at being Michael Palin anyway and with a convoluted route circum-navigating Abu Dhabi Airport, I touched down in Johannesburg little more than five hours before the off and pushed my knackered body – wedged between agitation and excitement – toward The Wanderers.

The scheduling of the final on a Monday afternoon seemed odd at first glance. It missed out the prime-time television audiences in just about all of the leading nations to embrace South Africa's Heritage Day, a public holiday, a welcome break from the broadcast-dictated norms of twenty-first century sport. It might have been a day off for the locals but the crowds of expectant families and friends eight, nine and even ten deep at the exit suggested that the route in to The Wanderers stadium would be a frustratingly stop-start one. It was nothing of the sort.

A big bear of a man by the name of Edwin defied his size and apparent lack of agility by leaping first from the posse of taxi drivers encircling the exit having been the first to spot the wandering tourist with the gormless expression writ large across his brow.

It wasn't just the long weekend that was producing Edwin's bashful and cheeky chuckle. He had relocated to the city from the northern province of Limpopo, leaving his family to earn enough to support his ten year-old son, whose saintly smile beamed up towards the father from the inside of his key fob. Softened up by the family-image, I fell headlong into his spiel about the positive image of the whole country, almost like a gullible first-time voter cast under the spell of Tony Blair rhetoric.

"When the cricket is finished, you have to see our country," Edwin instructed, ignoring the pressing engagement in Manchester three days later that I'd used as my unreserved apology for not being able to explore too much of his homeland beyond the trophy presentation. Edwin looked disappointed yet still decided that twelve hours or so in his taxi would be sufficient to see Sun City and take in the paradox of the parliament building in Pretoria and the township of Soweto. Soweto was important, reasoned Edwin. I could take photographs there. And if I did, then everyone in England would see that South Africa was a hospitable country with an exaggerated crime problem and they would all book their holidays there. Even with Edwin's taxi as my chariot, I didn't fancy a tour where my feet didn't touch the ground: it would have been like travel in a twenty20 style, with core lessons in culture and history smashed into tiny digestible pieces but still so much to make you lose the significance of it all. Contented at having devised a plan apparently to view all of South Africa in twenty-four hours, Edwin chuckled heartily, gave a friendly wave and rolled out of the hotel car park to wage combat with the platoons of amber-white-green flags under which huddled several thousand Indian supporters, in fine voice already before 10am and assembled in party mode on the Corlett Drive.

This was a major final but on the stroll down to wend my way through those throngs and collect my ticket, it would hardly have seemed credible. The winding pathways down from the Protea Hotel brought me to the stadium gates having passed only six or seven people and on arrival at the head of the queues, security were firm but light-hearted, showing that they were looking forward to this event as much as the paying punters were. Why couldn't all sports events be like this instead of the threatening tones so often all-pervading at British grounds where even working journalists are often subjected to interrogations that Torquemada would no doubt have dismissed as one step too far?

On the opening of the gates, pushing and shoving took precedence over all else. Everyone wanted an official tournament hard hat and the stalls offering free inflatable stumps became victims of a stampede. The only sanctuary appeared to be my temporary home at the back of the Tavern stand, a seat that had set me back the almost insignificant sum of £7. I perched merrily beneath the gaze of the sun with a similarly well-priced pint of Castle lager.

Crowds mingled just like any other party, rival supporters enjoyed banter. A group of six business associates and golfing buddies from Cape Town lined the row in front of me, claiming to be more excited by the prospect of an India versus Pakistan final than one involving South Africa. The masses squealed their excitement at the entrance of both teams for the warm-up, by the toss, they were far more attentive. Dhoni called heads and on winning the spin, decided to bat first. The Indian captain said 180 was the aim, Shoaib would settle for chasing twenty to thirty runs fewer.

The countdown was almost over. Ajay and his fiancée were roving around the area by our seats and just couldn't keep still. "I've been waiting for this for so long you know," he beamed, as if the match had been pencilled in his diary for a year and a half rather than a day and a half. The spirit of solidarity was strong, a bond almost unthinkable when troop numbers from both nations were building up around the Kargil conflict in 1999 or in the tensions of 2001. The thirty-odd youngsters who would decorate the on-field action with dancing in their teams of four around the boundaries, all came together carrying either the flag of India or Pakistan for a lengthy pre-match routine as if to emphasise that fact. This was more like NFL than cricket: fun for all the family. Even the umpires joined in the fun by punching fists to wish each other good luck before the off.

The anthems perfectly observed, the Indians filed back excitedly towards the dugouts, leaving Gambhir to head to the middle with a different opening partner. Pakistan were spared the unpredictable opposition of Virender Sehwag, whose groin strain was enough to give a Twenty20 international debut to Yusuf Pathan, the elder brother of seam bowling all-rounder Irfan.

Yusuf's heart rate had no time to normalise before he gave the sizeable Indian support some palpitations from the very first ball. Mohammed Asif's mild first ball was pushed to extra cover by Gambhir, who was initially indecisive about the single. When he did decide to take one, Yusuf was slow to respond and was fortunate to make his ground as Kamran Akmal disturbed the bails. It took the third umpire a few glimpses at the replay to be absolutely sure and our Indian-dominated block in the Tavern exhaled: a collective sigh of relief.

Asif was sacrificing his pace for accuracy and finding some light movement off the seam, leaving India wedged between two metaphorical stools. Teams batting first in the semi-finals had been conservative at the start of their innings, preferring to quietly accumulate and make sure they wouldn't be out of the reckoning altogether after ten overs and India were following the same model. Of course, Pathan hadn't featured in that game and took matters into his own hands, leaning into a ball of full length from Asif and dropping it into the stands at long-off for six. Ajay's smile widened and he was tempted to get out of his seat for the first of his in-game dances but an assertive glance from the fiancée was enough to keep him in his seat. The first over was worth thirteen runs.

Gambhir punished Sohail Tanvir's poor line in the next over by clipping him for four past short fine leg but Yusuf's inexperience was exposed soon after, looking to follow a square cut boundary with one through the leg side and managing only to sky a miscued pull shot for Shoaib to snaffle an impressive running catch with his eyes glaring into the sun. The rookie had managed 15 runs from eight balls but his dismissal allowed Pakistan to dictate matters, at least until the field restrictions were lifted. Only one more boundary would come in that time and Robin Uthappa's involvement was shortened when he looked to hit Tanvir inside out over cover but holed out to Shahid Afridi. 40/2 after six overs meant advantage Pakistan.

The action was intense and so finely balanced that bar takings seemed to be dented. The queue for a top up was so short during the seventh over that I only missed four balls from Afridi, part of a change to spin at both ends with the laboured Mohammed Hafeez wheeling away at the other end. Hafeez dropped short and wide with his second ball and was carved away by Gambhir who moved into the twenties by picking out the backward point fence.

Gambhir had realised what many had still not grasped about a Twenty20 innings: that like any other kind of cricket, it needs to be held together by at least one, if not two, knocks of real substance. Teams couldn't hope in vain for a monster over to just happen, like the one from Yuvraj that had slain England at Kingsmead so Gambhir had opted to rotate the strike and then look to open the shoulders later, hoping to be there as close as possible to the twentieth over.

The mature approach from Gambhir came with almost every person inside The Liberty Life Wanderers expecting Yuvraj Singh to go bananas at every opportunity. "Look out for that guy, he hits it absolutely miles," David Lloyd had said when I briefly ran into him outside the entrance gates that morning. "Any minute now, he'll smash it," added one of the Cape Town golfers in the Tavern.

Each delivery to the left-hander received a huge build-up from the crowd but he managed just a single from his first five balls, Pakistan cognisant of his strengths and starving him of the chance to go aerial by firing the ball in full and flat. Gambhir relaxed the tension with soft hands guiding the ball through mid-wicket off Afridi for four and then two boundaries following from the bowling of Hafeez to take the score to 69/2 at the end of the tenth over. Glancing over to the grass verge in front of the dressing rooms, I noticed several placards dividing the columns of India flags reading 'Chak de India' meaning India: let's start it or let's pick it up. Ironically, that is also the title of a Bollywood movie starring Shah Rukh Khan, the actor perched in the VIP section of the Bullring who would appear on the big screens inside the stadium to the biggest cheers of the day during the second innings.

The ball was hitting the bat slower than in Durban, where India had played most of their matches. But the outfield was quick and the notorious altitude in Johannesburg made the ball carry to different districts if the batsman made even a half-decent connection. India were still eleven runs an over away from the target set them by Dhoni at the toss. The captain cut a jittery figure on an otherwise jovial bench beyond the boundary.

Given the flailing arms, fluttering flags and general dissonance around The Wanderers, it's likely that Gambhir was perhaps the most level-headed person in the arena. Taking his lead from Yuvraj's confident lofted drive for four, he swatted Afridi away over wide mid-wicket with an ugly looking six two balls later. He then tucked into a decent Umar Gul delivery by manufacturing space outside the leg stump, freeing his arms up to carve the ball away over point for four more.

As had become the norm over the course of the fortnight, Gul had been brought into the attack well after the halfway point, Shoaib figuring that his strike bowler with the best discipline regarding line and length would be the best man to reign in a side looking to blast to all parts. "He's the bowler who's most impressed me over the last twelve months," asserted the former England captain Nasser Hussain from the commentary box, "he has the variations: the slower ones, the fuller ones, the yorkers and he looks fitter." Gambhir second-guessed his block-hole ball well enough to deflect it for four through midwicket in the fourteenth over but Yuvraj looked more agitated at the crease and didn't play the short ball well. Looking to get on with things, he aimed a flashy pull shot at a ball that bounced more than Yuvraj expected, splicing the ball horribly into the air for the bowler to pocket an easy return catch.

Dhoni walked in but found his timing tough from the off. Whilst much is made of "wickets in hand" in Twenty20, it is a false premise unless the team in question is made up of a series of players who can score quickly straight away. Every dot ball builds pressure much quicker than any other form of the game and one of the cleanest strikers in world cricket was in the process of finding that out. Gambhir had already acclimatised to The Wanderers and had 62 to his name but Dhoni couldn't give him the strike.

That was fodder for Umar Gul but the Indian supporters were happy to ignore that. Ajay whipped most of them up into the party mood with the first rendition of "Twinkle, twinkle, little star, India, you're my shining star," and nobody seemed in the least bit perturbed by the lack of acceleration out in the middle. Such were the festivities that the small grouping of Pakistan fans in the next block halted their cheering for an over or two, clearly believing that they must have missed something: was 130 a winning score after all?

Gul missed his intended target by a serious distance with the first ball of his third over and sent a beamer down to Dhoni who did well to swerve out of the way. The bowler was quick to get down the pitch and apologise but the India captain just couldn't settle afterwards and Gul approached the wicket for the next delivery with the disgruntlement of the partisan Indian support threatening to damage his eardrums. A well-directed bouncer had Dhoni bobbing around the crease again but it was to be his last exercise for the time being as the next ball cleaned him up: 111/4 with just 28 balls left.

Pakistan had the match in their hands and India were struggling for air, going 25 balls without a boundary before Gambhir gambled with the bigger back-lift and launched Umar Gul to the foot of the scoreboard at cow corner. Home run! The respite would only be brief though. Gambhir was premeditating the ideas of Gul pretty well and was down on one knee, anticipating the full ball. It was too late to readjust for the bowler who obliged with a low full toss but the paddle sweep was almost swallowed by short fine leg, where Mohammed Asif took the catch to send Gambhir on his way for 75 and give Gul his third victim. Silence engulfed The Wanderers and those Pakistan supporters in the next block waved a piece of card in front of the cameras: "This one's for you, Bob," in reference to their deceased former coach Woolmer. The side in green were now clear favourites with India 130/5 with just two overs remaining.

Rohit Sharma and Irfan Pathan took up the charge instead, the former fortunate to be sent two full tosses which he could manoeuvre to mid-wicket and delicately down to third man, chopping the ball from inches in front of the timber in the process. Those two fours cemented some self-belief amongst the Indians, whose whooping cranked up a decibel or two when Sharma's vigorous swing to deep long-on was parried over the ropes by Hafeez in the final over. In all, 27 runs were bludgeoned off the last twelve balls and India could claim respectability at 157/5.

The late afternoon sun had started to lose it's power by the time of the reply but I still had a pinkish glow as I sought further dehydration via another lager. The

South Africans in the queue weren't talking about the dancing, the music or the weather: it was all about the game. Did India have enough runs? Who held the advantage? Did anyone else care so long as it was fun? None of them were wearing the hard hats nor were they hitting each other over the head with branded inflatable stumps but they had still caught the bug.

Pakistan had an immediate setback when RP Singh removed Hafeez with his fifth ball, a subtle deflection that provided easy practice for Uthappa, stationed at floating slip. But their inconvenience was soon sliced away by the fearless Imran Nazir, who still appeared aggravated by the injury that had proved so controversial in the semi against New Zealand yet still played a remarkably flat-footed cameo. Width from Sreesanth offered up a first invitation in the second over and Imran accepted by biffing over the infield at cover. The next two sailed over midwicket and third man respectively, earning six runs each and Sreesanth looked lost when a half-volley was blitzed away square on the off side for four more. 21 came off the over and whilst a few were miscued slogs, the basic premise of cricket still held that when the bowler was "chucking pies" to give it the popular colloquialism, the batsman could tuck in.

Sreesanth's pricey first over meant that RP Singh had to drag things back and he took the challenge literally, the left-armer shaping one back in to Kamran Akmal to dethrone off and middle stumps after an unsightly swipe to leg. The Indian fans were now on their feet. The golfers chortled as the dancing in the stands built up and the national colours returned to dominant the back and fore-grounds. Even another handful of fours from Imran couldn't drown out the din, which became louder when Imran managed to run himself out before the sixth over was up. Younis Khan played drop and run to mid-off and Uthappa's sharp throw defeated Imran's dive after a 14-ball innings of 33. Pakistan were ahead on the runs comparison but the fall of their third wicket stuck them on the back foot in the match.

Indian out fielding has long been an embarrassment as indeed has that of Pakistan. So whoever won this competition, this was a revolution in itself and a joy to behold as a neutral. The perception of the lazy Indian cricketer more interested in honing his own individual technique than saving runs for the team had been half blown away in under two weeks. It was no isolated incident either. The standards in the Indian Cricket League later in 2007 were astonishing, especially as it was a competition derided in some quarters as a workhouse for the rookies and the retiring, the have-nots and the have-never-agains. It had been a story replicated around the world for over four years and the international scene was following suit.

Joginder Sharma was brought on to sleepwalk through the seventh over and Yusuf Pathan to lightly tweak in the eighth but Pakistan were in a period of restructuring their chase and after a series of singles, a frustrated Younis Khan whipped Joginder into the midriff of Yusuf for 24. Nobody seemed willing to apply themselves as Gambhir had to make a decent fist of the chase. As the pitch appeared to get slower, Shoaib perished to the bowling of Irfan Pathan and a few balls later, Afridi skied down the throat of Sreesanth. The only 'boom boom' came from the Indian fans, ninety per cent of the crowd twisting in ecstatic jubilation at a trophy they now believed to be theirs.

At six down, it should have been all over but then we had the thrilling climax: Indian excitement quashed by Misbah and then raised again by his casual flip down the throat of short fine leg, a stroke of impertinence where care and common sense was needed. As the tickertape and glitter shot up to the early evening skies and the recognisable tones of Ravi Shastri carried out the party preambles and post-mortems at once in front of the television cameras, it reminded me of a rugby league cliché you might hear a thousand times from defeated players and coaches over the course of a season: 'we didn't respect the game enough.' Misbah's dismissal came when six runs were needed off just four balls with just the one wicket left. By Twenty20 standards, the game was dead even – one mistake had been the difference, proof that this was a sport to rival any other in tension, skill, quality and uncluttered drama.

Indians sang and a good twenty thousand lingered at The Wanderers until the legs had grown weary on those taking the lap of honour to a third circuit. They were delivering their verdict on the most modern version of cricket with their dancing feet.

The Future

"For those who run cricket, the risk assessment is now very important. What is the downside and how is it managed?"

Dr Ali Bacher

IT TOOK A WHILE FOR THE glitzy presentation celebrations to die down at The Wanderers and when they did, the parties merely transferred elsewhere. Clusters of Indian fans chanted, sang, leapt and jigged around the television cameras neatly positioned at the exits to capture reaction – those stations whose access to match footage was limited or zero. With the chanting a long way from subsiding, a journalist back at the hotel remarked on what a shame it was that such a classic final had been settled by an error rather than a piece of world-class cricket but that was an endearing thing, not its downfall. Mike Gatting's misjudged reverse sweep had been the most telling factor in Australia's 1987 World Cup win but that wasn't to the detriment of fifty-over cricket, almost the opposite: after all when one mistake can lose a world final, surely that defines a sport in good health.

Misbah ul-Haq returned to Pakistan and immediately admitted that his premeditated attempt to flip the ball up and over the short fine-leg fieldsman had been a palpable error of judgment and those of the conviction that Twenty20 makes a mess of tried and trusted batting skills would use that passage of play as ammunition for their argument. That paddle shot perhaps represented the most popular way that batsmen had tried to improvise over the first five years of competitive twenty-over cricket to score in unusual areas and whilst appearing spectacular, it is no riskier a stroke than the sweep shot which has long been entrenched in the cricketing lexicon. Like with other shots in cricket of all shapes and sizes, the execution of a shot would determine whether a batsman survives or not and how well remunerated he is in the 'runs scored' column.

The conservationist fan or stakeholder in the game might have pointed to the potential for a ruination of technique in advance of Twenty20 and in the first year of competition, in England at least, they might have had a point. Bowlers were timid and wary of variety, their opponents heaved away with the head mechanically flinging up towards the skies and basically slogging. As the jokey feel dissipated so plans emerged and were developed sufficiently to give credence to the entire competition.

Even had the substance been lacking to the sport then the financial side meant that Twenty20 has a solid future in domestic cricket whatever would happen in the international arenas. Yorkshire had just one quarter-final berth to show from their first five appearances in the Twenty20 Cup yet the leading reactionaries in the county game still publicly proclaimed ahead of the 2007 domestic series in England that they hoped to raise half a million pounds from the competition. These are staggering figures. "The average County Championship attendance is around 2,000," Chief Executive Stewart Regan told the *Yorkshire Post*, "so if we have a full house for the Lancashire game on Monday and get fifty to sixty per cent capacity for the other two home games then we will have an attendance of 45,000 people coming through the gates." Regan went on to add that the home fixtures would yield sixty per cent of gate receipts from just under nine per cent of the playing days available to Yorkshire in the competitive summer.

Yorkshire weren't so lucky in the end because the Lancashire game was swept away in a mini-monsoon at Headingley and two other games were played in such farcically wet conditions as to almost ruin the spectacle. But the generation of the kind of interest alluded to by Regan brings additional opportunities to inflate the coffers from people with higher disposable income than the average county member.

The supporters who faithfully plonked their cooler bags and sandwich boxes in the pavilions of the county circuit when I was growing up were not the type to splash out on merchandising and often saw the purchase of a programme as the height of their weekend expenditure. The influx of the new breed of cricket fans brought parents with disposable income and regulars at football matches in the winter months who were in the habit of latent displays of affinity to their chosen club by buying shirts, baseball caps, car stickers – all subsidiary items that gather dust on the shelves for Championship cricket when crowds are sparse and fans wanting to splash out are even more rare. "We will take more in the shop on Monday night [home game against Lancashire, 2007] than what we take from 25 per cent of our Championship matches," added Regan before the Roses Twenty20 was sunk by cricket's traditional enemy: the weather.

That situation shows no sign of abating and despite the gradual proliferation in support base and the move towards a football-style element in the crowd, it still seems as though the success or lack of it for a side seldom affects their ability to attract the paying punter through the turnstile. The warning for the future comes directly from football in that people can only fork out so much money so the golden goose can't be strangled.

The England and Wales Cricket Board upped the ante for the 2008 domestic summer, resetting the calendar so that each county would face the other five in their regional sections both home and away rather than the preposterous structure that saw teams play some rivals twice and others just once. The new draft means that over a three-week period, families wanting to see every home fixture would be obliged to stump up for five rounds of tickets and give up five of their evenings as well. Will the novelty be lost? There is certainly every chance. The new format boasts common sense and accessibility to youngsters (and indeed, any fan new to the game) but at what cost? A degeneration into lapsing public interest and the same arid atmosphere that surrounds contemporary fifty-over competitions would leave one-day cricket with just about nowhere to go.

Whether five games, eight or ten per county in England, the apparent desire to strengthen the shelf-life of Twenty20 is bizarrely undervalued at times as schedulers refuse to acknowledge the financial advantages of pencilling in reserve days. One chronic downpour lasting a couple of hours often wiped out entire fixtures especially in the saturated summer of 2007 and whilst counties could insure themselves against the lost gate receipts, warding off the unquantifiable losses from merchandise, food sales and alcohol in particular has proved a tougher proposition.

"The thing is that Twenty20 is the cornerstone of the county game right here and right now," analysed Claire Hughes in her blog on the *Yorkshire Post* website, "because if it was pulled from underneath the counties, they would collapse headfirst into financial chaos ... there may be no accounting for the weather, unless like Yorkshire and Leicestershire you employ a no-refunds policy to hang on to some of your sell-out revenue, but the nuts and bolts of it is that no play equals no money, if not in terms of bums on seats, in terms of pints from bars and hot dogs from stands."

Her point was that "Christmas should never be cancelled". What is the point of wrapping up an entire genre in cotton wool if it never gets to see the field of play? It's one of the anomalies that must be refined before Twenty20 can be said to be the finished article.

Still, there is a bandwagon growing in English domestic circles, carting dangerous portents to the future. Those with their fingers on the game's financial pulse want to press on with Twenty20 and after the Schofield Report emphasised the madness of playing 'Pro40' cricket, corridors are lined with those who want a Twenty20 league of some description. Forty-over cricket has long been a tool to attract people to cricket for an afternoon on a day off - that's what the creation of the first Sunday League was all about. Yet times have changed and with no international version to act as a big brother to aspire to, there hardly seems a point in messing around for forty overs when the game looks pedestrian following the main event of Twenty20 in the height of summer. There will be some who argue that with a World Twenty20 now seemingly a permanent fixture in the inter-national calendars of the near future, that emerging players need as much exposure to it as possible to hone the nuances and expand their skills. But to make Twenty20 a regular event through the summer would reduce its mystique in the eyes of the public and once the honeymoon period is over for fans, they might divorce cricket altogether in an era where such plentiful competition exists as an entertaining alternative.

Short-termism has often blighted the administration of cricket in the past but it is in the long-term treatment of the fifty-over version that will have the biggest ramifications for the sport as a whole over the next half-decade.

Limited overs internationals have been far from appetising since the last decent World Cup competition in 1992. After the ICC World Twenty20, the govern-ing body were still meddling with the laws and playing conditions to artificially create a format capable of retaining its status as "the financial driver of the game", in the words of the Chief Executive Malcolm Speed. Substitutions were temporarily introduced, flawed and removed again, power plays were constantly tampered with but only exacerbated the problem of the stultifying middle overs and the free hit was eventually imported from Twenty20 to punish a bowler for overstepping. Even a mandatory ball change was introduced after 34 overs – the most bizarre innovation of the lot. The only thing consistent in fifty-over cricket was confusion and inconsistency but still Speed defended the future of one-day cricket's longest and most-established form.

"What we have now is a new phenomenon to go along with fifty over cricket," says Speed, "we need to make sure we blend the two and the pie gets bigger rather than remaining the same size, but is divided among the three forms of the game. Our priority will be to preserve Test cricket. We need to make sure that Test cricket remains strong and that is the iconic form of the game."

With all of the manipulation and desperation measures to lure any semblance of enjoyment kicking and screaming from the diaphragm of fifty-over cricket, day-long limited overs cricket already seems to be surviving only by life support machine. Speed's utterances prove that administrators want to keep the electricity drip-feeding that machine for as long as possible with all of the obvious ramifications for advertisers in-stadia and also through television, whose love for Twenty20 may forever be tempered by its limited commercial value when matches are in progress. Not as comprehensible was Speed's apparent fear about the future of Test Matches.

Upon the induction of Twenty20, there existed an 'I told you so' bunch of conservative cricket fans waiting for their moment to espouse the virtues of grafting batting and probing bowling both unhindered by razzamatazz. The membership of that club might have dwindled with the success that brimmed from excess but some pundits echoed Speed's sentiment and screamed 'caution' at the end of the ICC World Twenty20 anyway, accepting that the glories of the tournament had been great but worrying about what lies around the corner.

The whole point emanating from these comment pieces appeared to be that Twenty20 could spell the end for Test cricket and on the face of it, that could be construed as a valid and weighty argument. If people are struggling to afford the time to watch seven hours of sport on five consecutive days, then why would they stick with that when the same sportsmen were wedging exhilarating contests into a three-hour bash and satisfying the same appetite?

In the *Times*, John Woodcock recalled a Test he had covered half a century before when England had laboured for six hours to reach 157 for 3 against South

Africa, an event "more a penance than a pleasure to be watching. England went on to win the match and make many friends on the tour but we all know that the formalism with which they did so has long had its day."

What Woodcock appears to be railing against is a change in the social climate around cricket rather than the actual fabric of the sport. In the fifty-year interim, Apartheid had stung and then been flattened in South Africa changing perhaps forever the outlook of a whole generation of peoples. India and Pakistan had developed individual identities upon partition, technology had opened up consoles and computers to the youthful and workers worldwide. It seems arrogant to believe that cricket exists as a standalone empire, impervious to the changes in social fibres around it. Such transformations had created a desire for Twenty20 but that doesn't mean Test cricket should be as a neglected older brother when a new sibling arrives on the scene.

Indeed, why should the two wildly contrasting beasts be construed as being from the same family anyway. Few similarities exist between Test and Twenty20 aside from the presence of blokes with bats, a ball and stumps. Of course, the two share the broad title of 'cricket' but then league and union are both considered rugby but few would think the expansion of one would be at the cost of another.

"That the majority of budding players and fringe followers may now see Twenty20 cricket as the ultimate form of the game, rather than the "quick fix" that it is, is inescapable," Woodcock deliberates. "Generally speaking, and at the top level, more lively and entertaining Test cricket has been played during the past few years than probably ever before, its conformation still very much as it was when Peter May's side mistook Christmas Eve for Good Friday almost half a century ago. Yet, quite suddenly, the more familiar forms of the game are under threat from something substantially dependant on gimmickry."

Woodcock is right on one thing – that the quality bar of Test Matches had been forced ever higher in recent years. The England v Australia series of 2005 was almost unprecedented in intensity and evenness of battle between the bat and the ball. The drawn tests – a concept that non-believers take as evidence of cricket's futility after five days of action – were among the most dramatic sporting moments ever. The fifth day in Manchester saw almost ten thousand people locked out of a ground that had struggled to attract people at all ten years before. Interest was accelerating in some places rather than disappearing altogether. "Those of us who followed England and Australia in the summer of 2005 will always be certain of the primacy of Test cricket over other forms of the game," opined Simon Barnes, also in the *Times*.

Neither was that series a one-off. India's phenomenal comeback in a three-game series against Australia in 2001 had emboldened the sport's durable side, whilst India also had fantastic battles in South Africa at the end of 2006 and in England in the northern hemisphere summer of 2007. None of this tallies with a downgrading of the importance of first-class cricket, which seems to be scare-mongering, of a fashion. And what is the gimmickry of which Woodcock speaks? Most of the actual regulations of Twenty20 are in keeping with the laws of pyjama cricket of any length. Leg-side wide deliveries are still punished with the same rigidity and fielding restrictions are governed in the same way. The 'gimmick' tag was applied with liberalism bordering on a reckless streak at the conception of Twenty20 but the only things I could sense as gimmicky at the World Twenty20 final were dancing troupes hip-hopping away on the boundary edges and what do they have to do with the on-field 'product', to steal a marketing phrase?

Test cricket has supporters but the steadfast refusal of some to believe that any renegade type of the sport is fit to lace it's boots could have repercussions down the line, when the current Test-goer gets too old to rise from the armchair and continue pay through the gates. Twenty20 is an access route to the sport. If youngsters don't use it as a starting point now for their interest in the game then maybe they'll never get to the more verbose and intellectual bit at all.

The intellectual side of Test Match cricket comes in the art of captaincy, the ability to attack and retreat with your field settings at the right time, the use of bowlers at the right ends at the right times, the mental strength in the marathon rather than the sprint. It is glorious and all-embracing. Big hitters can prevail as the great Sir Ian Botham once found to his credit and to the appreciation of the sporting world. Accumulators can excel. There are multiple ways to skin multiple cats in multiple environments. The key is to harness those together.

"Change is inevitable," wrote Barnes, "but unlike evolution it is not a blind process. We do actually have some kind of control over the nature and the quality of those changes. That, it might be said, is the definition of the task of the sports administrators. Examples: Wimbledon and the Olympic Games could make billions with perimeter advertising. Instead, the administrators have declined to take that route, believing that it is more important (and probably more profitable) to maintain the mystique of these events. That then is the challenge to sport's administrators: to make the right changes and only the right changes. To accept that your sport has room for improvement, or at least, adjustment, but also to accept that your sport has areas in which change has to be resisted."

The pragmatic approach is often left untouched during media scrutiny. Forecasters of the impending apocalypse for cricket are plentiful but few push forward ideas to make sure the elongated versions would be safeguarded against the prevailing changes. One person who has stuck his neck out with a resolution for balance is Clive Lloyd.

Lloyd knows more about the changing face of the sport than most. At the zenith of his splendid and often scintillating career, he led West Indies by the hand into the first ever ICC-approved one-day international tournament in 1975 and lifted the World Cup trophy despite the national side only having ever played a couple of games before the competition in England. The following summer on the same soil, he led West Indies into a new era of hostile, bullying pace bowling, enough to excite and terrify in equal measure. Respected as a coach, a match referee and a general authority on the game, (as well as a former member of the Stanford 2020 'Legends' group) his words of advice carry a great deal of gravitas.

"Twenty20 is just like when the forty-over game started," recalls Lloyd, who had been exposed to an almost insufferable diet of one-day cricket in his days with Lancashire. "Eventually, I think it may die out. You can't groom your young cricketers in Twenty20. Your younger cricketers are going to grow in the longer game, there they will learn the rudiments of the game. This is a game for people at the higher level. There will become a time when you come to Twenty20 and the guys get bowled out for 30 – you will have to go home after five overs each side. That can happen. It's just entertainment."

Lloyd indirectly raises a vital question when determining what kind of a role twenty-over cricket should assume in the jostling for prominence in the next half-decade or so: what are youngsters coached to do exactly when it comes to batting? It is true that aspiring players can be susceptible to mirroring their idols in their choice of shots and the way they are played but how is that harnessed through coaching? When I was trooping to midweek nets as a schoolboy, I loved to play the cover-drive and the lofted straight drive because it was the shot with which Richie Richardson and Carl Hooper, my two favourite batsmen, gave me so much pleasure whilst I sat mesmerised in front of the television set on school holidays. Yet whoever coached me always taught me to get in line with the ball and gave me the tools with which to build a decent defensive shot to keep me at the crease in the first place. Whether in Twenty20 or Tests, you can't score runs in the pavilion. The old proverb holds.

I'm not sure that the mentoring of any youthful cricketers is ever blurred with an endgame in mind: a distinction between being readied for Test cricket or a shorter game. Yet for two reasons, Lloyd's insistence that Twenty20 is accepted primarily as entertainment is a compelling argument.

Firstly, young players don't tend to possess the brute force needed to send the ball huge distances so they could easily become disenfranchised at an early stage before any natural aptitude for the game is allowed to blossom. That ties in with the second reason: if Test cricket were to drop down the pecking order in terms of being financially rewarding and were to lose prestige, then the incentive to learn the basics of defensive stroke play and the patience and mental composition to be able to build an innings would be lost. Even if Test cricket were to stay in the calendar in such a hypothetical scenario, some of it's basic traits would be undermined to such a degree as to ultimately devalue it. Between evolution and revolution, the best course is difficult to chart.

"It's a really good spectacle at the moment," continues Lloyd, "but it's just like anything else in terms of lifespan. As a young cricketer, you are only judged by what you do in a Test Match or what you do in a one-day game: how you have fought when things are down, when you have lost three wickets or maybe five on a turning pitch. It is exciting, there is no doubt about that. Young people are coming to games and they are enjoying it and any amount of people we can get watching cricket, we have to be thankful for that."

In the sporting world and the wider world, a heavy emphasis is placed on youth in any true assessment of progress or the lack of it. Yet to do that for Twenty20 would be insular for the reasons stated earlier in this chapter and also because of the limited reach of cricket in the world as a whole. The stereotypical view of the sport as something played by the landed gentry on village greens of England on picturesque fields in the backdrop of a castle or some other such nonsense has helped make the game exclusive down the years in the minds of some and the all-white clothing of first-class and Test match cricket is part of that ancient perception. Kerry Packer bulldozed some of those barriers with the advent of World Series Cricket and pyjama kits but

Twenty20 has the potential to carry cricket to different countries in it's new and refreshing birthday suit.

"I believe that Twenty20 cricket is the way to develop, promote and popularise the game in those countries where little cricket is currently played," former head of South Africa Cricket Board, Dr. Ali Bacher told *The Star*. "This is surely the ideal form of cricket to ignite great interest in nations like the United States and China, and open up new markets that cricket needs." The ICC have long voiced their belief that cricket can become a peripheral sport in America where 'fast food' sport has the potential not only for crowds but the kind of lucrative investment from sponsors to match that of Indian markets if it was to become a big hit. The perception that they were trampling all over the stereotypical sport for the English upper classes might bizarrely help Twenty20 – or a brand more akin to Cricket Max – become accepted and even admired in the US.

At the other end of the scale, four teams actually competed for a Twenty20 competition in Nepal in October 2007, showing that the sport can prosper even in places you don't expect.

The growing feeling among cricket circles heading into 2008 is that the days are numbered for fifty-over matches, a demise hastened by Twenty20. Among the most vocal cheerleaders for that would be Shane Warne.

"Twenty20 is how the minor nations, the likes of Canada and Holland, can improve and promote the game," Warne told the *Herald Sun*. "One thing I believe is that 50-overs is gone. I believe that Twenty20 should be one form of the game, keep that to a minimum and keep it special because it is entertaining." Warne's comments come as something as a surprise from someone who had only twice stepped onto a Twenty20 field in competition and the man with almost three hundred wickets in one-day internationals was to compound that with a recommendation to change fifty-over cricket to forty to mirror the event held in England, saying that it keeps up the entertainment factor and lops an hour and a half away from the game time to mean that more people would be prepared to watch it.

Whatever the future holds for forty overs, fifty overs and Test Matches, hard cash will mean that Twenty20 will continue to hold a lofty stature. The inauguration of a 'Champions League' in India in 2008 will almost inevitably mean that states, franchises and counties the world over will have one eye on a major jackpot if they get towards the business end of their respective competitions.

Whether the concept will work and produce decent cricket or not is another matter. Whilst the image conjured up by the titling is of the classic European football brand that brings together the 32 best sides on the continent, the reality could be very different. The Australian teams invited will not have played short cricket in match situations for nine months and the English domestic summer will have been over a month before. The important thing is that its existence should help the domestic game to progress as a lucrative entity. The pot of gold at the end of the tunnel will generate stronger Twenty20 competitions and surely, better players.

The concept has been tried before, when a World Club Championship was trialled in Leicester in September 2005. Like the footballing equivalent the idea flumped but mainly because it was ahead of the times and peppered by unsuitable weather at the end of what had been quite a hot and euphoric English summer. The slow take-up of Twenty20 in Australia, West Indies and India meant that those three vibrant and exciting nations were left unrepresented. Leicestershire and Somerset flew the flag for England but despite strong squads from Titans (South Africa), Faisalabad Wolves (Pakistan) and Chilaw Marians (Sri Lanka), a PCA Masters XI had to be hastily thrown into the mix as well to fit the format of the event. Faisalabad won a low scoring final on a cold evening. Rather like Martin Crowe's Cricket Max, it might never have seen the light of day again but the idea would be replicated when the time was right. Furthermore, as a trump card of the BCCI over the breakaway ICL, the governing body would make sure the new 'Champions League' would be a triumph come hell or high water.

With the investment pouring into Twenty20 at the highest levels of the game, the future is a bright one at domestic and international level but some are aiming higher and delving deeper.

"If we are told that international cricket is the only important thing to us," asks Kapil Dev, "then what happens to the other five thousand people who want to play cricket? The BCCI do a fine job with so much in the Indian game but we are ready for a new era now where other people can choose to play cricket as a career like people can do with sport in European countries. In India and Pakistan and Sri Lanka, players have never been able to live a life out of cricket but we [Indian Cricket League] want to change that and the Cricket Control Board must understand that."

As with any revolution, what happens next depends almost entirely on the ruling authority. If the BCCI are unable to counter the very reasons behind the birth of the ICL (no international telecast rights for the Zee network and better pay for players without a realistic aspiration of representing their country in the near future) then there will be no reason to scrap the breakaway league and indeed, it can be expected to grow still further.

"I see this as a very good opportunity for the BCCI to pick up their act," former India international Sanjay Manjrekar told *CricInfo Talk*. "They have been less than disappointing in the last few years and now if the BCCI doesn't raise their professionalism and the way they have looked after Indian cricket then there is tremendous scope not only for ICL but also for similar enterprises to come into Indian cricket. But if the BCCI learns from this lesson and they have that motivation then they will make sure the ICL can never replace the BCCI."

Manjrekar's words came before the start of the first edition of ICL, which was stronger as a product than many expected and cannot now merely be shooed away by the Board if they get their own house in order. Too much momentum had been gained by the ICL's achievements just outside Chandigarh. Furthermore, suppression alone will not make the so-called 'rebels' just pack up their kit and go home, a point not lost on the West Indies Cricket Board when they decided to work with Allen Stanford rather than against him, to improve the infrastructure of the sport in the Caribbean. Had they taken the proverbial long-handle to his plans, the Board would have done nothing but expose their own frailties and toughen the resolve of those for whom money was no major object.

Whether or not it can and will be a success is beyond argument. Many can – and do – thrash out the positives and negatives for technique and tacticians but those are things that would become peripheral anyway if the game beneath international level sunk without trace because of low interest. The biggest threat to the existence of Twenty20 will come when that golden goose plumps up and gets ripe for killing. Domestically, the continual addition of matches year on year gives the potential for the public to get bored and the formula to become tired. Internationally, the goalposts are moving at such a rate as to suggest that lip service is being paid to the cynics: rather than cancelling Christmas, Santa could be set for the biggest shift of overtime.

"We've said for the last two years, and our members agree with us, that the focus of Twenty20 should be about counties and provinces and states where we've had great difficulty filling grounds in the past" said ICC Chief Executive Malcolm Speed during the World Twenty20 event.

"We now know that people will come to watch domestic cricketers play Twenty20. We will play it sparingly at international level and our members have agreed to a self-imposed limit of three matches at home in any year and four matches away in any year so the South African team will be limited, for example, to seven matches in any year so long as no more than three are in South Africa – apart from ICC events.

"The next one [ICC Twenty20] will be in England in 2009 and it will be short and sharp. Thereafter, following the World Cup in 2011, we need to make a decision on whether to have two Twenty20 competitions in the years 2012, 2013 and 2014 or whether there will be two Champions Trophies and one Twenty20. The indicators from this event are though that Twenty20 will continue to be very popular and I wouldn't be surprised if we had those tournaments in 2012 and 2014 as long as we can continue to develop the quality of Twenty20 in the counties, the states and the provinces."

In less than three years since New Zealand and Australia pitched up in fancy dress and facial hair for the first ever Twenty20 international, the rules had been stretched from two matches in a year to seven – an enormous switch. More than that, Speed innocently betrayed one of the big follies of sporting administrators down the years in admitting that the concept of regular World Twenty20 events would be popular rather than what is right for the game.

What Speed forgets, and what many of the rest of us forget in the hurly-burly of modern life, is that you can have too much of a good thing. Too much Twenty20 could easily become a fad and be tossed away like an obsolete games console. Then what do we use to showcase the beautiful sport of cricket to the Xbox generation? Test Matches are wonderful things but they need introducing to a mass audience and Twenty20 is that doorman at present. Let's preserve Twenty20 and keep it special: a treat. To shoot the doorman at the top of his art would be a crime we may already be in the act of committing.

Epilogue:
When Hari-Kari Met Sari

*"Only those expecting the apocalypse
could feel disappointed."*

Alan Lee,
The Times (Saturday 19 April 2008)

CRICKET USED TO BE A SPORT of refining field settings, honing techniques, marginalising those with even the smallest mental weakness. By March 2008, it had become alphabet spaghetti that sports fans across the world would find either deliciously palatable or morally repugnant. Looking out over the unlikely pre-season setting of Abu Dhabi's Sheikh Zayed Stadium, Sussex captain Chris Adams just about summed it up. "It's all quite confusing at times," he jokingly ventured, "because we have the ICL, the IPL, the ECB and the PCB and I suppose the ICI and the B and Q." Well, perhaps he was joking.

His was a problem mollycoddled by the kind of politics that sport was designed to leave well alone. Sussex's overseas wizard Mushtaq Ahmed had penned a deal with Lahore in the breakaway ICL, so the combined authorities were muddling through some kind of ruling on whether or not he would be permitted to feature in county cricket, without any kind of coherence. Whilst ICL was publicly paraded as a Satanic creation by as many people as possible, jamboree after publicity-strewn jamboree hailed the arrival of the Indian Premier League: 59 matches in 45 days of franchise fantasy-cricket; the closest to dream-teams away from those devilishly difficult computer games of *Cricket Captain.*

Indian cricket had finally cobbled together its latent genes of modernisation and created some genetically modified cricket with a difference, that difference being that cricketers at the top end of the scale would be paid the kind of money that would render life after sport to be one of hobbies rather than meaningful employment for most of those concerned. This was the same India whose showing at the inaugural ICC World Cup in 1975 was shrouded in sulky negativity, the same stubborn-beast that had stuck fingers in their ears at the very mention of Twenty20 until they had been awarded the 2011 World Cup staging rights, before which they had even threatened to boycott the first international tournament, only to then go and win the first ever World Cup.

As if to prove that Indian cricket does nothing by halves, their Premier League would be all-singing, all-dancing. Franchises were rolled out across eight major cities and won by people from vastly contrasting backgrounds. Mukesh Ambani, the Chairman of the Reliance Industries conglomerate, tabled over $111 for Mumbai over a ten-year stretch, but whilst businessmen were at the core of the bidding, Bollywood stars couldn't wait to get in on the act. Shah Rukh Khan, whose appearance on the big screens during India's World Twenty20 win over Pakistan had caused widespread delirium at the Wanderers in Johannesburg, pitched in for Kolkata Knight Riders and actress Preity Zinta would co-own Kings XI Punjab. So certain was she that IPL would not become a wet fish and fizzle out that she seemed to endorse a partial suspension of all cinema releases across India.

"I'm going to tell all my producers not to release any movie between April 19 and May 30," said the 'Bollywood Babe' on the eve of the competition. "It would be suicide."

Zinta would charm the media with her rather unrestrained glee at putting so much back into the grassroots of Indian cricket which is the point at which, to steal an analogy from American Football, we should throw a flag in on the play and actually try and match such statements up with a bit of real life.

For a start, the grassroots would not be greatly represented and neither would they be immediately advantaged from the Indian Premier League, which would showcase the highest-profile stars that the world had to offer in a soccer-style scenario. Those players were flogged in a quite remarkable auction process on 20 February 2008 that was akin to the picking of teams on a school playground with a few unlimited chequebooks thrown in for additional spice.

Like a day out at a sporting Sothebys, each player had his base rate – the lowest possible acceptable figure. Eighty-nine players had put pen to paper on a deal with the BCCI to play in the Premier League and were sold off one-by-one, with each franchise limited to eight international cricketers each.

"The auction is an unusual situation and I don't know whether it has ever happened in sport," said Shane Warne who fetched $450,000 from the Jaipur franchise. "We're going to have different players alongside each other in the same sides with eight World XIs. It's an exciting new development."

The bizarre notion of auctions were such that having splashed out hundreds of millions just to acquire the franchises, the owners were happy enough to have an open bidding process. Market forces would then be at work rather than having to second-guess what pie in the sky would be scribed inside a sealed envelope. How much would Hyderabad's Deccan Chargers want Andrew Symonds, for example? The answer was mammoth as the man they call Roy became Roy of the Rovers with $1.35m burning a hole in his wallet. It was a remarkable turnaround in the Indo-Symonds relationship after the Australian fell out of favour with every Indian national having accused Harbhajan Singh of racial remarks during India's tour of Australia the preceding winter. With almost $200,000 a week on the table, it was a rift worth healing.

But not everyone was happy with being auctioned off like cattle.

"I think it does not sound nice to your ears when you hear a cricketer being auctioned or sold," said Inzamam ul-Haq, the former Pakistan captain peering at events over the fence after transferring from the Hyderabad team to the Lahore venture in the Indian Cricket League. "I would not like to see it happening with myself." Other high-profile players on both sides of the political divide voiced similar concerns.

The Indian Cricket League could feasibly have claimed to dig closer to the grassroots than the IPL because it gave the players in the strata beneath international level the chance to make a living in cricket without simultaneously being tied to local, regional or national businesses. How can a nation have such concerns about their second tier of cricketing talent when Mahendra

Singh Dhoni was having his services commissioned for $1.5m over little more than seven weeks? Whilst IPL further raised the profile of the whole sport, it does have more than mere potential to broaden the gulf between the haves and the have-nots in India, automatically rubbishing the claims of Zinta to be a bastion for the future of the game.

Far be it for cricketers to be regarded as human beings when such ridiculous sums are being bandied about but few people considered the psychological effects of being herded into a bidding war. For those who were selected and remunerated handsomely, the million-dollar tags would prove the ultimate status symbol. But what about those who were ignored or felt their talents unmatched by the bounty they attracted?

"Obviously it hurts when you compare the price of some others to what I got," Wasim Jaffer told *CricInfo* after Bangalore Royal Challengers signed him up for a cut-price $150,000. "I have proved myself on the field and I have made my runs in Test cricket, over 2,000 of them. But other players who haven't scored enough have got much more, because people think they will be a big hit in Twenty20. That's what public image does."

Jaffer's case is not a tough one to find sympathy for. Since scratching around for 4 and 6 on Test debut against South Africa in Mumbai in February 2000, the opener had chalked up 31 caps and shown signs that his maturity was helping the transition from talented, precocious youngster to a hard-to-dispense-with batsman in a team that has had a top-heavy look about it in the middle order for the best part of a generation. His double hundred in Antigua against West Indies in June 2006 was a mark of sustained quality and whilst not living up to the same level, 202 against Pakistan in Kolkata in the yawnathon series of late 2007 would secure him the much-craved bounty of a place in the hearts of the Indian public. Yet when the wallets were opened, he was deemed to be worth more than half a million dollars less than Gautam Gambhir, a sixth the value of South African all-rounder Jacques Kallis and just a tenth that of Dhoni, the IPL's most significant purchase.

"Today's generation of players is keen to develop a rock star image," Jaffer added. "They give a lot of attention to their looks, their clothes and their hairstyle. Ten years ago, nobody used to care." It was precisely that they didn't care that meant that private tournaments such as the IPL couldn't flourish a decade earlier but the point is no less salient. After all, Rahul Dravid, who

Jaffer credits with being selected at all, had taken tedium to new depths in the winter in scoring 5 off 66 balls in Melbourne against Australia followed by an equally painful-to-witness 16 off 114 at the second time of asking. It was hardly the type of charismatic innings of which Twenty20, as a modern form of mass entertainment for our Playstation generation, is undoubtedly made, yet still, Dravid would be Bangalore's "icon" captain.

Dravid's lack of suitability to the form of the game seemed to have escaped the Indians and in pointing it out pundits almost managed to inadvertently convince people outside the sub-continent that this was a different game to the Twenty20 that had been played in every other Test-playing nation thus far. The difference was that dollar bills were more readily available and so, the field boasted more thoroughbreds than elsewhere. Nothing about the cricket itself would prove to be in the slightest bit revolutionary but the hype and drama in mere discussions about IPL before a ball had been bowled intimated at a change in the world order unseen since Metternich picked up his P45 in Vienna back in 1848.

In England, debate was zealous and hyper-active but also counter-productive and often conservative. Radio phone-ins wanted to know the ins and outs but seemed to get ridged around the altogether different issue of whether Twenty20 would spell the end of Test Matches – the same arguments that had been whirling around in circles back in 2003. As always, the sentiment seemed to centre around the preservation of the county game despite the fact that it remained gloriously inefficient as a sporting business for all bar three weeks in the domestic summer, those three weeks being the ones crammed with twenty-over cricket. On the very same broadcasts and the same pages as often denounced foreign and Kolpak-qualified cricketers in the county game, the headlines were now screaming about their absence due to the IPL and the detrimental effect it would have on the improving of young English players: an outrageous case of double standards, although that isn't to say that both viewpoints maintain more than the odd grain of credibility. English fans had been largely passive whilst two overseas players had been permitted at any one time for their counties in 2007 but when a bigger fish with a bigger cashcard came calling in another competition, then the hands of appeal were gesturing towards some moral arbiter somewhere, presumably crying foul.

Some of the oft-heard complaints seemed to be nothing more than sulking at the lack of English representation. Trapped between the desire to win international caps (the 2008 Test Series against New Zealand would start at Lord's on May 15 – over two weeks before the IPL's conclusion) and the need to stash away some big bucks for the wettest of rainy days, the dithering of the uncertain ECB lasted long enough for England's stars to miss the boat. Kevin Pietersen, England's most marketable product on the world stage, rejected an offer, quite probably under sufferance, and in the end, only his county colleague and captain Dimitri Mascarenhas landed a deal in the second auction. As a fringe international specialising in short forms of the game, Mascarenhas was unhindered by the red tape of a central contract, which bound Pietersen to England, but was restricted to two weeks with Jaipur-based Rajasthan Royals in 2008 owing to his county duties as captain. Full stints were planned in 2009 and 2010.

"I saw that loads of stars had joined early on and didn't think too much else of it," Mascarenhas would recall. "I didn't really think it was too much of a possibility for me because of the times that it was being played, in the English season, but after the first auctions it had obviously become a huge talking point. I first became aware of it through Warney after he had seen the people who would be in his team. He got on the phone to me and really it all went from there. If it wasn't for Shane Warne, I wouldn't be playing in the IPL."

The Aussie leg-spinner had long been an advocate of Mascarenhas' credentials during his time at Hampshire and was in the privileged position of being able to put someone else's money where his mouth was. But Mascarenhas would hardly be a gamble. His athleticism in the field would assist a team whose signings hardly oozed elasticity and his wide, beaming smile would fit in nicely to the carnival atmosphere of the Indian Premier League. His playing style is pretty well suited too – especially the bowling once affectionately described by Andrew Flintoff as "putting it in the right places and wobbling it about a bit." If people in India hadn't known before the late English summer of 2007 that Mascarenhas was a ferocious hitter with the bat, then the five consecutive sixes off Yuvraj Singh at The Oval would have helped.

"The last six months have been a dream come true for me and to play for

England is everybody's dream," adds Mascarenhas. "People always ask me what I was thinking hitting those sixes and it could have been different. If I'd have taken a single off the first ball of the over then it wouldn't have happened and if the catch had been completed off the first one that I hit, I would have been out for five and nobody would have been talking about it. So I suppose there has been a lot of luck involved in everything but then again, you have to be in the right place to take advantage of that. It's the old saying: the harder you practice, the luckier you get."

With Warne choosing to leave Hampshire to pursue a small town's worth of other avenues, Mascarenhas was made county skipper and that complicated the issue. The IPL would start in the same week as the English County Championship and end two and a half weeks into the Test Match summer, so the county would have to be pretty amenable to Mascarenhas playing there for him to take a break from his contract on the South Coast of England.

"Hampshire have definitely been understanding but at first it was a difficult position to be in. Having been given the opportunity, I wanted to play out there for all six weeks – the whole tournament – but I had to agree to do otherwise because without Hampshire, I couldn't have gone at all. I had no choice but the county have been good to me and very supportive so I'm happy to go there for longer over the next two years.

"In the dressing room, everyone has been happy for me and all the lads are very excited. I watched a few of the early matches including a great win for my team, the Rajasthan Royals, and it looked fantastic. Of course, a few of the boys have had a few jibes in about the money! But I haven't had one piece of bad press and everybody seems to be really positive on it."

Shane Warne characteristically put English cricket in a spin, describing the absence of leading players such as Pietersen and Flintoff as "a shame". Michael Vaughan proclaimed that England's stars couldn't be left on the periphery of the IPL for too long whilst simultaneously assuring the ECB of his commitment and pride to pull on the Three Lions. Still, for the first four weeks of IPL, it would be an Englishman-free zone out in the middle.

* * *

BY 18 APRIL 2008, THE PLAYERS were in place and the publicity could be substituted in favour of real action. Just what did we expect from the Kolkata Knight Riders' visit to meet the Bangalore Royal Challengers at the Chinnaswamy Stadium? I for one did not have a clue. Do Bangalore-dwellers have such a loyal bond to their city of residence that they can, for example, cheer if Australian Ashley Noffke were to bowl their very own Sourav Ganguly? Indeed, what would happen at all once the novelty wore off – especially if one of the multi-million dollar franchise owners found his/her investment to be worth only a pile of defeats?

"Walking round the stadium in Bangalore before and after the match, I saw a single flag – an Indian flag – and that was furled," reported Scyld Berry in the *Daily Telegraph*. "The vast majority of spectators were in their twenties and thirties, almost 15 per cent female, almost everyone dressed in jeans and slacks and T-shirts, wearing or carrying nothing more, illustrating their social mobility. And they were being asked to support a cosmopolitan team, representing their city, in which only a couple of players, notably Bangalore's 'icon' player, the captain Rahul Dravid, could be described as local."

Questions of allegiance were posers for another day but there would be an eleven-minute long exhibition at the opening ceremony that marked out in no uncertain terms that even if the cricket proved to be Twenty20 with a few noughts added onto several bank accounts, the IPL would offer up cricket's biggest firework showing – burning of dollars in the truest sense.

"The opening ceremony was in itself worth the entrance fee," wrote an enthralled Laurence Booth in the *Guardian*, "notably the laser show and firework display which provided a devastating counterpoint to the feeble efforts at Lord's before the 1999 World Cup. And if the officials' speeches dragged on rather too long for the spectators' liking, the catcalls seemed understandable in the circumstances." Fifty-five thousand had long been camped inside Karnataka's premier cricket venue, wailing so crazily that the television set would occasionally start to crackle with displeasure. Not a ball had been bowled but rather than the delirium brought about by sport, it seemed the fans were merely exhaling on behalf of a nation forced to hold it's breath for too long.

The flamboyant crowd was new, the concept new, the evolution of cricket continuous but where so many things change, elements that remain the same only become more noticeable. Whereas in England, David Lloyd had been lured towards the hot-tubs, the cowboys and the Bucking Broncos by some kind of invisible yet irresistible gravity, Laxman Sivaramakrishnan studiously surveyed the wicket in Bangalore as if it were the first day of a Test, his wiry frame squatting towards terra firma to tell us all that it was a firmly rolled strip, likely to produce "a run feast." The only difference from his usual broadcasting style was that he had to shout to hear himself think but in that he was outshone by Ravi Shastri at the toss. Shastri belted out his lines to the crowd as if each person clung to each one of them, perhaps forgetting that as few harboured anything but the faintest allegiance to either the Knight Riders or the Royal Challengers, they could have done it all in the relative piece and solitude of the dressing rooms without any hullabaloo.

"It has been fantastic, having everyone together here for two days," said Dravid at the toss after winning it for Bangalore. "We have prepared well and want to put on a good performance for our home crowd; a real spectacle because we want them to witness some great cricket." Hang on, was this really not a Test Match? The words sounded just the same but Dravid had exchanged the whites for an eye-catching bright red number with liberal dashings of amber that were far from fetching. IPL seemed to have better kits than their rebel rivals but the designers had the misfortune of dressing Bangalore like a team of Power Rangers. Kolkata were one up in the fashion stakes as Ganguly sported the sleek black number with gold trim and in the early style-over-substance exchanges, perhaps that will have been noticed more than the outcome of the coin-spin, where Dravid inserted his opponents, believing the dew factor would make it harder to bowl as the evening progressed following the 8pm local-time start. Ganguly said he would have batted anyway, so everyone got what they wanted.

Ganguly faced up to Praveen Kumar for the first ball in IPL history – an all-Indian face-off to marginalise the multi-national build-up. Kumar, perhaps nervous, allowed his opening salvo to slip down leg side, Ganguly brushed it off the pads and Brendan McCullum careered through for a leg bye. Only one more and a wide followed from the opening over. All that money and Kolkata had mustered a pyrotechnic-free 3/0. Doom-merchants the world over let out a monster sigh of relief as they realised that the IPL was real Twenty20 after all.

McCullum was reminded from the commentary box that "there's no time to get your eye in in this game" after welcoming Zaheer Khan 's spell from the BEML End with a dot ball, slashing wildly outside off stump and the message was received loud and clear. Second up, the New Zealander walked towards the bowler and with a crunch, deposited him to the ropes at mid-wicket for 4. The next ball saw an adjustment in length which proved to be an over-compensation from the left-armer who dropped too short and disappeared in the same direction, only quicker. This is what the hordes had come to see and, led by Shah Rukh Khan, the Kolkata owner, the crowd danced and cheered to celebrate each boundary the way Bollywood intended.

In the *Times*, Alan Lee would remark that McCullum looked like "a toy spaceman" with his garish gold helmet and pads and by the fourth ball of the second over, he appeared to have landed on a model village. Zaheer was already fed up of being smashed to leg so cut down his angle of attack to go around the wicket. McCullum decided not to mess with a winning formula so looked for the same again after swooping his body to the off side and miscued amusingly over slip to the third man barriers for the IPL's first maximum from the tenth ball of the innings. Four more followed and a bemused Zaheer skulked off with eighteen runs chalked up against his name from just one over.

From there, McCullum demonstrated an ogre-like mastery of all he surveyed. Having flayed attacks belonging to Bangladesh and England over the southern hemisphere summer, he had already built a hunger for racking up runs and wasn't about to stop after his smashing of Zaheer. His aggressive punch down the ground off Praveen in the third over for four was made all the more aggressive by the fact that he was three yards closer to the bowler by the time he struck it. Ashley Noffke was pressurised out of the reckoning, spraying his first ball a long way down the leg side for five wides and the extra ball was helped over the long leg fence as McCullum made the waiting Ganguly a spectator. The cheerleaders acquired from NFL side Washington Redskins had little to shake their pom-poms about; those in Kolkata gold bopped in time with the music at the end of the fourth over with the visitors 50 without loss and the home team on the end of a good hiding.

The fact that the crowd didn't care whether it was the Kiwi or the Bengali who was biffing the ball around was a tick both in the positive and negative columns. The acid test for the whole sustainability of city cricket in India was to see how many would actively cheer against the same heroes who pulled on the sky blue of their nation in international cricketers. On the departure of Ganguly for 10 – edging Zaheer to the hands of Kallis at second slip – Ricky Ponting bounded to the crease and was booed by enough folk to suggest that recent wounds from the Indo-Australia series had not had time to heal. The IPL was proving evolutionary rather than revolutionary: perceived impostors would be incidental to the popularisation of Twenty20 in India as far as some were concerned, for the time being at least.

Ponting played a golf shot to end the time with the fielding restrictions in place and Kolkata were left at 61-1 after six overs; quite unremarkable by the standards of twenty-over match play. Overs seven and eight passed without boundary-slapping incident before Ponting irked Jacques Kallis with a slog over the slips for four and a more measured clearing of long leg for 6. Almost expecting the burst, the gold-foiled girls on the sidelines were quickly in position to shake their respective booty.

Events at the opposite end of the Trans-Tasman partnership indicated that McCullum had an urgent engagement to get to. The first ball of the twelfth over was a hopeless slog belonging to parks cricket but the ball narrowly passed by the off stump: a warning sign. Just in case anyone had missed the point that the New Zealander enjoyed to live dangerously, he took one hand off the bat next ball to swat the ball down the ground for six. Ponting's demise to the bucket hands of Kumar in the next over didn't disturb anyone too much – by this time they all wanted to watch McCullum – whether barracking for Bangalore or the Knight Riders. All eyes were on the Kiwi creating carnage.

He didn't disappoint by bashing Kallis twice to the boundary in the thirteenth and then taking apart the hapless Victorian leggie Cameron White with a collection of strokes best attributed to a baseball-esque technique. Stepping into the last delivery of the over and dispatching it some distance over the leg-side fence, McCullum reached 99 and brought up a ton off 53 balls with an extra cover drive for two runs from a low full toss from Noffke in the next over. Adulation was unconfined, even among Bangalore fans. This is what they had come to see and it almost mattered not that a New Zealander had achieved the first century of the IPL. Shah Rukh Khan wiggled his hips in jubilation that McCullum's was already a justified pay cheque.

At the fall of Ponting, David Hussey had wandered out to play second fiddle to McCullum and justifying a pay cheque was something of a family affair for the Victoria all-rounder. He had been involved in a protracted wrangle with county side Nottinghamshire as his two deals overlapped, so the pay-off just to be in Bangalore joined the bounty on his head from the auction, where his $625,000 signing dwarfed that of his brother Mike, who as well as being more experienced at the highest level of the game, had earned the nickname "Mr. Cricket," partly because of his aptitude for it.

Still, McCullum carried on regardless as Kolkata racked up 68 runs from the last five overs. Zaheer Khan came back over the wicket and with a strong bottom hand, McCullum welcomed him by shovelling him over his left shoulder, clearing short fine leg for six. Kallis was butchered over the on-side and then savagely dismissed to the second tier down the ground for McCullum's tenth six of the innings. From 100 to 200 had taken just 48 balls for the Knight Riders. Praveen Kumar came back for the last over and witnessed his full ball, the slower one and the low full toss all clear the ropes; Brendan McCullum walked off with 158 not out off 73 balls and all-round admiration from everyone who witnessed it.

"I just couldn't feel my legs for the first eight or nine balls," he told the waiting television crews. "It's such a big tournament and such a big crowd that I was just happy to get through that. Sourav, Ricky and Dave all helped with that. The boundaries out there are pretty short and I'm just lucky they came out of the middle. I'm absolutely ecstatic with a score like that."

"To achieve serious recognition globally," Alan Lee wrote in the *Times*. "The IPL needed its overseas players — with their head-spinning salaries and the merest suspicion of "take the money and run" — to perform at least as well as the local Indian heroes … McCullum quickly sorted that one out."

McCullum's contribution was well and truly unmatched on the opening day as the Royal Challengers limped to just 82 — just over half of the Kiwi's personal contribution. The asking rate of over 11 runs an over for the victory target of 223 was never a realistic concern and the match petered out with everyone talking about *that* innings.

That they could talk about it around the world was not a formality. The IPL had generated so much excitement and hype at the inception that every cricket fan in the world wanted to see the birth and, as always seems to happen around the time of a major series in India, the media found life tough going to relay the messages from this quite unique occasion. The IPL administration demanded the right to use all photographs taken at their events for free and forever, an unusual curb on press freedom that didn't go down too well. Furthermore, news and sport websites were forbidden to upload pictures in-game as rights had been sold to a portal in North America. Accreditation guidelines were resolved two days before the first match but many media outlets were still unhappy about a raft of other issues that would hinder their reporting of the Indian Premier League. *CricInfo*, the bastion of all things cricket online, were unreasonably told to pay for their images from the IPL but retained the moral high ground by giving the competition as much coverage as they would have done had there been no issue.

In the UK, Setanta Sports won the five-year television rights to show the live matches and thus gained an entry into the cricket market that was perhaps their one early failing in their battle for control of the digital airwaves with Sky Sports. In Australia, Channel Ten would use the competition, and the curiosity surrounding it, to prise viewers away from their major free-to-air rivals at Nine, who'd had the fortunes of the Baggy Green to themselves almost since the days of the World Series in the late Seventies.

* * *

VIEWERS DIDN'T GET EARLY contests of a tight and nervy nature but they had plenty of teeing off to enjoy, even after McCullum's seventy-five minutes of fame were done. Mike Hussey made a century on the second day as the Chennai Super Kings ran riot against Punjab in a match of almost 450 runs. Virender Sehwag bashed 91 not out off 41 balls as the Delhi Daredevils out-charged the Hyderabad franchise, with one over from Andrew Symonds near the end depatched for 4 6 4 6 4 6. With the ball, Warne bowled with finesse and his former international co-conspirator Glenn McGrath controlled with the same guile with which he had made his name over 14 years of Test match cricket.

From the first week of the Indian Premier League, it was clear that this would be a crash-hot competition and one with enough stars to almost guar-antee top quality cricket. As if the point had been laboured over a ten-day spell, Zee TV had been broadcasting their triangular series of so-called rebel cricket the previous week in which the ICL World had taken on the ICL India and Pakistan teams in a format aping that of World Series Cricket. The talents on show were endless, the actual quality far lower than that of IPL. They had been strange broadcasts to keep an eye on too. Several banners popping up proclaiming ICL to be "the only Indian league" or "the best in India" almost seemed to verge on attempts at Soviet-style propaganda just days away from all the hype of IPL kicking into gear.

"Am I the only one who couldn't give a toss whether the Bangalore Royal Challengers beat the Kolkata Knight Riders?" asked George Dobell in his column for *SPIN World Cricket Monthly.* "Oh, I know the concept is important. But so is soil erosion, tax law and the impact of asbestos on the Vietnamese community in Cardiff, but I'm not hugely concerned with any of that either."

He makes a good point. If people cared at the start, would they at the end? The ICC World Twenty20 had previously been the globe's most successful event in the format and that had lasted just thirteen days. The IPL would go on for a month longer. Outside of India, we have seen it all before because the actual cricket is true to the same principles as turned up at The Rose Bowl in June 2003 and have been sprouting up across the world since. Yet part of the reason for Twenty20 being such a revolution for cricket as a whole is in the ability to turn a pastime into a business. Elsewhere, potential remains but the wallet-speed of the moguls in charge of the Indian franchises means those prospects are increased around the IPL, whatever that may mean for lower strata of the sport. It may lead to a world league that pits Manchester against Mumbai, Lahore versus Leeds or Cape Town against Kingston, but somehow I think sporting traditions elsewhere will restrain any move to worldwide city cricket.

There is also the chance that IPL might just fail and that the owners will slip away with respective tails between their legs. Like the players they employ, they have one chance to make a difference by doing things well. One wrong decision and the whole tent will deflate on the circus. It underlines the fact that whatever you think of Twenty20 cricket around the world, it has turned cricket into a not-wholly-unwelcome game of roulette with a bigger ball and plenty of bats. Five years in, the bets are getting bigger.

BIBLIOGRAPHY

Magazines

The Wisden Cricketer (South African edition)
August/September 1997

The Wisden Cricketer
March, April, September 2007

SPIN World Cricket Monthly
October 2006, October/November 2007

Websites

www.telegraph.co.uk
Comment pieces from Steve James and Mark Nicholas from the website of the *Daily Telegraph*

www.cricinfo.com
Terrific in-depth analysis from cricket correspondents across the world as well as hosts of the CricInfo Talk podcasts

www.listener.co.nz
A reference to a post-mortem of Cricket Max in New Zealand

www.bbc.co.uk/sport
News, comment and analysis on the history of Twenty20 in the UK since 2003

www.nzherald.co.nz
Reaction, comment and reportage from the first ever Twenty20 international at Eden Park, Auckland

www.smh.com.au
Reflecting the views of the Australian establishment towards Twenty20 through the news of international and KFC Big Bash Twenty20 competition

www.timesonline.co.uk
Comment and news pieces from *The Times* in London

www.worldtwenty20.com
The excellent and updated official website of the ICC World Twenty20 tournament

www.thetwenty20cup.co.uk
Constantly updated news and statistics source for domestic Twenty20 all over the world

www.pro20.co.za
News and statistics from the Pro20 competition in South Africa

www.twenty20cricket.co.nz
News and statistics from the Pro20 competition in New Zealand

www.theargus.co.uk
In-depth reports and news from Sussex CCC

www.dailyecho.co.uk
In-depth reports and news from Hampshire CCC

www.ypn.co.uk
Yorkshire Post powered news and reports from Yorkshire CCC plus the Cricket Talk weekly podcast during the domestic summer.

Books
The Packer Affair
Henry Blofeld
Collins, 1978

Twenty20 Vision: My Life and Inspiration
Mushtaq Ahmed
Methuen Publishing, 2006

Wisden Cricket Almanac 2007

Pundits from Pakistan
Rahul Bhattacharya
Picador, 2005

A History of West Indies Cricket
Michael Manley
Andre Deutsch, 1990

ABOUT THE AUTHOR
MARTYN HINDLEY

MARTYN HINDLEY HAS BEEN the Cricket Correspondent in the North-West for BBC local radio since 2006, charting the fortunes of Lancashire. He learned his trade as a freelance journalist working on football and rugby league, covering his first cricket match in 2002 when England played India in the Headingley Test match.

In 2008 he joined the reporting team of the BBC's *Test Match Special,* alongside such luminaries as Boycs, Aggers and CMJ, all of whom have hardly suffered from short forms of their names.

Reporting on the game is seen as an adequate compensation for having no talent at it, having featured briefly for Astley and Tyldesley under-13s in the Bolton Association during his youth.

Martyn has a broad interest in European football as well and is a regular commentator on Champions League matches for UEFA.com, for whom he has also presented regular podcasts.

His passion for Leigh RMI Football Club is unfathomable but admirable given their status as a side in the Conference North, but he has plenty of non-sporting pursuits to occupy his spare time including travel (favourite places include Kiev, Ukraine) and swimming.